FIGHTING FOR
THE PRESS

FIGHTING FOR THE PRESS

THE INSIDE STORY OF THE PENTAGON PAPERS AND OTHER BATTLES

JAMES C. GOODALE

The City University of New York
CUNYJOURNALISM
PRESS

CUNY JOURNALISM PRESS IS THE ACADEMIC IMPRINT OF THE CUNY GRADUATE
SCHOOL OF JOURNALISM, PART OF THE CITY UNIVERSITY OF NEW YORK
219 WEST 40TH STREET, NEW YORK, NY 10018
WWW.PRESS.JOURNALISM.CUNY.EDU

© 2013 James C. Goodale

Visit our website at press.journalism.cuny.edu
First printing 2013

Cataloging-in-Publication data is available from the Library of Congress.
A catalog record for this book is available from the British Library.

ISBN 978-1-939293-08-4 paperback
ISBN 978-1-939293-12-1 hardcover
ISBN 978-1-939293-09-1 e-book

Typeset by Lapiz Digital, Chennai, India.
Printed by BookMobile in the United States and CPI Books Ltd in the United
Kingdom. The U.S. printed edition of this book comes on Forest Stewardship Council-
certified, 30% recycled paper. The printer, BookMobile, is 100% wind-powered.

Congress shall make no law respecting an establishment of religion, or prohibiting the free exercise thereof; or abridging the freedom of speech, or of the press; or the right of the people peaceably to assemble, and to petition the Government for a redress of grievances.

FIRST AMENDMENT, UNITED STATES CONSTITUTION

To my wife Toni, Ashley, C.J., Tim, Clay and Ricki and the next generation: Will, Lizey, Paloma and Celeste.

TABLE OF CONTENTS

ACKNOWLEDGMENTS

I want to thank Stephen C. Shepard, dean of CUNY Journalism School, and Tim Harper, publisher of CUNY Journalism Press, for publishing this book, and an equal thanks to John Oakes, co-publisher of OR Books, for agreeing to distribute it. More particularly, I want to thank John for serving as my understanding editor.

My thanks to Victor Navasky, who urged me to write this book; if he had not, there would not have been a book. My thanks also to Kofi Annan, Ben Bradlee, Richard Cohen, Clifton Daniel (posthumously), Jimmy Finkelstein, Kris Fischer, Max Frankel, Pete Gurney, Warren Hoge, Victor Kovner, Tony Lewis, Tom Lipsomb, Shirley Lord, Peter Matthiessen, Sidney Offit, Dan Rather, Bob Sack, John Sicher, Bob Silvers, Paul Steiger, Mike Wallace (posthumously), and Tom Winship (posthumously), all of whom have supported my writing, and to my fourth-grade teacher Jane Woodman (Chapin) and her husband E. Barton Chapin (posthumously) for teaching me how to write.

A special thanks to those who read the book before publication and gave me their extremely helpful comments: Clay Akiwenzie, Erik Bierbauer, Jeffrey Cunard, Harry Evans, Fred Gardner, Lynn Goldberg, Ashley Goodale, Tim Goodale, Toni Goodale, Al Hruska, Bruce Keller, C.J. Muse, Paul Steiger, and Jim Zirin.

I also wish to thank Trevor Timm, now a lawyer with the Electronic Frontier Foundation, who served as my invaluable research assistant for two years, and special thanks to my agent Ike Williams.

Finally, my thanks to Devi K. Shah who assisted me in every aspect of the book. She made suggestions on every chapter, found material I had long forgotten, and was a major force in organizing all the publishing.

I have been saving the inside story of the Pentagon Papers for the right time. That time has come. The WikiLeaks matter has made the Pentagon Papers case more relevant than ever before.

When the *New York Times* published the Pentagon Papers, it was accused of treason, damaging national security, and violating the Espionage Act. All these claims are being made against WikiLeaks and other whistleblowers and leakers today. The First Amendment was under attack then, and it is under attack today. The principles underlying the great First Amendment victory the *Times* won for the press in the case of the Pentagon Papers should protect reporters and the news media today.

But to understand what the Pentagon Papers were all about, it is important to know what actually happened inside that story and inside the *New York Times*.

That case came in the middle of Nixon's war against the press—a war that began before Nixon was elected and continued through his presidency. His vice president called the establishment press "nattering nabobs of negativism." His attorney general tried to jail *New York Times* reporter Earl Caldwell. And that was before the Pentagon Papers. But the pressure on the press did not end when Nixon resigned. Reporters went to jail for decades after. And succeeding presidents have tried to use the Espionage Act to stifle free expression.

The Pentagon Papers case was especially sensitive because it came in the middle of the Vietnam War. On its front page of June 13, 1971, the *New York Times* published a series of Defense Department documents and other information that was classified top secret, which outlined U.S. government policy on the war in Vietnam. These documents (the "Pentagon Papers") had been leaked by Daniel Ellsberg, a researcher who had access to the Pentagon Papers at the Rand Corporation, a think tank serving as a consultant to the Defense Department. Ellsberg passed the documents to reporters at the *Times*.

There followed a period of intense debate, carried out in the board rooms of the newspaper, the offices of its legal counsel, and ultimately the law courts of the nation. The questions were clearly defined: whether publishing these documents would be in the country's interest, and whether their publication was protected by the First Amendment. On June 30, 1971, the Supreme Court decided the First Amendment protected their publication. This decision was the first of its kind by the Supreme Court, and put new weight behind freedom of the press.

This is the story of those weeks in June when the press's freedom of speech came under its most sustained assault since the Second World War. It is also the story of efforts by the government to silence the press since that time, and the response of the press to those efforts.

Beyond the inside story of the Pentagon Papers, this book will look at the freedom of the press today. In many respects, President Obama is no better than Nixon. Obama has used the Espionage Act to indict more leakers than any other president in the history of this country. His Justice Department is threatening to indict Julian Assange. Obama is ignoring the Pentagon Papers case at his peril— and the nation's peril. It is a case for the ages and matters as much, or more, today.

CHAPTER I

THE OTHER STORY THAT SUNDAY MORNING

On Sunday June 13, 1971, a story was published on the front page of the *New York Times* under a three-column headline: "Vietnam Archive: Study Traces 3 Decades of Growing U.S. Involvement."[1] I thought it was the most boring headline I had ever read; no one would read this article.

It was the first installment of the series of articles that became known as the Pentagon Papers. When we published it, my colleagues at the *Times* and I had been expecting all hell to break loose. It was the first article in a planned series based on leaked Defense Department documents showing decades of deception and duplicity: how the American people had been misled about our involvement in Vietnam. But with this boring headline, I wondered if all our expectations of a huge explosion following publication would be wrong. All that day, I kept waiting for the other shoe to drop, but it didn't.

Indeed, the nation's press on that Sunday was more interested in Tricia Nixon's wedding the previous evening. I had watched excerpts of it on TV. I noted with interest some of the high-placed dignitaries who were there, and wondered how they would react to the bombshell story right there on the front page the next morning, next to coverage of the wedding.

I took a radio with me out to my dock on the lake next to my house and turned it to the news stations to see what sort of commotion the publication had created. None to speak of. The news broadcasts were all about Tricia's wedding, with a word or two about the *Times'* publication of a Vietnam archive.

The White House had no reaction. President Richard Nixon had not even read the article. Attorney General John Mitchell hadn't read it either. The headline, apparently, had put everyone off.[2]

General Alexander Haig, the president's deputy national security adviser, *had* read it, however. He reached Nixon in the afternoon to discuss the progress of the Vietnam War. Nixon asked him, "Is there anything else going on in the world today?" to which Haig replied, "Yes sir—very significant—this, uh, goddamn *New York Times* exposé of the most highly classified documents of the war."

In his phone call with Nixon, Haig called it, "a devastating...security breach of the greatest magnitude of anything I've ever seen."[3] Nixon was much more worried about the leak than the story. He suggested an easy solution: he would just start firing people at the Department of Defense—whoever could be held responsible.[4]

Secretary of State William Rogers was next to call Nixon. Their conversation was mostly about the coverage of Tricia Nixon's wedding.[5] Admitting that he hadn't read the story yet—wedding coverage was a higher priority—Nixon brushed it off as a story about the former administration of President Lyndon B. Johnson, not his. A few minutes later, Henry Kissinger, Nixon's national security advisor, called the White House. Perhaps Nixon had read the story by this time. He agreed with Kissinger that printing the Pentagon Papers was an unconscionable thing for a newspaper to do. "It's treasonable, there's no question—it's actionable, I'm absolutely certain that this violates all sorts of security laws," Kissinger said.[6] He told Nixon not to ignore the story: "It shows you are a weakling, Mr. President."[7] Nixon told Kissinger to call Attorney General John Mitchell to discuss what to do.

I was the chief counsel for the *New York Times*. As the newspaper's top lawyer for all its business, including journalism, I had been closely involved in our internal discussions with editors, reporters, and the publisher about whether we could or should publish the Pentagon Papers. I had told the *Times* that in my view there was a high probability that Secretary of Defense Melvin Laird would call for Mitchell or Nixon to take action against the *Times*.

But on Sunday, Laird called neither Mitchell nor Nixon. He did, however, prepare for a TV appearance on *Meet the Press*, assuming the program would be entirely devoted to the Pentagon Papers. He did not receive one question on the story. It may have been because the producers of that show hadn't read the story, either. Laird did, however, call Mitchell the next day. That call set off a chain of events that led to one of the most important Supreme Court cases ever.

Let's go back to the beginning. My first inkling that there was trouble brewing had come several weeks earlier, on March 13, 1971, at the annual Gridiron Club dinner. There was hardly a more important dinner for politicians and journalists in Washington, D.C. than the Gridiron Club. The greats of the political and journalistic world attended in tails. The President of the United States was usually the main speaker, expected to create hilarity at both his own and the media's expense.

On this particular evening, however, Nixon was with his pal Bebe Rebozo in Florida. Vice President Spiro Agnew stood in for him. Most of the members of Nixon's cabinet were there, as well as governors, senators, publishers, Supreme Court justices, and the like. I was thirty-seven, one of the younger men in attendance, and one of the few without a national reputation in government or media. I was there because I was vice president and general counsel of the New York Times Co. It was an impressive title, but among the glitterati at the Gridiron, it counted for little.

There were only limited invitations to the event held at the Statler Hilton Hotel. The Gridiron had only fifty members then; all were male. My wife, Toni, had come with me to Washington, but not to the dinner. Women were barred. In fact, thirty-five women, including the *Washington Post* writer Sally Quinn, picketed the dinner.[8] Limousines for Spiro Agnew, Henry Kissinger, Chief Justice Warren Burger, and Teddy Kennedy rolled through the picket line.[9]

With limited invitations, the *Times* parsed them out to those it wished to impress. Sharing this prized invitation in-house was unusual, so I was surprised when I was invited by Arthur Ochs "Punch" Sulzberger, the publisher of the *Times*.

I had two theories about why I was there. First, I was being thanked for several successful years. I had been leading the press's fight against Nixon's attempts to subpoena reporters and it had been my idea to take the New York Times Co. public while retaining the control of the *Times* in the Sulzberger family.

I had conceived of a corporate structure of Class A and Class B voting stock, which many media companies subsequently copied word-for-word. I had also led a large acquisition of Cowles Communications designed to solve the company's financial problems.[10] With a huge asset base, the New York Times Co. could negotiate with the unions and protect the financial integrity of the *Times* newspaper. This led to the prosperity the overall company and the newspaper enjoyed in the 1980s and 90s.

The second theory I had for my invitation was that Punch Sulzberger had decided to introduce me to the greats of the world. That was, of course, pure fantasy. While I had the respect of journalists and others in New York, I was not part of the New York power scene and certainly didn't know any congressmen or senators. More to the point, Punch had no interest in making me part of that scene.

I was a young family man with a three-year-old son, Timmy, and a twenty-nine-year-old wife about to give birth to my second child. In fact, while I dealt from time to time with the famous *New York Times* reporters in Washington such as James "Scotty" Reston, Tom Wicker, and Max Frankel, those contacts were few and far between.

I was more friendly with the news people in New York: Abraham "Abe" Rosenthal, the volatile editor of the *Times*, Arthur "Artie" Gelb, the managing editor, Seymour "Top" Topping, the foreign editor and Eugene "Gene" Roberts, the national editor.

It turned out that I was not in Washington for any of the reasons I imagined. I was there to learn a secret that would change my life, and set in motion a chain of events that would ultimately contribute to the resignation of the President of the United States.

I did not know that as I stepped into Punch's limo to go to the dinner. I was uncomfortable in my first pair of tails. I had checked them out with Punch and his wife Carol in their hotel room, and Carol had given me a barely passing grade. Punch's limo stopped short of the picket line and we walked across and entered the main ballroom for my first experience at a high celebrity event.

The place buzzed with importance. Punch was immediately mobbed by senators and such. I knew I had to navigate on my own or end up talking to the bartender.

Max Frankel, the *Times'* star foreign reporter, had me at his table, alongside Roger Mudd, the CBS anchorman. Amid the banter and the dining, I really thought I had hit the big time. Before dinner, Max Frankel said, as an aside, "Have you heard about the classified documents we have on Vietnam?" I said I hadn't, placing little significance on his remark. He did not elaborate, and changed the subject.

Agnew rose to speak. He had for the last three years been attacking the press for Nixon, calling them "nattering nabobs of negativism" and worse. He was introduced as "that ferocious, fulminating fireball of the far-flung fairways."[11] Agnew sang a song with the line: "Politics is a rough game—when effete snobs rule the airwaves, someone had to set things right."[12] The guests roared. After the dinner, Punch took me to a small party in a room in the Willard Hotel, only about fifty people. The door opened, and there were Senators Ted Kennedy and Hubert Humphrey.

Suppressing my awe, I turned from listening to one conversation to bump into Supreme Court Justice Potter Stewart. What in the world was I going to talk to him about? He was standing there with his Yale classmate, Downey Orrick, a partner of the well-known firm in San Francisco that bore his name.

With a few pops under their belts, they thought it was great fun to encounter a young lawyer who was vice president and general counsel of the *New York Times*. They wanted to know how in the world anyone so young had got such a plum. They kidded me at great length about my good fortune. "You must be related to the Sulzbergers," and so on. Potter Stewart then started talking about the *Sullivan* decision, from the famous *Times* libel case that went to the Supreme Court. In *Sullivan*, the Court applied the First Amendment in a libel case for the first time.[13] I told him that I had worked on that case at Lord, Day & Lord, the outside counsel for the *New York Times*.

L. B. Sullivan was a County Commissioner in Alabama during the civil rights movement. He had sued the *Times* in Alabama for an ad that untruthfully accused him of mistreating civil rights demonstrators. The Alabama court entered a $500,000 verdict against the *Times*. There were other similar cases pending which, if successful, would have put the *Times* out of business. The U.S. Supreme overturned the verdict, creating a new rule for libel under the First Amendment. The other cases disappeared. The *Times* was saved.[14]

Stewart smiled at me and said, "We won that one for you." I thought to myself, "Gee, is this what goes on in Washington? Supreme Court justices say which side of the press they're on at cocktail parties?" But I said nothing, smiled and changed the subject.

The next day, I went with Punch Sulzberger and our wives for lunch at Max Frankel's home. I discovered that lunches and dinners are the staple of Washington life. Once, when I asked Max how he rated a particular Washington denizen, he said disparagingly, "Oh, he goes to all the wrong dinner parties." For this lunch, Max had invited Israeli Ambassador Yitzhak Rabin to talk with Punch.

Somehow Rabin got separated from Punch and ended up eating by himself in Frankel's living room. Meanwhile, Punch, Carol, Max and I were eating out on Max's terrace enjoying the early spring sunshine. Our terrace luncheon dragged on. By the time we walked back into the living room, Rabin had departed in a huff, insulted by not being invited to the terrace. As I said goodbye to Max, it became clear why I had been invited to the Gridiron dinner. Max and his colleagues had a tranche of classified documents. I was being let in on a secret, and I was to keep it secret. I didn't yet know exactly what the documents were, but I was supposed to figure out how to publish them.

While I may have been naïve about how the social world of Washington worked in terms of lunches and dinner parties, I was not a naïf about Washington politics and the relationship between the press and the government. The *New York Times* had been fighting Nixon since the 1968 election. Nixon had gone on national television to threaten the *Times* with a libel suit for an editorial entitled "Mr. Agnew's Fitness." This marked the beginning of Nixon's war against the press which continued until he resigned. Nixon was the first president in memory to use or threaten to use the legal process to get his way with the press. It is one thing to engage in a verbal attack against the press, another to convert that animosity to legal action.

The Pentagon Papers case cannot be understood without fully understanding its context. And its context was that Nixon, a lawyer, looked to the courts for redress. He accompanied this approach with withering attacks on the press in an attempt to create a favorable climate for his administration.

In the Watergate tapes, Nixon bragged to his national security advisor Henry Kissinger several times that he brought down Alger Hiss by attacking him in the press.[1] I had followed Nixon carefully ever since that case. Hiss was a diplomat and, once, the Secretary General of the United Nations Charter Conference, who was accused of being a communist by Whittaker Chambers, a renounced communist American writer and defected Soviet spy. Chambers had shared this information with Nixon's House on Un-American Activities Committee when Nixon was a congressman.[2]

When on December 2, 1948, Chambers produced microfilm of State Department documents given to him by Hiss, which Chambers stored in a pumpkin, Nixon crowed that the "Pumpkin Papers" showed the perfidy of liberal democrats. Hiss, having denied knowing Chambers, was indicted for perjury. Hiss won the first perjury trial with a hung jury.

Hiss was tried again, and in the second case he was convicted of perjury and sent to prison. As a teenager I followed the Hiss case as carefully as an average kid might follow his favorite baseball team. I knew all the players and all the events. In the liberal circles of Cambridge, Massachusetts, where I grew up, Nixon and Chambers were viewed as villains. They were out to destroy the liberal establishment.

My mother, a professor's daughter, had gone to Europe on a student trip with "Algie" Hiss. Family friend James Garfield, grandson and namesake of the late president and a partner in the law firm of Choate Hall & Stewart, knew Hiss when he worked for that law firm.[3] No one in Cambridge could believe that Hiss had been a spy. Almost everyone seemed to believe that someone else, like Hiss' wife Priscilla, must have copied the government's papers, and that Hiss was protecting her.

For whatever it's worth, I thought Hiss was guilty because the Pumpkin Papers were typed on a Woodstock typewriter that had once belonged to Priscilla Hiss. Strangely enough, when I arrived at Debevoise & Plimpton, the firm that had handled the first trial, I learned something interesting: Hiss' own lawyer, Edward McLean, had sought the typewriter on the theory that it would exonerate Hiss. McLean thought he would find that Hiss did not own the typewriter.[4]

Nixon seemed to be right in this particular case, but I developed an extraordinary loathing for him. He symbolized for me everything that was wrong with the Republican Party. He was extremely threatening to what I thought was the best part of America—the liberal Eastern establishment.

His campaigns against Congressman Jerry Voorhees and Congresswoman Helen Gahagan Douglas were liberal nightmares. Nixon was accused of using every dirty trick imaginable against Voorhees and slandered Douglas with gutter tactics. For example, Nixon pioneered an early version of "robo-calls" during his campaigns in 1946 against Voorhees.[5] In these calls, an anonymous person would call a household, say "we just wanted to inform you that the congressman who represents your district, Jerry Voorhees, is a communist," and then hang up. In his campaign against Douglas, Nixon insinuated she was a communist by referring to her as "the Pink Lady" and cited her supposedly communist-leaning voting record in Congress.[6]

I was particularly sensitive to the attacks of right-wing Republicans such as Nixon and Senator Joseph McCarthy. A close friend of my family, George Faxon, who ran a camp I attended, was driven out of his teaching job because he refused to say under oath whether he had been a member of the Communist Party. Additionally, my friend from grade school, Louisa Edsall Kamin, and her husband, Leon, were forced to flee to Canada by Senator Joseph McCarthy for the same reason. Kamin was a Harvard researcher who also refused to say whether he had been a communist. He later became chair of the Department of Psychology at Princeton University.

I am not a radical liberal and never had been, but my attitude to Nixon informed every move when I advised the *Times* in the Pentagon Papers case. I thought I knew what he would do, how far he would go, what his legal strategies would be. It turned out I was right.[7]

On October 26, 1968, a week before Nixon won the Presidency in a landslide, the *New York Times* ran an editorial accusing Nixon's running mate Spiro Agnew of various misdeeds. The *Times* said Agnew was party to questionable land deals. It charged that his position as a director of Maryland Bank while Governor of Maryland involved "clearly repeated conflicts of interest." The editorial concluded: "In his obtuse behavior as a public official in Maryland as well as in his egregious comments this campaign, Mr. Agnew has demonstrated that he is not fit to stand one step away from the Presidency."[8]

Nixon himself responded to the editorial the next day on CBS' *Face the Nation*. The editorial was "the lowest kind of gutter politics that a great newspaper could engage in," he said, and "a retraction will be demanded at the *Times* legally tomorrow." Yet Nixon refused to go into detail about which, or any, of the allegations he thought were incorrect, stating "I am not going to do anything that might injure Mr. Agnew's case with regard to the *Times*."[9]

The next day, Agnew's campaign manager, George W. White, Jr., called Harding Bancroft, the executive vice president of the *New York Times*, demanding a meeting about the editorial. Bancroft, who was then running the *New York Times* and for all practical purposes its CEO, asked me to attend the meeting. White was a well-fed, red-faced lawyer from Maryland who was very angry and blustery, and nothing like the distinguished Wall Street lawyers who then controlled the New York City legal establishment. Bancroft was a gentlemanly, waspy ex-diplomat who had hired me with the thought that I would succeed him as the de facto CEO of the *Times*.

White said Agnew had no conflict of interest and was not involved in questionable land deals. Later it turned out that Agnew was indicted for taking bribes and had to resign as vice president. White wanted a retraction and if he did not get it, Agnew would take appropriate action. He said that Agnew had also sent a lawyer for the Nixon-Agnew campaign committee, Everett I. Willis, a partner at Dewey Ballantine, to meet later that day with Louis Loeb of Lord, Day & Lord, who had been the *Times'* outside general counsel for years.

There was no question in my mind the *Times* had not libeled Agnew. The statement in the editorial was merely the *New York Times'* opinion. One generally cannot sue a newspaper or anyone else for an opinion. Furthermore, the Supreme Court in its great *Sullivan* case, which I had discussed with Potter Stewart at the Gridiron Club, made it almost impossible for someone like Agnew to win a libel case against a newspaper. He would have to show the *Times* was acting recklessly, that is, entertaining serious doubt about the facts of the editorial before it published. The *Times'* editorial board did not doubt it was correct.

This didn't mean, of course, that Nixon and Agnew wouldn't sue, and if they did sue the *Times*, Louis Loeb and Lord, Day & Lord, would have to defend it. I had started at Lord, Day & Lord in 1959, a year after graduating from the University of Chicago Law School following a stint in the U.S. Army, where

I served in intelligence. I was extraordinarily grateful to Lord, Day & Lord for hiring me as a Chicago graduate and "sending" me up to the *New York Times*, its client. Strange as it seems today, the University of Chicago Law School did not then have a national reputation. It has one now since, among other reasons, President Obama and Justices Scalia and Kagan were members of its faculty. But then, there were only a handful of graduates in New York City. When I interviewed with New York law firms, the comment frequently was, "I didn't know they had a law school out there."

I was on a fast track at Lord, Day & Lord, although I didn't realize it at the time. After only two years I had my own clients, enormous responsibility, and the respect of those with whom I worked. Ferdinand Eberstadt, a client who had his own investment firm, had taken a shine to me and had told Lord, Day & Lord I was "the hottest young lawyer on Wall Street."[10]

Loeb's office called me to say Willis had requested a meeting with him at two o'clock. I said I would meet with them to discuss the next steps to take. Loeb had been outside counsel for the *Times* for decades. By the time I got to his office he said, "You don't have to tell me very much about that meeting this morning, I am reading about it right now in the newspaper." He pulled out the front page of the *New York Post*, which covered the story.

It suddenly struck me that I was now in a different league. I could meet with Ferd Eberstadt ninety-two times and no one would know about it except a few at Lord, Day & Lord. But in my capacity as chief counsel at the *New York Times*, when I had a meeting near Election Day, it was plastered all over the paper with my name mentioned. This was my first experience with high publicity threats against the press. I would be less than candid if I did not say I was taken aback.

I went over my analysis of Nixon and Agnew's threat with Loeb and we agreed it was not libelous, and told Willis that. It seemed to me to be a political ploy. Nixon and Mitchell were making unsupported allegations. These allegations were similar to the ones Nixon made against Voorhees and Douglas and the same as Nixon would later make against the *Times* during the Pentagon Papers case.

Nixon had smeared the *Times*, accusing it of libel as he had smeared Voorhees and Douglas. There was no way for the public to know the *Times* had not libeled Agnew. If a presidential candidate takes time on a national TV show a few days before the election to accuse the *Times* falsely, there was realistically no way for the *Times* to defend itself.

I drafted a letter which I sent to John Mitchell, who was then the head of the Republican campaign. I said our editorial was not libelous and that we would not retract it. Agnew's lawyer would not give up. The next day, October 29, 1968, he said that the editorial was "absolutely libelous" and recommended Agnew sue the *New York Times*. In a blistering statement to the press, Agnew denied all allegations of wrongdoing, called the information inaccurate, and demanded a retraction.[11]

He accused the *Times* of being prejudiced because it had endorsed Nixon's Democratic rival, Hubert Humphrey, for president. "Everyone knows that the *Times* endorsed Vice President Hubert Humphrey and is actively supporting him," his statement read. "The fact that the *Times* waited until a week before the election to distort the facts and make its inaccurate charges against me compounds the libel."[12]

Agnew continued his attack on the *Times* through the election. He repeated his allegation of libel and continued to demand a retraction. Republicans, thinking they had gained an advantage by attacking the liberal media, kept the criticisms going.

At the end of the week John Mitchell, head of the Republican campaign, demanded another retraction from the *Times*. James "Scotty" Reston, the *Times'* executive editor, had written a column that said "Nixon's radio and television appearances with citizen-interviewers were 'nearly always in a controlled situation, with the questioners carefully chosen, the questions solicited from the whole states or regions, but carefully screened.'"[13]

I sent a letter addressed to Mitchell saying that we wouldn't retract what Reston had said. Throughout the rest of the campaign, the libel suit against the *Times* was mentioned frequently by Republican candidates. Many who covered the election for the press said they felt under threat with everything they wrote.[14]

At that point Agnew became Nixon's attack dog against the press even before inauguration. In a speech before the Republican Governor's Conference, he accused the *Times* of distortions and inaccuracies. Smiling, he described the *New York Times* and *Newsweek* as "executionary journals." He said there were other publications that were "fit only to line the bottom of bird cages."[15]

Once in office, Agnew enlisted Pat Buchanan and Bill Safire as his speechwriters. By the end of 1969, they were crafting whole speeches around Agnew's hatred for all forms of media. Agnew barnstormed cities across the United States, delivering these speeches as if he was still campaigning against the Democrats.

In Des Moines, he criticized mainstream media for the "narrow and distorted picture of America [that] often emerges from the television news." The press was a "tiny and closed fraternity of privileged men elected by no one." While denying he had any interest in "censorship," Agnew implied that newspapers and television news programs should not be allowed to "wield a free hand in selecting, presenting, and interpreting the great issues of the nation."[16] [17]

In San Diego, Agnew reached his apex. The press was, he said, "nattering nabobs of negativism." With the success of that alliterative phrase, the press also became "Pusillanimous pussy footers," and "vicars of vacillation," as well as "the hopeless hysterical hypochondriacs of history." The *New York Times* did not take this sitting down and called him a "functional alliterate" and mocked him in headlines such as, "Traveling Agnew Volubly Verbalizes Viewpoint."[18]

But Agnew rejected calls to tone down his rhetoric when he was criticized for being too incendiary. Nixon told the press he would not censor Agnew, and Agnew himself defiantly declared, "I intend to be heard above the din even if it means raising my voice."[19]

Realizing he was touching a nerve, his criticism started to get more personal, calling out not only the institutional press, but individual reporters. For example, in just one speech, he managed to insult the editorial writers of the *Washington Post*, *New York Times*, *Atlanta Constitution*, *New Republic* magazine, and *I. F. Stone's Bi-Weekly*, as well as *Post* cartoonist Herblock,[20] *Times* columnists James Reston and Tom Wicker, *Life* magazine's Hugh Sidey, the *New York Post's* Pete Hamill and Harriet Van Horne, and syndicated columnist Carl T. Rowan.[21]

Agnew then touched off one of the great media battles in early 1971, leading a furor over the CBS TV documentary, *The Selling of the Pentagon*. CBS had charged that the Pentagon was engaging in a pro-Vietnam War "propaganda barrage" at the taxpayer's expense, and explored the corrupt relationship between the Pentagon and its defense contractors.[22] This did not go down well with the Defense Department, Congress, or Agnew.

Agnew's argument was somewhat convoluted. He said the producer and writer of the show were not to be trusted because the previous shows they had done on Haiti and hunger in America were false. It therefore followed *The Selling of The Pentagon* was false.

CBS agreed to run comments by Agnew and three defense officials in edited form. Yet, instead of feeling vindicated, this made Agnew furious. "It's rather unusual to give you the right of rebuttal and not allow you to decide what you're going to say in rebuttal. They edited some of my previous remarks and [remarks of] two other administration officials and showed only the ones they wanted to show."[23]

But Agnew's threats against the press were not empty rhetoric. Rep. Harley Staggers, head of the House Armed Services Committee, followed up on the criticism of the editing of *The Selling of the Pentagon*. He subpoenaed outtakes from CBS.

Staggers wanted to know what CBS edited out and what it kept in its show. Frank Stanton, the president of CBS, appeared before Staggers' Committee and effectively told Staggers to stuff it. He said the First Amendment protected CBS' right to decide what it should include and exclude on its network. He said he would go in contempt of Congress if Congress enforced its subpoena against him.[24]

The Armed Services Committee voted to hold him in contempt, but the entire House then voted down the contempt citation 226–181.[25] It was a great triumph for the press. It was, however, before the case involving *New York Times* reporter Earl Caldwell reached the Supreme Court later that year.

The *Caldwell* case was a dramatic stage-setter for the Pentagon Papers case, and it was a central part of Nixon's war against the press. As soon as Nixon was inaugurated, his Justice Department started subpoenaing the press for its sources and other unpublished information. This was unprecedented. The reverberations from this fight can be felt to this very day.

CHAPTER III

NIXON FIRES A SALVO

In the middle of Nixon's war against the press, he fired a salvo at the *New York Times*. On January 30, 1970, his Justice Department sued *Times* reporter Earl Caldwell for his notes about his coverage of the Black Panthers. The Black Panthers were a black revolutionary group, and Caldwell, one of a very small number of black reporters then at the *Times*, had managed to gain their trust.

As fate would have it, I had to make the decision to fight Nixon, since there was no one else at the *Times* around to do it. The suit was brought against Earl Caldwell, not the *New York Times*. In the world of politics, however, it was, for all practical purposes, a suit against the entire paper. The *Times*, after all, employed Caldwell, and Nixon, of course, could have kept his Justice Department from going after the press.

But at that time, Nixon's war against the press was on full throttle. He had no intention of calling back the troops. That would have been a sign of weakness. In the several weeks before Nixon sued Caldwell, there had been rumblings that Nixon's Justice Department had been issuing subpoenas to the press.[1]

Furthermore, there were stories saying that certain members of the press had worked out a compromise with the Justice Department over producing information the department requested. It was reported that the TV program *60 Minutes* and its producer, CBS, had settled a subpoena for a program they had done on the Black Panthers.[2] In today's world, such a salvo would set off alarm bells. Today, major members of the press would band together in unified resistance. But back then, before the Pentagon Papers case, there was no organized group of media lawyers, either in or out of media organizations, to do that.

On Sunday, February 1, 1970, reporter Henry Raymont broke a story for the *Times* that said that Nixon's Justice Department had subpoenaed the files of major news entities. He also reported that these entities were not fighting the subpoenas. They were complying with them.[3] Raymont pegged his story on the report, earlier in the week, that *60 Minutes* had complied with a Justice Department subpoena that sought outtakes from a segment on the Panthers that was broadcast on CBS

January 6, 1970. The Justice Department was investigating alleged death threats made to Nixon by a Black Panther named David Hilliard.[4]

CBS received a second subpoena for all its calls, memoranda, correspondence, and notes relating to the production of the program. CBS, while criticizing the subpoena, said it would comply. It claimed it had no alternative but to cooperate in a criminal case involving an individual accused of threatening the life of the President of the United States.[5]

Raymont disclosed that *Newsweek, Time,* and *Life* magazines admitted that in October, 1969, they had received subpoenas from the Justice Department for "all photographs and interviews" they had concerning members of the "Weatherman faction of Students for a Democratic Society." That group had allegedly incited four days of riots and disorder in Chicago. *Time* and *Life* said they had complied with the subpoena and *Newsweek* was negotiating an agreement as well. The *Chicago Tribune, Chicago Today, Chicago Daily News, Chicago Sun Times,* and NBC had made similar agreements without fighting the subpoenas.[6]

Raymont said of press compliance with subpoenas, "The disclosure came amidst growing concern among newspaper editors and television network news executives across the country about what they believe to be an increasing effort by the authorities to collect intelligence about radical movements from the news media."

Raymont got in touch with J.G. Trezevant, president of the Chicago Newspaper Publishers Association, and Norman E. Isaacs, president of the American Society of Newspaper Editors. Trezevant referred to the legal actions as "dragnet subpoenas" and "reckless fishing expeditions" that amounted to "harassment" of the editorial staffs of newspapers. Isaacs similarly said he was "deeply disturbed" by the growing trend.[7] Neither, however, proposed any action to deal with this "harassment."

Instead, across the media world, editors and executives were permitting the Justice Department to get away with a wholesale assault on the press. Without protesting, the press had permitted the department to operate under the radar. Between January, 1969 and July, 1971 CBS and NBC had received a total of 122 subpoenas for films or reporters' testimony in grand jury or court proceedings without raising a finger to resist.[8]

Before the *Caldwell* subpoena, the *Times*, during my tenure, had never been subpoenaed to provide sources and other unpublished information. Civil rights groups during the 1960s had asked the *Times* to cooperate with their lawsuits and I had advised Clifton Daniel, then the *Times'* editor-in-chief, to deny all such requests. Reporters were not to serve as witnesses for civil rights groups, or for the government, or any other group. To do so would inhibit their ability to cover stories, and it would also compromise their independence.

After reading Raymont's article, I asked myself what would happen if the *Times* got a subpoena from Nixon's Justice Department for our sources. I concluded that the *Times* had to resist. We could not let Nixon get our sources. We must not cave, as the rest of the press had. I thought I would have the luxury of time to convince my colleagues of the wisdom of my position. It turned out that was wishful thinking.

The following day, Monday, February 2, I received a frantic call from Wally Turner, the San Francisco Bureau Chief for the *Times*. He told me the Justice Department had subpoenaed Earl Caldwell for his notes. Earl had not told him about it, and was supposed to be in court within forty-eight hours.

I told him the *Times* would "resist," even though the *Times* was not technically part of Earl Caldwell's case. It would find a lawyer to defend him. That lawyer would get a time extension from the Justice Department, and we would begin an all-out war against Nixon.

I had no business telling Wally Turner the *Times* would do all this: that was a decision that would have had to be made by Punch Sulzberger, advised by me, in association with Harding Bancroft, the company's sole executive vice president. The problem was they were not available. They had gone off on an executive retreat with other members of the *New York Times* masthead, including Abe Rosenthal and John B. Oakes, the editorial page editor. They were closeted in an unknown locale in North Carolina, unreachable by phone.[9]

Had I taken the time to find them, it would have been too late. While other media companies had decided to cave into the government, I had decided to fight. I was sure they would agree with me. This initiated a fight against attempts to obtain reporters' information that continues to this day.

While it was clear I needed a lawyer to represent Earl Caldwell, none of the lawyers in the media world knew each other. No one had any particular experience dealing with this kind of issue. No one had any First Amendment experience.

The *Times* had to hire a Columbia law professor, Herb Wechsler, to make its First Amendment defense in the Sullivan case. My own view was the First Amendment protected sources since sources were the lifeblood of the press. The difficulty with my position, however, was that no one had ever articulated exactly what that First Amendment interest was. Only one court of any consequence had decided a claim by a reporter to protect sources. That was the Marie Torre case.

Torre was a reporter for the *Herald Tribune* who had written a story in which an anonymous CBS executive said that the singer Judy Garland did not do a television special "because she thinks she is terribly fat."[10] Garland sued CBS for libel and subpoenaed Torre, but Torre went to jail rather than disclose her source, citing the First Amendment. Future Supreme Court Justice Potter Stewart, who was then a visiting Second Circuit Court of Appeals Judge, affirmed Torre's contempt conviction. He said that "The duty of a witness to testify in a court of law has roots as deep as the guarantee of a free press."[11] He suggested Torre might have some First Amendment defense in a different situation.

But Torre's situation was a civil case. Stewart gave us very little to go on. The *Times*, however, could not worry about that now. It had to jump to Earl Caldwell's defense. Virtually the only lawyers I knew in the press world were Gabe Perle, the general counsel of Time Inc., and Al Hruska, a partner at Cravath Swaine & Moore, who was an outside counsel for CBS. I called Hruska, who gave me the name of Jack Bates, a lawyer who represented press entities at the firm of Pillsbury Madison & Sutro. This turned out to be a big mistake, although I didn't know it at the time.

While I was familiar with the First Amendment rights of the press, media lawyers generally tended to a paper's business interests. At that time, newspapers made lots of money (although the *Times* did not) because they were monopolies. As the profits rolled in, most families who owned these companies were interested in insuring that the profits continued to flow. Lawyers for press companies were therefore knowledgeable about issues affecting the business of the press. This meant they knew about advertising, circulation matters and union problems, since all newspapers were unionized. They gave scant consideration to what First Amendment rights reporters might have.

This position was aided by a long tradition: that the government and other parties did not seek sources or otherwise harass reporters. This was particularly true in those states where there were so-called "shield laws" that shielded reporters' sources.

Caldwell had published stories in which he said the Black Panthers threatened to kill President Nixon. If he had to disclose his notes or testify to what he saw, the Black Panthers would no longer let him in their headquarters, nor would they talk to him. This meant that both Earl Caldwell and the *New York Times* were through covering the Black Panthers. The *Times* had few black reporters and none would be able to get up to Earl Caldwell's speed.

I arranged for Caldwell to meet Bates. This was a disaster. Bates, who had no feel for the sanctity of reporters' sources, allegedly berated Caldwell for not cooperating with the government. A threat against the president was a serious thing, he said. Caldwell fled from the offices of the establishment Pillsbury firm and into the arms of Anthony Amsterdam, a brilliant lawyer who counted the NAACP among his clients. At one time he had argued more death penalty cases in the Supreme Court than any other lawyer.

Amsterdam was intense and had a reputation in law school for appearing behind the stacks of the library in the wee hours, bleary-eyed, seeking answers to highly abstract questions.[12] I had not met any lawyer like him before. He was a real civil rights lawyer and bore scant resemblance to the blue-chip lawyers from the "best" law firms. Amsterdam took Caldwell in tow.

I believed, strongly, that the *Times* should act as a buffer between Nixon's war against the press and Caldwell. I came up with a theory that while the government sought Caldwell's notes, those notes really belonged to the *New York Times*.

As owner of the notes, the *New York Times* could intervene in Caldwell's case to protect him. While my theories sounded heavy-handed to some reporters, it made sense legally. The *Times* owned the articles reporters wrote and the work that underlay them (i.e., their notes).

If the court let the *Times* into the case, the question would then be what our position was under the First Amendment. I initiated conversations with Abe Rosenthal. Our position should be one to protect all reporters, I thought, not just Caldwell, and one which would not sell out the press.

The First Amendment really is a simple concept: "Congress shall make no law respecting an establishment of religion, or prohibiting the free exercise thereof; or abridging the freedom of speech, or of the press; or the right of the people peaceably to assemble, and to petition the Government for a redress of grievances."[13] The government cannot stop you from speaking. This, of course, is what Nixon aimed to do. If reporters had to disclose their sources, no one would speak to them. If no one speaks to them, reporters would not publish anything, and their speech would be curtailed. The First Amendment should protect this.

But the question was whether reporters could refuse to testify under any circumstance. Were there circumstances in which everyone would agree they should testify? Abe and I would have to work this out.

Abe Rosenthal was a legendary *New York Times* editor. He was brilliant, irascible, energetic, emotional, comedic, paranoiac, competitive, impatient, intellectual, creative, instinctive. And I loved being around him. He pretty much was the whole show at the *Times*. The two of us would have to figure out how to respond to Nixon.

He should have had the title of executive editor. But he didn't. He was "managing editor" because he was in purgatory of sorts. Punch could not make up his mind whether he should give this volatile son of immigrants the top job. Abe did not easily fit the image of a buttoned-down *New York Times* editor.

While Punch was making up his mind about Abe's prospects, he asked Scotty Reston, the most prominent of all *New York Times* writers, to come to New York to oversee the news operation as vice president. Both Scotty and Abe were to play prominent roles in the Pentagon Papers case.

As a Pulitzer Prize-winning reporter, Abe had covered Poland and Japan.[1] He did not arrive permanently in New York until 1963, the year I started at the *Times*. We got off to a rough start: on his first day he called me for libel advice. In the middle of my long-winded explanation, he hung up saying, "I can't stand this anymore." But Abe and I became very close during the *Caldwell* case. The *Times* would not take a position in the case unless I could explain it adequately to Abe and unless he embraced it. My experience in *Caldwell* paid off the next year in the Pentagon Papers case.

Abe had a great sense of humor. Every conversation, no matter how serious, ended in a joke. A serious subject was always surrounded by much laughter. Abe was smart as hell. You had to race to keep up with him and he did not suffer fools gladly. We both knew we were in a battle against Nixon to the end.

The dialogue I had with Abe was an extremely important one for the *New York Times*, but also a significant one for the future of journalism. The position the *Times* took would with some probability be followed by others in the press. Our conversation had significance beyond the four walls of the *New York Times*.

If you walked up to a *New York Times* reporter sitting at his desk and asked him whether he should disclose his sources, he would say, "No." Why? "Because the

First Amendment protects me." But which First Amendment? The First Amendment that's in the Constitution which says there are no exceptions to the right to speak freely, or a real life First Amendment which has exceptions?

In short, our discussion was one common to most constitutional debates. Simply put: Is the First Amendment absolute as is stated in the Constitution, or does it have exceptions? That is to say, is it qualified? It would not be an easy thing for the *Times* to say the First Amendment was not absolute. Why should the *Times* admit there are any exceptions to the First Amendment when the *Times* carries the flag of the First Amendment and free speech daily?

But the more Abe and I thought about it, the more we thought the *Times* could not say the First Amendment was absolute.[2] There would be some exceptions when reporters had to disclose their sources. For example, if reporters had secretly been told about 9/11 or a plan to assassinate the President, surely a reporter would have to testify. The issue was, how do we articulate this exception so that it did not swallow up the First Amendment?

Abe and I felt particularly isolated in thinking through our position. Our peers, such as *Time, Newsweek,* and CBS, had been cooperating with Nixon for several years by complying with subpoenas. When we "woke them up" by taking the First Amendment position that we did, their responses were not particularly helpful.

Time issued a statement that it would examine each subpoena as it came in and refuse to supply any material that was not "relevant" to the main thrust of the subpoena. "Should we believe that there is no immediate relevance and that a law enforcement body is on a 'fishing expedition' for information, we will take appropriate legal action to contest the subpoena."[3]

That was a mealy-mouthed statement. Not one mention of the First Amendment. *Time* would fight the subpoenas if not "relevant," but all defendants fight subpoenas that are not relevant. A subpoena issued for "irrelevant" information should not have been issued in the first place.

CBS said it would "confront" subpoenas, but did not say how. Oz Elliot, *Newsweek*'s editor, was somewhat better. He said that "We may be legally compelled to submit our files, but we believe that all confidential sources must and will be protected," but that still suggested that *Newsweek* wouldn't protect their reporters' unpublished notes.[4]

The *Times* statement Abe and I drafted was the only one that referred to the Constitution: "The *Times* intends to use all its resources to make sure no judicial action violates the constitutional guarantees of a free press and the rights of newspapers to carry on their work freely and without coercion."[5] Apparently, I was one of the few who thought there were constitutional guarantees under the First Amendment for the protection of sources and other unpublished information.

Reading these statements many years later still makes me slightly apoplectic. The business side of these major companies and their lawyers did not have a clue about the First Amendment. It seemed highly unlikely I could get them all on the same page to follow our First Amendment argument.

Prodded by Anthony Amsterdam, Caldwell's lawyer, we came up with our First Amendment position. *Times* reporters could reveal sources or notes if the government could show a particular need for a reporter's sources which could not be served by alternate means. In other words, if the reporter's information was not absolutely essential to the government, the government did not get it. To get the information, the government had to show that it was very important or "material" to the government's case, that it was "demonstrably relevant" to a defined governmental inquiry, and that the information sought was not obtainable elsewhere. This became known as the *Times* "three-part test."[6]

In Caldwell's case, this meant he would win. There were plenty of other people in the Black Panther headquarters who saw what was going on. Why pick on Caldwell? Unless the government could show what Caldwell had to say that was unique was highly important to its investigation, he was not needed.

The *Times* and Caldwell filed a joint brief in the federal district court in California. The *Times* intervened on Caldwell's behalf because it owned his notes which the government sought. In our brief, we said Caldwell would appear in the grand jury room and tell the jurors he had written the articles in question and verify the quotes in them. He would, as lawyers say, "authenticate" his articles.[7] If he was asked questions beyond "authentication," he would decline to answer unless the government could show a genuinely compelling justification.

I then began the task of trying to get the United States press on the same page as this brief. I asked the Associated Press, *Newsweek,* and CBS to file amicus curiae briefs in support of my First Amendment position.[8] This turned out to be just as daunting as I anticipated. The AP and CBS more or less followed my lead, but *Newsweek* and the ACLU went off the reservation. *Newsweek* admitted in its amicus brief it had folded for years when subpoenaed for unpublished material. It said it now realized that was wrong, no doubt prodded by the hardline stance I was taking at the *Times.* Its new position was that reporters should have absolute protection for sources and notes no matter the circumstances, a complete 180 degree turn from its previous stance.

Newsweek's position was mind-boggling. It was the very position Abe and I had rejected. We were not the fount of all wisdom, but we had taken a long time to think through our position. *Newsweek*'s lawyers never asked us what our reasoning was.

This was the beginning of a less-than-cordial relationship between the legal arm of the *Washington Post* (the owner of *Newsweek*) and the *Times* on First Amendment matters. This lack of cordiality continued through the Pentagon Papers case, where the *Post*'s lawyers took inconsistent First Amendment positions.

The ACLU took the same absolute position as *Newsweek*, which was that under no circumstances should reporters be required to testify.[9] I found this position fairly disappointing. I decided the ACLU had other fish to fry, and they were not mine.

Again, this was the beginning of a relationship where I consistently saw the First Amendment one way, and the ACLU another.[10]

*   *   *

On April 3, 1970, Caldwell won a landmark ruling from Judge Alfonso Zirpoli in the Federal District Court, a trial court of the Ninth Circuit in California. It was a front-page story. I was very excited. I had led resistance to Nixon's war on the press and I had won. Zirpoli had adopted the test we proposed for protecting reporters in even stronger terms than those we used.[11]

While Zirpoli ruled that reporters still had to physically appear in front of a grand jury, under the First Amendment, they did not have to answer questions about confidential sources or other unpublished information (e.g., notes) unless there was a "compelling and overriding national interest that cannot be served by alternative means."[12]

For me and Abe, this was an important moment. It prepared us for the Pentagon Papers case. In that case, the *Times* also had to propose a First Amendment test that would be acceptable to the courts and to our peers. Like the *Caldwell* case, the Pentagon Papers case involved an issue never decided before by the Supreme Court.

The *Times* was therefore setting precedents, with much at stake not only for itself but for the future of all writers, journalists, and press organizations. In both cases, it fell to me to be responsible for the articulation of the press' position.

After the *Caldwell* decision, the *New York Times* ran an editorial saying the decision was the best possible outcome for the public at large. "It upholds the grand jury's right to summon a journalist to testify," the *Times* declared. Yet "at the same time it upholds a journalist's right to protect private information and associations that, if revealed, could drastically curtail his ability to function under the First Amendment."[13]

Amsterdam declared that Caldwell's rights were now protected. "This is important," he said, "because it allows Mr. Caldwell to give assurances to the Black Panthers or any other persons who are willing to speak confidentially to him that he will not disclose—and can't be required to disclose—what they tell him."[14]

Then Earl Caldwell surprised us all. He was going to appeal to the Court of Appeals of the Ninth Circuit in San Francisco. How could he appeal from an enormous First Amendment victory, the first of its kind? He now said he did not want to go into the grand jury room at all.

He believed the Black Panthers would think that if he went into the grand jury room he would tell all. Since the grand jury was a secret proceeding, no one would ever know what he had said. I had several solutions. "When you get out of the grand jury room, hold a press conference and tell them what you said." "Oh," he said, "they will never believe I am telling the truth."

All of this was more than Abe and I thought the *Times* could support. We had said in our brief Caldwell would "authenticate" his article in the grand jury room.

Now he said he would not. His position threatened the institutional integrity of the *Times*. We had told the court we would stand behind our article. Caldwell said he would not.

And so we decided not to intervene in Caldwell's appeal to the Ninth Circuit. Instead we filed an amicus brief to the Ninth Circuit where we appeared as a friend of the court but not one of the parties in the case. The *Times* supported Zirpoli's impressive decision to protect sources, but not Caldwell's far-out position that he didn't have to appear at all before a grand jury. Surprisingly, Earl won his appeal in the Ninth Circuit.[15] The government immediately appealed to the Supreme Court. But why had Caldwell taken the position that he would not go into a grand jury room at all, particularly after saying in his brief that he would?

I got an answer thirty years later at a party given by former *Newsweek* reporter Kevin Buckley and his wife Gail in their New York apartment. I ran into Earl Caldwell and John Kifner, a *New York Times* investigative reporter. When they saw me they both started grinning. "Kif," as he was known, said with an impish grin, "Come into the next room so we can talk to you privately." We walked away from the throng. Kif said, "Earl wants to tell you something." Caldwell looked at me and said, "I never had any notes, I destroyed them."

I was shocked. Here the *Times* had made a major issue over protecting reporters' notes, namely Caldwell's notes, and he didn't have any. When we intervened in the case on behalf of Caldwell to protect him, we did it on the basis that we owned his notes. But there were no notes. Unwittingly, we had lied to the court. We were wise not to intervene in the Appeals Court in San Francisco on the basis of owning his notes. That would have been a lie, too.

From Caldwell's point of view, if he had destroyed the notes after he was told to bring them to court, he was in contempt of court and subject to a fine.[16] Had the government found out, all hell would have broken loose. The fact that he had destroyed his notes helped explain the incredible position he took in the case. He didn't want to get near a court or a grand jury for fear he would be found out, and so he concocted this theory that he didn't have to go to the grand jury at all.

On May 3, 1971, the Supreme Court said it would take Caldwell's case. It said it would take two other cases at the same time and would hear them together under the name of *Branzburg v. Hayes*.[17] This is how Caldwell's case became known as *Branzburg*.

Paul Branzburg was a reporter for the *Louisville Courier Journal*. He had covered some hippies manufacturing and using hashish and was subpoenaed by a grand jury in Louisville. He refused to say what he had seen.[18] Paul Pappas was a Fall River, Massachusetts reporter. He was invited to Black Panther headquarters, which he thought was going to be raided by the state police. The raid did not happen, but he was still subpoenaed and asked to testify about what he saw.

I was convinced that Earl Caldwell's case, now joined by Messrs. Branzburg and Pappas, would be one of the more important Supreme Court press cases.

It has proven to be just that. While in the popular imagination the word "Branzburg" does not have the same ring as the "Pentagon Papers," for press lawyers, when you say "Branzburg," everyone knows exactly what you mean. It's a little bit like the two Catskill comics who have told each other's jokes so often that the jokes have numbers. One comic says to the other "number one" and they both start laughing. The other says "number two," more laughter. And so "Branzburg" for press lawyers means the case where the Supreme Court decided what rights reporters have.

Since this was an extremely important case, I decided that what the press needed was a so-called "Brandeis brief." The brief is named for Louis Brandeis. Before he was a Supreme Court Justice, Brandeis wrote encyclopedic briefs for the Supreme Court on behalf of social causes. They were not legal briefs so much as they were briefs urging a change in social policy through Supreme Court action. A "Brandeis brief" suited the Caldwell situation. For all practical purposes, there were no precedents in the federal courts for making reporters cough up their sources. In a sense, the court would have to decide whether to make a new law or not. They would look to those who filed briefs to help them.

In order to create such a brief, I had to find a world-class scholar to write it and then persuade the media industry to sign it. Herb Wechsler was my first choice. He was a Columbia University scholar who had argued the Sullivan case for the *Times* in 1964. He, however, had a teaching commitment. My next choice was Paul Freund of Harvard, who many thought to be the premier constitutional scholar in the country. He said, as a matter of principle, he never took a position in an active constitutional case. He thought it would compromise his academic reputation.

I was stuck. The only thing to do was to go to the list of media lawyers I had created following Caldwell's initial victory. I used it to mail them our brief so that they might follow it. I called several, even though I didn't know them. They cheerfully admitted little knowledge of the First Amendment, nor did they know who the experts in the field were.

I had no interest in calling NBC or its lawyers. They were not on my list, since they, along with CBS, had been folding on subpoena cases. I was particularly upset because NBC had folded in a case called *Patco* over unpublished information.[19] The *Times* was also subpoenaed in that case, and I had advised a *Times* reporter not to bring the unpublished information which the subpoena required. This was a very dangerous tactic, but emboldened by the furor over the *Caldwell* case, I decided to do it anyway.

When the *Times* reporter was called to the stand, the lawyer had asked him for those notes. He said he didn't bring them with him. The judge looked at the lawyer and said, "Well, he didn't bring them with him, so it looks like you're not going to get them. So go on to the next witness."

The next witness was from NBC. He had brought his notes and forked them over. He was represented by a Cahill Gordon lawyer named Floyd Abrams. I did not know Abrams. I was not eager to call him to discuss an industry-wide brief because I couldn't understand why he had "let" NBC cave.

I called him anyway. He was the most knowledgeable press lawyer I had talked to since the *Caldwell* case began. He had a natural appreciation and knowledge of the First Amendment. I asked him if he had a recommendation for a lawyer to write the industry-wide brief. He said "Alex Bickel." Bickel had been his professor at Yale Law School and had an excellent reputation as a constitutional scholar.

I thanked him for the recommendation; however, I thought Bickel was too conservative for the *New York Times*. He had been highly critical of the liberal majority on the Supreme Court. I called some of my friends at the Bar who knew Bickel and would be sensitive to the perception that he would be too conservative. They said that I was wrong. While he was conservative, he would be an excellent choice.

I also thought that the "optics" of having a conservative, distinguished, constitutional scholar taking a novel position with respect to reporters' sources were excellent. Alex was always difficult to reach, as he would famously demonstrate in the Pentagon Papers case. I tracked him down in California and he agreed to write the brief. Several weeks later, Abrams brought him to the *Times* to meet me.

I opened the door of my office to greet them. I stuck out my hand to Floyd Abrams and said, "How do you do, Professor Bickel," and turned to Alex Bickel and said, "How are you, Mr. Abrams." Floyd looked like a distracted professor and Bickel, dressed immaculately in Wall Street garb, looked like a Wall Street lawyer. They both laughed.

From that moment on, I got along with Bickel famously. We had several meetings to write the *Branzburg* brief. We agreed immediately on the position that we would take. It would be substantially the same as the position that I had taken at the beginning of the *Caldwell* case.

We wrote the brief before asking other media companies to join us. They wanted to meet Bickel and read his brief before joining. We scheduled a meeting for Monday lunch, June 14, 1971, to meet with broadcast companies to persuade them to join. June 14 was a fateful day in newspaper history. That morning, the *Times* published the second installment of the Pentagon Papers, following publication of the first installment the day before. Alex had planned only to come to New York for a working lunch. It turned out he had to stay a lot longer than he had expected. Nixon's war against the press was about to take a new turn. Not only would he seek reporter's sources, he would now seek to censor the press with prior restraints.

CHAPTER V

DRESS REHEARSAL FOR THE PENTAGON PAPERS

Almost a year to the day before the Pentagon Papers hit the headlines, the *New York Times* went through a dress rehearsal of the proceedings that would prove a useful testing ground for our arguments. A federal judge in Baltimore, Roszel C. Thomsen, tried to stop the *New York Times* from publishing a story in its Sunday edition.[1] I told the *Times* to disobey the Judge's order. The order amounted to a "prior restraint." The First Amendment simply does not tolerate prior restraints.

When I went to the *New York Times* in 1963, I heard about the phrase "prior restraint" for the first time. *Time*'s General Counsel Gabe Perle had taken me under his wing when I arrived at age twenty-nine. He took a modicum of pleasure from throwing around publishing words he knew I probably wouldn't understand, one of which was "prior restraint."

It means simply censorship. The court orders you not to print something. You can't print it. You have been censored. You have been restrained before (prior) you've been allowed to speak. As we all know, censorship can take many forms. In the 1600s, during John Milton's time, one could not publish a book unless one received a license from the British Crown. In the 1930s and 1940s in Nazi Germany, publications had to be submitted to the Nazis for approval before publication.

The simplest form of prior restraint in America, however, is a court order not to print. This is what the Pentagon Papers case was all about. Nixon attempted to stop the *Times* from publishing classified information. Prior restraints are different from subsequent punishments. Just because you can't be censored before you publish doesn't mean that you can't subsequently be held responsible for what you publish.

The difference between the two is important. If you are censored, you can't get the words out of your mouth. But if you are free to publish, you can face penalties, if what you publish is libelous or even criminal. For publishers, the name of the game is to get everything published that is possible and then to face the consequences.

At the time of the Pentagon Papers, no federal court had ever enjoined a publication in the history of the country with prior restraint, although state courts had occasionally attempted to do so.

The newspaper industry, however, has had a peculiar history with censorship orders, that is, prior restraints. In Minnesota in the 1920s, a scurrilous newspaper, *The Saturday Press* run by Jay M. Near, had been enjoined by a state court judge. The paper was anti-semitic. The state court stopped it from publishing and put it out of business. The case is known as *Near v. Minnesota.*[2]

Near's newspaper wanted to appeal to the United States Supreme Court but didn't have the money. It could not find any supporters in the American press establishment to help. Publishers were more interested in making profits than in protecting the First Amendment.[3] Finally, Robert McCormick, the publisher of the highly conservative *Chicago Tribune*, stepped in and financed the case.[4] The Supreme Court decided in favor of the newspaper, as scurrilous as its publication might be.

It decided that the prior restraints were generally forbidden under the First Amendment regardless of whether what was printed was truthful or not.[5] It was a major First Amendment victory, one of the most important of all time. The Supreme Court said that there might be some circumstances in which a prior restraint could be granted. A court might, for example, stop a newspaper from printing the date a troop ship sails during time of war.

The Supreme Court never decided that such an exception had the force of law. It just pointed out that effectively the protection under the First Amendment for prior restraints was not absolute. There could be exceptions to it.

The only issue the court actually decided in *Near v. Minnesota* was that it could not enjoin a newspaper for libel and other slanderous language. Its comments about the exceptions to the First Amendment were what lawyers call "dictum." This is a sophisticated way of saying that statements that are not directly germane to what the court is deciding are not to be taken as binding the next time around.

The *Near* case was also relevant to the discussions I had with Abe as to whether the First Amendment was absolute. If there might be rare exceptions to prior restraints, then the First Amendment must be "qualified," not absolute. If it was not absolute, there might be a rare circumstance in which a prior restraint might be granted against a newspaper.[6]

I believed such circumstances were rare indeed. My view was that a prior restraint could not be granted against a newspaper, except in the most extraordinary circumstances, such as the publication of the secrets of a hydrogen bomb. Generally speaking, other prior restraints should be disobeyed. If the press didn't disobey prior restraints, its publishing schedule would be in the hands of the courts.

Suppose the *New York Times*, right before election day, knew that Agnew was as corrupt as he turned out to be. (After all, he resigned the vice presidency because of corruption.) His lawyer asks a court to enjoin the *Times'* story. The court agrees. The election is held. Agnew wins because the public does not know what the *Times* knows. After the election the *Times* publishes. It is too late. By censoring the *Times,* the judge has taken the ability to decide the election away from the public. Neither the *Times* nor any other part of the press should obey such an injunction, because it is clearly unconstitutional.

Indeed, when Agnew's lawyer first came to the *New York Times'* office and threatened to sue for libel, he did not run to court to stop the *Times* from printing more allegedly libelous items. He was, as most lawyers had been for many centuries, content to use "subsequent punishment." He threatened a libel suit rather than a prior restraint.

When I first arrived at the *Times*, pushed by Perle, I became fascinated with this subject, trying to prepare myself for what I would do if I ever got in a position where a judge ordered the *Times* not to print.

In theory, orders not to print are not that hard to obtain. All a lawyer has to do is go to court, allege the world is coming to an end if secrets about his client are printed and then ask the judge for an order to stop it. These orders are known as temporary restraining orders (TROs). In some circumstances, a lawyer can get a judge to sign such an order without even telling the other side.

While thinking this subject through, I had a chance to research what courts had done historically in the U.S. when asked for orders not to print. I could not find any federal courts that had ever enjoined the press.

State courts, in a few instances, had enjoined papers from publishing. In all such cases newspapers disobeyed the injunction. Uniformly, such states did not punish the papers for such disobedience. These state courts decided that prior restraints were, for all practical purposes, simply not an acceptable form of judicial behavior.[7]

I therefore resolved that if the *Times* was ever served with a prior restraint, I would not (generally speaking) cause the *Times* to obey it. I never checked my thinking with anybody at the *Times* or, if the truth must be known, anywhere else. There was no one at the *Times* who would appreciate what I was talking about. And there were no other lawyers I knew of (and I didn't know many, if any) that had given the subject that much thought. A year before the Pentagon Papers, on Saturday, June 20, 1970, I got the chance to test my theories.

I was in the middle of a tennis game in Northwest Connecticut when the club pro yelled my name across the courts. I had an urgent phone call. I rushed to the phone. It was the Washington Bureau correspondent, Fred Graham.

Fred was a Harvard Law School graduate and had been to Oxford. It is not easy to give advice to another lawyer and Fred sounded very concerned. He said that he had received an order not to print a story set for Sunday's paper, the next day.

Before he got the words out of his mouth, I said we weren't going to obey any order not to print. He said, "Slow down and get the full story." A runaway grand jury had issued a report that four members of the House of Representatives, a senator, and a former senator had been offered bribes by a contractor who was under investigation for defrauding the federal government.

The jury had "run away" because it was not following the instructions of the U.S. Attorney Stephen H. Sachs, who had convened it. The grand jury wanted to indict the senator and continue investigating one of the congressmen.[8] A grand jury doesn't really have power to indict without the cooperation of the U.S. attorney supervising them. And so what it had done was to deliver to a Judge its views on the facts of the case or, in short, a "presentment."

Fred had gotten a copy of the presentment. He said he did not get it from the grand jurors. He had gotten it from another source, probably someone in the U.S. attorney's office. With the help of other *Times* reporters, he prepared a story on the presentment, which was about to go to press. The attorney for one of the congressmen called Fred to say that the judge had ordered the *Times* not to print the story. I said, we're not going to obey that order. He asked me again, was I sure? I said I was sure.

In theory my advice could have been checked with a superior at the *Times*. In the real world there was simply no opportunity to do that. By the time I had checked, the deadline would have passed and the story would have been lost. I was dead sure this kind of order, relayed through an attorney, was so informal that it was not worthy of any respect.

Later that evening, about 7:30, Fred called again. This time I was at a cocktail party and was on my second whiskey sour. Fred had discovered that Judge Thomsen signed an order for the *Times* to appear in court the following Monday and justify why it should not be enjoined from publishing this story. The judge had told the lawyer for the defendants that the *Times* should not run the story that night (Saturday night) for Sunday's paper, but rather wait until the next Monday when he had a chance to decide whether to enjoin the *Times*.

Fred was now worried that if the *Times* went ahead and published, he would be held in contempt and the *New York Times* would also be held in contempt. Again, I told Fred the answer was the same, we are not going to obey an order not to print. He didn't want to take no for an answer but finally rang off, quite disconcerted.

On Sunday, June 21, 1971, the *Times* published his story under the headline, "6 on Capital Hill Figure in Secret Inquiry On Builder's Action in $5-Million Claim."[9] On the Monday following publication, the court was upset, to put it mildly. It called a hearing to hold the *New York Times* in contempt. I said we were not going to attend. The judge had no ability to tell us not to publish.

After thinking it over, the judge decided he hadn't issued an order after all. All he had done was to tell the defendant's lawyers that he agreed with them that the story should not be published. I thought the court's reaction was hogwash and that we were right to risk contempt since a prior restraint is so clearly forbidden by the First Amendment.

When the government threatened the *Times* with a prior restraint a year later, in the Pentagon Papers case, it was not a novel experience. I had been threatened before and prevailed. I knew of no lawyer who had a similar experience. This was understandable. Very few prior restraints against the press had ever been issued in this country and they were all issued in state courts. Before the Pentagon Papers case, no prior restraint in the history of the United States had ever been issued against the press in the federal courts.

Nixon used a prior restraint order to stop the *Times* from publishing classified information in the Pentagon Papers. But the *Times*—and other publications—had published classified information before. That fact, together with my own experience in classifying documents in the army, greatly influenced the advice I gave the *Times* about publishing the Pentagon Papers.

Out of all of those involved in the Pentagon Papers case, I was the only lawyer with intelligence training. Judge Murray Gurfein, the trial judge in New York City, was an intelligence officer in World War II. We shall see later how that background affected his views.

When I arrived at the *Times* in 1963, I had been cleared for access to "secret" classified information since 1959. I was a member of an elite intelligence unit in the Army Reserve. I held this clearance for the first seventeen months I was at the *Times* until my tour of duty ended. This experience formed my view that stamping documents "secret" has little meaning, and that leaks of highly secret information should be expected.

While the system of classified information is supposed to protect the nation's secrets, it is a broken system because information is classified indiscriminately. Consequently, it leaks, in some large part, because no one has much respect for the system. While it exists to protect the nation's secrets, it ends up attempting to protect too much trivial information. For example, for years the Marine Corps stamped the menus for its annual dinner "secret."[1]

The unit I was in, a Strategic Intelligence Research and Analysis Unit (SIRA), was located in New York City. There were three officers and four enlisted men per unit. The units were largely made up of lawyers, although there were some bankers as well. The senior lawyers were typically partners in major Wall Street law firms. The bankers were officers of banks such as Chase Manhattan and J.P. Morgan. Three of the units, including mine, were cleared to read "secret" documents. The fourth was cleared to read "top secret" documents. (Steve Rockefeller, the son of the Governor and future Vice President Nelson Rockefeller, was in this latter unit.)

We were trained as intelligence analysts and required to work on reports during the year, which we completed during our two weeks' summer training. It is fair to say that as reservists we may not have taken our duties as seriously as we would have had we been full-time intelligence analysts for the CIA.

Nonetheless, early on, I became fascinated with the classification system. More to the point, I tried to understand why I was classifying documents as I did. I wrote reports on matters of strategic importance entirely from "open sources," such as the *New York Times, Wall Street Journal,* and the like. I learned that "intelligence" was not at all what I thought it was before I joined the army.

I think this is true for most people. When you think of someone who is employed by the CIA, for example, the thought immediately springs to mind that such a person is a spy. In fact, if someone is "in intelligence" the average person thinks of him as cloak-and-dagger. This is one of the great misconceptions about intelligence. Intelligence covers the gathering of information that is useful for the defense of the country. It is true that some of this information is gathered by spies.

Such information (human intelligence or "Humint") is, however, infinitesimally small when compared with the total intelligence gathered by the United States. We learned that a substantial portion of the intelligence gathered by the United States was from "open sources."

Important intelligence, not generally available to the public, was also collected through Communications Intelligence (Comint), which included information obtained by breaking codes and listening to uncoded intercepts. We were given lectures about how Comint and code breaking was the province of the National Security Agency (NSA), located at Fort Holabird, Maryland.

Some of the senior members of the four SIRA units had been trained at Fort Holabird. But as a general rule, most of us were not. We were given general training about NSA and code breaking.

The analysis applied to strategic intelligence was no different than analyzing history. Indeed, the manual for such analysis had been written by a Yale history professor Sherman Kent, who later worked for the CIA.[2] Having once aspired to be an historian, I had read Kent's work on historiography.

While I enjoyed intelligence analysis, particularly strategic intelligence analysis, I became increasingly disenchanted by the fact that the work I did was classified "secret." Typically, we would write reports on such topics as the movement and location of immigrant groups and threats, if any, to national security. In fact, we did not write a report on such groups and threats, but it is illustrative. The reports we wrote probably remain classified to this day. I have no intention of disclosing them, even as trivial as they may be. I took my oath of secrecy seriously.

These reports were not that much different from the materials in the Pentagon Papers. While the Pentagon Papers, as will be shown, consisted of a history of decision making with respect to the Vietnam War, the methodology, particularly the use of historical analysis, was identical to what I was doing.

I dutifully stamped each of my reports "secret." The principal source of my reports was the *New York Times*. I would clip stories from the *Times* daily and keep them in a special folder in the unit's safe which was stamped "secret." Other sources I used for my report I would find by doing library research.

While not every analyst in my unit concerned himself (there were no women) with the propriety of stamping their reports "secret," it bothered me that I was doing it. How in the world could items taken from the *New York Times* be secret and not disclosed to the public when they were intended for and already read by the public?

I had concluded, in some part, the intelligence system was nonsensical. I constantly had before me the World War II cartoon of the soldier who held a pack of matches on which the word "secret" appeared on each side. It seemed to me the only justification for my use of the classification stamp was that because we were interested in a particular subject, say, the security implications of immigration, the simple fact of our concern would be of interest to an adversary.

The intelligence services justify over-classification with what is known as the mosaic theory.[3] This theory was used, perhaps for the first time, in the Pentagon Papers case. Under this theory, each bit of intelligence, although insignificant by itself, becomes significant when the whole mosaic is put together. And so while a *New York Times* article may be of little significance, when put together with other information, it provides tips to our adversaries.

I didn't think giving the name "mosaic" to this theory made it any more convincing. My bottom line was that those who controlled intelligence were hopelessly paranoid. While my sample was small and insignificant, this was nonetheless my view.

Because I was an intelligence analyst, I paid close attention to matters in the news which involved obvious leaks of classified intelligence. I was particularly fascinated by an article that appeared in *The Saturday Evening Post* on December 8, 1962, titled "In Time of Crisis,"[4] which described the decision making process of the Kennedy Administration during the Cuban missile crisis.

A U-2 spy plane photographed Russian missile emplacements in Cuba. On Monday, October 22, 1962, President Kennedy addressed the nation to say Russia planned to deliver nuclear missiles by sea to Cuba. He announced that we would place a blockade to stop Russia's ships two days later.

The blockade was successful. It turned away Soviet ships steaming towards Cuba. Nikita Khrushchev, the Soviet Premier, then sent a letter to the president effectively offering a trade. If the United States were to remove its missiles in Turkey, the Soviets would remove their missile emplacements in Cuba. The deal was struck. The crisis ended.

Six weeks after the crisis, *The Saturday Evening Post* reported the details of the decision making process. The President convened an inner circle of advisors: Dean Rusk, the Secretary of State; Robert McNamara, the Secretary of Defense;

S. Douglas Dillon, the Secretary of the Treasury; Robert Kennedy, the Attorney General; Maxwell Taylor, Chairman of the Joint Chiefs of Staff; McGeorge Bundy, National Security Advisor; and Ted Sorensen, the president's speechwriter and close friend.

According to the *Post*, they concluded "that the blockade was only a first step and that if Soviet missiles were not removed 'further action' would be taken."[5] This action might be a total blockade, air strikes against missile bases, or even an invasion of Cuba. When Khrushchev made his offer of a trade, the *Post* reported that Secretary of State Dean Rusk said famously, "We're eyeball to eyeball, and I think the other fellow just blinked."[6]

The article consisted almost entirely of classified material. It included an in-house paper written by CIA Director John McCone. It included reports of previously undisclosed phone calls and evaluations of the strengths and weaknesses of the Russians from a strategic viewpoint.

It communicated what amounted to an intelligence estimate of the Russians. I was fascinated by the article, which I read on the 86th Street crosstown bus on my way to work at my law firm. I was stunned at what I read. I couldn't understand how all this information could be leaked to the public when I was stamping my inconsequential intelligence reports "secret" so they could not be leaked to the public.

In April 1961, eighteen months before the Cuban missile crisis, the *New York Times* ran a front page story on a possible invasion of Cuba at its Bay of Pigs. It said that the U.S. was training Cubans in Florida to make an invasion against Cuba and told how many Cubans were being trained, what their equipment was and other matters of military interest.[7]

The article said that 5,000–6,000 troops were ready to storm the beaches but speculated whether they would be wiped out no matter how much training they had. The article closed by saying "The Columbia Broadcasting System issued a report last night saying that there were 'unmistakable signs' that plans for an invasion of Cuba were in their final stages."[8]

On the following Sunday, in "The News Of The Week In Review" section, the *Times* printed an article titled "Cuban Alarums."[9] This article stated that "from a score of points around the Caribbean last week came reports, statements, and rumors: the invasion of Cuba by anti-Castro exiles might be launched at any time. The Cuban people, Premier Castro said Friday, were impatient to have it come."[10] The Bay of Pigs invasion, which began on April 17, 1961, was a disaster. It was one of Kennedy's worst mistakes.

It turned out later, once I got to the *New York Times*, that each of these stories had a particular provenance and were part of *New York Times* history. I also learned they were not the only notorious stories the *Times* had published based on classified information. Scotty Reston had won the Pulitzer Prize for one such story and received further national acclaim for another.

The first was a story on the Dumbarton Oaks Conference in 1944. This conference set up the structure for the United Nations. A former clerk at the *Times*, Chen Yi, leaked to Reston complete texts of proposals for the conference from the US, British, Chinese, and Soviet delegations. Yi had become a member of the Chinese delegation and thought highly of Reston. The *Times* published these proposals in installments to the great ire of the governments at the conference, and Reston won the Pulitzer Prize.[11]

In 1953 Reston got hold of the Yalta Papers, which had been classified since the Yalta conference in 1945. The *Times* published all of the report, totaling more than 200,000 words. The report took fifty pages in the paper. Within the halls of the *Times*, the Bay of Pigs story was particularly famous. When the story was shown to publisher Orvil Dryfoos, he was worried. He thought the story might cause the invasion to fail. If it did, the *Times* would be blamed. He was particularly concerned the story said the invasion was "imminent." He asked the editors to cut the last paragraph which contained the word "imminent." They substituted a quote from CBS News which said there were "unmistakable signs" for an invasion of Cuba.

At first, President Kennedy was very upset with the *New York Times*. At a meeting on April 27, 1961, before the American Society of Newspaper Editors, he told them it was insufficient to ask only whether a story was newsworthy. "I suggest …that you add the question: 'is it in the interest of national security?'"[12] He warned that newspapers were giving great comfort to the enemy publishing information which could not otherwise be acquired unless by "theft, bribery or espionage."[13]

He went on to say that newspapers had published "details of this nation's covert preparations to counter the enemy's covert operations that were available to every newspaper reader, friend and foe alike…[and] that the size, the strength, the location and the nature of our forces and weapons, and our plans and strategy for their use, have all been pinpointed in the press and other news media to a degree sufficient to satisfy any foreign power."[14]

A year later, however, Kennedy changed his tune. On September 13, 1962, in a conversation with Orvil Dryfoos at the White House, Kennedy remarked on the Bay of Pigs story, "I wish you had run everything on Cuba."[15] If the *Times* had published everything, perhaps the U.S. would not have invaded, saving lives and saving Kennedy immense political embarrassment.

The Cuban missile crisis story also had a particular *Times* twist. The day before President Kennedy went on television to tell the nation he was going to blockade Cuba, he called Reston. Kennedy had heard that the *Times* knew that the Russians had placed nuclear emplacements on Cuba. He said that he understood Reston had been talking to National Security Advisor McGeorge Bundy. He knew from Reston's line of questioning that the *Times* knew the critical fact that emplacements for Russian missiles were in Cuba.

As Reston later said, "The president told me that he was going on television on Monday evening to report to the American people. He said that if we published the news about the missiles, Khrushchev could actually give him an ultimatum before he went on the air...I told the President I would report to my office in New York and, if my advice were asked, I would recommend that we not publish."[16] Kennedy then telephoned Dryfoos in New York and repeated the request. Dryfoos talked with Reston and others on the staff. The story was not published.

It is a mistake to think that newspapers publish everything they're told. Newspapers have editors primarily to decide what should and what should not be published. Many stories end up getting shelved. This is because they're inappropriate for publication for one reason or another. The reasons may stretch from grammatical changes to matters of greater importance such as the two examples seen in the *Times'* handling of the Bay of Pigs and Cuban missile crisis.

Editors with Washington experience are required to make judgments on material which impacts national security and may be classified. What both the Bay of Pigs and Cuban missile crisis examples show is that when there is an issue of imminent danger to national security, publication should be weighed carefully.

In both of these stories, the *Times* censored itself. The issue was the same in each. When the *Times* determined there was imminent danger to national security, it did not publish. Whether this was correct or not was debated internally for many years to come.

Kennedy's remark about the Bay of Pigs could be taken as evidence that the *Times* made a mistake taking out "imminent." On reflection, he may have concluded the *Times* story did not damage national security, despite what he had rather testily told the American Society of Newspaper Editors.

It's hard to see why such publication would have damaged national security. Fidel Castro knew the invasion was coming. As the head of a small Caribbean island, his ability to retaliate and damage the United States was nonexistent.

The Cuban missile crisis might have been a different case. A misstep in the handling of this crisis could have precipitated a nuclear holocaust. Russia did have the capacity to destroy the US. As President Kennedy said at the time, the moment could "mark a turning point in the history of relations between East and West."[17]

In any event, both of these examples were different from the story the *Saturday Evening Post* published. That was history. It posed no imminent danger to the United States. While these examples of past actions by the *Times* and the *Saturday Evening Post* rattled around in my head for many years, it was not until after returning to New York, following the Gridiron dinner, that I was able to pin down when a newspaper could legally publish classified information, or information affecting national security and when, if ever, it could not publish that information.

CHAPTER VII

CAN CLASSIFIED INFORMATION BE PUBLISHED LEGALLY?

The Gridiron dinner was my first glimpse of the huge legal case that was to come. When I returned to New York on Monday, March 15, the first thing I did was to consider the legal consequences of publishing classified information. What I discovered astounded me. There seemed to be no law covering such publication.

Max Frankel had told me the *Times* had "documents relating to the Vietnam War." I did not know what was in those documents. In fact, I did not know anything about them, except that they were classified. I discussed the matter with Joe Aman, a young lawyer who worked with me. He was the principal researcher in my law office of four. I wanted to know what the law was with respect to publishing classified documents. There must be a simple legal statement somewhere which said "classified documents cannot be published" or "classified documents can be published only under the following circumstances."

This was a new issue for me. I had been the *Times'* chief counsel for eight years and had run across every conceivable publishing problem, but never once had the issue of publishing classified information come up. I knew from the *Saturday Evening Post* article on the Cuban missile crisis and the *Times* articles on the Bay of Pigs invasion that classified information had been published. But I didn't know how the press published it legally.

Joe came back the next day and said he couldn't find anything. I told him that could not be possible. More loudly than needed, I said, "I can't believe there are no laws covering the publication of classified information." I was irritated that he had not done a better job. Sharply, I told him to go look again.

Several days later he came back with the same answer. There was nothing. There had never been a court decision concerning the publication of classified information. He did, however, think the government could possibly assert, although erroneously, that the Espionage Act,[1] an Executive Order 10501, authorizing classification[2] and a federal law § 641 that made theft of government property a crime, might apply.[3]

Of the three sources of law brought to me by Joe, the Espionage Act became famous in the Pentagon Papers case. It was the law on which the government brought suit. I immediately focused on this Act. I had heard of it once before. Earlier in the year, antiwar activists had broken into FBI files in Media, Pennsylvania. Attorney General John Mitchell had warned the press not to publish the files. If they did they would face prosecution under the Espionage Act. Mitchell's remarks were reported near the back page. No one took him seriously. I never gave it a second thought.[4]

Section 793(e) of the Espionage Act states, "Whoever having unauthorized possession of, access to, or control over any document...relating to the national defense ...which information the possessor has reason to believe could be used to the injury of the United States...willfully communicates, delivers, [or] transmits ... the same to any person not entitled to receive it...shall be fined under this title or be imprisoned not more than ten years or both."

I immediately focused on the fact the action it penalized was "communication," not "publication." I had seen laws somewhat like this before when advising the *New York Times*. If lawmakers wanted to control publication they had to say so specifically.

For example, every publication in New York State is required to publish a list of its officers and directors. The law says that, particularly. It does not say every publication in New York must communicate to the public who its officers and directors are.[5] Communication has much larger meaning than publication. It includes conversations, broadcasting and the like. One only publishes when one uses a printing press—at least in those days.

Furthermore, the Espionage Act was a criminal law that punished people *after* a crime was committed. It was hard to see how this law could be used to stop publication which takes place before the crime (of communication) is committed. Lawyers are fond of saying "you can't enjoin a crime." One has to wait for the crime to be committed before taking legal action.

The *Times* did not intend to commit the crime of espionage. It was trying to inform the public. Espionage required delivery of secret information to an enemy with the intent to harm the United States. The *Times* did not intend to harm anyone with its publication.

Generally speaking then, because the law was written to apply to espionage and not publication, it seemed to be too vague to fit our situation. When a law is vague, it is unconstitutional. I thought the Espionage Act was unconstitutional.[6]

Joe had, however, found a regulation that covered classification. This regulation was first issued by President Dwight D. Eisenhower. It authorized documents to be stamped "top secret," "secret," "confidential." This regulation explained why I had stamped copies of the *New York Times* "secret."[7] It did not explain what to do if documents were misstamped.

Joe said he could not find any action Congress had ever taken to authorize such classification. Since Congress had taken no action, a president's order authorizing classification applied to people working for the president and executive branch. It did not apply to newspapers.[8]

This regulation justified, for example, the classification I stamped documents with when I was in Army intelligence. But the regulation had no power beyond that because Congress, which acts on behalf of the people, had not passed any laws covering classification.

So the bottom line was that a classified document had no legal impact at all on newspapers. All that classification meant was that the government thought a particular piece of information was secret as far as it was concerned. But if someone got hold of it, such as the *New York Times* or a member of the public, there was nothing the government could do about it. The government could discipline a leaker, but not a leakee, like the *Times*.

In a sense I was astonished at this conclusion. It was similar to the law for reporter's privilege. There was no law there either, other than the First Amendment. At least I now understood how classified information had been published in the past and why the government took no action.

I thought the reason no law had been passed was probably because Congress did not want to violate the First Amendment. This turned out to be true. I did not, however, know it at the time, because I did not have the legislative history of the Espionage Act available to me. It turned out Congress was quite careful not to use the word "publish" in the Espionage Act. It chose communication not publication to cover espionage.

I did note there was one particular part of the Espionage Act that did punish publication of codes, Section 798.[9] I was struck by the fact that Congress had a specific rule against publication of codes (and atomic secrets[10]). I could understand that. Publication of codes and atomic secrets might possibly not be protected by the First Amendment. While the Espionage Act covered crimes, I still was more concerned with prior restraints. It did not seem possible a criminal law could authorize prior restraints.

I remembered that scarcely eight months ago I had advised Fred Graham (and the *Times*) to publish a story about a runaway jury, even though Fred and I believed a judge had ordered the *Times* not to do so.

Orders not to print, i.e., prior restraints, in my view, were not permissible under the Constitution unless they covered some extraordinary event such as publishing the secrets of the hydrogen bomb. This was because *Near v. Minnesota*, the case the *Chicago Tribune* paid for involving a state court's attempt to issue a prior restraint, decided the First Amendment generally forbids the issuance of prior restraints.

I returned to this analysis many times following the Gridiron dinner. I continued to reach the same conclusion that there was no law that applied, other than the First Amendment. In that period, I had not heard one word from Frankel or anyone else as to what was up, if anything. I still had no idea what it was Frankel wanted me to review. I thought perhaps he had received classified papers of some sort from Vietnam protestors who had broken into the State Department.

I reported to Punch Sulzberger, the paper's publisher, and Harding Bancroft, the paper's executive vice president, but I did not tell either of them what I had been told by Frankel. In the first place, I did not know enough about what Frankel possessed to communicate anything. In the second place, it was my practice not to tell anyone in management about publication matters. This was an ancient tradition at the *Times*. No one was entitled to meddle in what the *Times* published except its editors.

I was a lawyer for those editors. I would lose their confidence if I squealed to management every time I knew what they were up to. It was an obvious conflict of interest since I also represented management. But I handled it as best I could.

If, in fact, some extraordinary matter came up with the newsroom, I would feel obliged to tell management. None had ever previously come to my attention, however. My view generally was that the editor of the *Times* could tell the publisher of the paper which stories raised legal problems which I could then confirm.

Bancroft had hired me in 1963 with the implicit promise I would succeed him as the sole executive vice president of the *New York Times*, in other words, as the *New York Times'* CEO. But there had been a management shakeup in 1970 and Harding's job was split into three parts with two other executives taking over his operating responsibilities.

That left Harding with time on his hands and he spent a great deal of it arguing with me about my structure for a major acquisition by the *Times* which was to be completed on March 24, 1971, eleven days after the Gridiron dinner. It was the acquisition of Cowles Communications, the company that published *Look* magazine and owned TV stations, magazines, and book publishing entities. This acquisition was then the panacea for the *New York Times'* financial woes.

Harding was a former lawyer, as was Amory Bradford, his predecessor, who had been general manager of the *Times*. Each had worked at major Wall Street law firms before coming to the *Times* to assist the Sulzberger family in running the company. My background was identical to theirs, but I wanted to continue to practice law. They did not. Harding had asked me to set up a legal department, which I did with the title "general attorney."

Bancroft had nothing but the best interests of the *Times* at heart. He had worked at the State Department and the United Nations. He had been general counsel to the International Labor Organization headquartered in Geneva. Generally, he was a great person to work for. He was, however, like many aging lawyers, no longer interested in doing the grunt work to make himself knowledgeable about the law. He would analyze legal questions such as an acquisition, but without any specific knowledge. For example, when he queried the structure for the Cowles acquisition he was told the reason for the structure was because the Treasury Department demanded it.

He responded, "the Treasury can't be right on that one." This approach to legal questions put him at a great disadvantage in making appropriate judgments for the *New York Times* in the Pentagon Papers case. But at this stage of the story the Pentagon Papers had not yet reached the *New York Times*.

On April 21, almost six weeks after the Gridiron dinner, I walked back to the *Times* with Abe Rosenthal from a stockholders meeting. Abe said, "Have you heard about the papers we have?" I replied, yes, I had them briefly described to me, but I did not know what they were all about. He asked, "Would you like to come to a meeting we are having tomorrow to discuss them?" I said, "Yes, of course." I spent the afternoon reviewing the Espionage Act to prepare.

The next morning, I met Neil Sheehan for the first time in Reston's office. We were joined by Abe Rosenthal, Jim Greenfield the foreign editor, Turner Catledge, the former *Times* editor-in-chief in town for the stockholders meeting, Sydney Gruson, Punch's assistant, Gerry Gold, a New York editor assigned to the project, Bob Phelps, a D.C. editor, and Peter Milonas, the administrative editor.

This meeting took place at the height of the Vietnam War. A week-long anti-war protest was taking place at that time in Washington D.C. involving thousands of Vietnam veterans.[11] At the same time there was a 10,000 person peace march in Providence, Rhode Island.[12] In the two days before our meeting, the *Times* had published forty-two stories on Vietnam.[13]

In the meantime, Nixon's war against the press continued unabated. Spiro Agnew viciously attacked the press the month before over the CBS documentary *The Selling of the Pentagon*. A day before the meeting, CBS President Frank Stanton had told Congressman Harley Staggers he would not give Congress outtakes for the TV show.[14] Two weeks after our meeting, the Supreme Court decided to take the appeal in *Branzburg* and set argument for February 23, 1972.[15]

Sheehan was a serious and driven Harvard graduate. He reminded me of the Harvard faculty children I had grown up with who took their philosophical beliefs very seriously. He was very much opposed to the Vietnam War, and had written a *New York Times Book Review* article in which he had questioned whether those responsible for the war were war criminals. What he was about to say was shocking.

He told us the government knew the Vietnam War was built on a tissue of lies. It had prepared a secret history, which showed the government had lied about the war consistently since the 1940s. This history later became known as the Pentagon Papers. It was classified "top secret sensitive."

Neil first described how he got the documents. He said a "source" had made them available to him. He did not identify the source, and no one asked him to. The source had made photocopies of the papers and had shown them to him. He had been examining them for some time and decided to xerox the xeroxes, so that he had a copy. He had done this, unknown to his source. I asked whether anti-Vietnam protestors had broken into the Pentagon and stolen the history. He said "no."[16]

Neil's presentation was riveting. Unlike other *Times* meetings I had been to, there were no interruptions, no arguing back and forth. Neil held the floor for two and a half hours. Scotty Reston sat at his desk smoking his pipe.

He went into a long story of how Secretary of Defense Robert McNamara had gathered a group of people, all of them with scholarly achievements, some of them academics and some within the Defense Department itself, to compile a complete history of the United States involvement in Vietnam from 1945–1967.[17] He said the history was massive. It consisted of 7,000 pages. It would take some time to turn the study into publishable stories. The study consisted of two parts. The first was the history itself and the second consisted of verbatim documents attached to each of the chapters. He said there was a chapter about the ongoing peace negotiations, which he did not have. He was glad he did not; if he had, he would not have published it.

Neil went into some detail about his reasons for publication. The government had lied about the origins of the war, it had lied about the assassination of Ngô Đình Diệm (the President of South Vietnam); Johnson had lied that he did not seek a wider war when he ran for President in 1964, and this was just the tip of the iceberg. He wanted to publish the articles as a series. The documents would be reprinted verbatim where relevant.

I learned later that the Pentagon Papers did not reach the newspaper's offices in New York until April 17, a few days before our meeting. The source of the documents was, of course, Daniel Ellsberg. Some of us did not know that for sure until many years later. To this day, no one at the *Times* has directly told me Ellsberg was the source.

Ellsberg worked for the Rand Corporation, a think tank that provided strategic advice to the United States government, and still does. It had a copy of the Pentagon Papers to enable its analysts, such as Ellsberg, to read and use as a source for the advice the Corporation gave to the United States government on the Vietnam War. McNamara never said publicly why he commissioned the study. I have always assumed that he wanted the history prepared in order to learn about our mistakes in Vietnam.

He asked Leslie Gelb, who was then Director of Policy Planning and Arms Control for International Security Affairs at the Department of Defense, and who had a PhD in history, to run the project. McNamara initially asked him for answers to 100 questions about the war in Indochina, e.g., "Did the U.S. violate the 1954 Geneva Accords on Indochina?"[18] Later, Gelb got McNamara to approve transforming the answers to the questions into a forty-seven volume history of decision-making by the U.S. in Vietnam from 1945 to 1967.

Ellsberg had, in fact, worked on the project when he was at the Department of Defense and had written one of the chapters. He had copied the papers when he was at Rand with his colleague Tony Russo. Ellsberg first took them to Senators J. William Fulbright of Arkansas[19] and George McGovern of South Dakota[20] so that they would read them into the congressional record. Fulbright asked Melvin Laird, Secretary of Defense, to release the papers, but he refused.[21] Both senators, despite initially showing interest, ultimately declined to release Ellsberg's copies publicly.

Frustrated by this experience and convinced that the Pentagon Papers showed the duplicity of the United States government with respect to the Vietnam War, Ellsberg decided to approach Neil Sheehan of the *Times*.

Ellsberg knew Sheehan from the time Ellsberg was working for the Defense Department in earlier years: he had leaked one of its documents to Sheehan. In January 1968, Sheehan wrote a story based on another leaked document, although not from Ellsberg, that said that General William Westmorland, then the commander of U.S. forces in Vietnam, was about to request an additional 206,000 troops for Vietnam. The story "opened [his] eyes" to the idea that "leaking could be a patriotic and constructive act."[22]

Ellsberg subsequently sought out and leaked another document to Sheehan about how General Westmoreland had underestimated North Vietnamese troop strength by as many as 100,000 troops in the lead up to the Tet Offensive. The *Times* ran the story without naming Ellsberg as the source, and it caused a great stir.[23]

Ellsberg had first told Sheehan about the Pentagon Papers several weeks before the Gridiron Club dinner. He did not show Sheehan the Pentagon Papers themselves until the day before the dinner. Ellsberg kept his copy of the papers at a friend's apartment in Cambridge, Massachusetts, where Ellsberg lived and worked. He invited Sheehan to Cambridge to take notes on the Papers, but he did not allow Sheehan to have or make a copy for himself.

Ellsberg left Cambridge for a weekend at the end of March. Sheehan, who already had a key to the apartment in which the papers were stored, copied the entire study while Ellsberg was out of town. According to Ellsberg, Sheehan copied the papers without his permission.[24]

Sheehan took the copy of the papers back to Washington. There, he and Gerald Gold, a *New York Times* editor, started reading them at the Jefferson Hilton Hotel. Gold did not permanently bring copies to New York until shortly before the meeting of April 21.[25] The day after the meeting, Gold took the copies to the New York Hilton where the *Times* set up a secret headquarters. James Greenfield, the foreign editor, was put in charge of the project. E.W. Kenworthy, Fox Butterfield, and Hedrick Smith joined the team there as well.

When it came time to express my legal views at the meeting, I said I was concerned that Nixon and Mitchell would try to enjoin publication. I said I wanted to know more about a law "I found" called the Espionage Act, which I briefly referenced. I therefore asked if it would be possible to publish the article all at once and not in installments. I asked how important it was to publish the documents as well as the text.[26]

I did not get direct answers to these questions. Sheehan said the documents were important and Frankel said he wanted to think about my suggestions. I had made these comments to get those present to start thinking about the risks of publication. My hope was to get them to adjust their expectations through a series of meetings focused on my suggestion to publish all at once. I could then bring the package to Punch Sulzberger and Harding Bancroft in a way they would approve.[27] I never had that chance.

CHAPTER VIII
A STRATEGY TO PUBLISH

Following the meeting with Sheehan, I knew I was on top of an explosive situation. If I called Bancroft immediately to say the *Times* had the Pentagon Papers, he would be very upset. He would want to know more about them than I knew. I had yet to see them. I was promised a set the next day.

Such a call would also breach my relationship with those present at the meeting. I had told them I would continue discussions on how to publish legally. The greater risk, however, was that Bancroft would insist I call Louis Loeb, the distinguished former general counsel of the *New York Times* and partner of Lord, Day & Lord, the *Times'* outside counsel. If I did this, I knew Loeb would go ballistic. The risk would be that he would blow up the whole project.

Louis Loeb was a legendary figure in New York City's legal circles.[1] He was everyone's favorite after dinner speaker. Primed with a few martinis, he would tell more jokes than you could shake a finger at. His peers at the New York Bar had elected him to the Presidency of the New York City Bar Association.[2] This was not any old bar association. It had the greatest minds of the legal profession in its membership. Its reports commanded national attention. Many thought it was the most important bar association in the country.

Loeb had been a partner at Cook, Latham & Lehman, which used to represent the *New York Times*. Cook was Louis' father-in-law. When Cook died, Louis moved the *Times* business to Lord, Day & Lord, then one of New York's largest firms with a sterling reputation. It was thought of as a "white shoe" firm. One friend asked me jovially whether I had to wear a tuxedo to work. It also included Carolyn Agger, the cigar smoking wife of the Supreme Court Justice Abe Fortas.[3]

Loeb and his father-in-law had represented the *Times* for over fifty years. He was an important voice in its affairs. He was particularly well respected by all for his fairness in dealing with the white-collar union at the *Times*, the Newspaper Guild. As with most lawyers for press companies, his experience centered on the business activities of the *Times*. He had no experience in dealing with First Amendment matters.

For fifty years the *Times* would look to Louis Loeb and his firm for advice in any crisis. It was a different legal world then. Today, law firms are significantly larger and clients look to a variety of firms for advice. Then, an established organization such as the *Times* had only one set of lawyers, and that was that. The *Times* followed the advice of its lawyers, and to do otherwise was unthinkable.

Herbert Brownell was Lord, Day & Lord's most prominent partner. He too had been a president of the New York City Bar Association. He was the former Attorney General of the United States under Eisenhower and a prominent Republican, who knew all the members of the Nixon Administration, particularly John Mitchell, Nixon's Attorney General, and the president himself. Both Brownell and Loeb were centrist Republicans and played major roles in the Pentagon Papers case.[4]

I was given enormous responsibility for a young lawyer. It was, by today's standards, a small firm, which made it easier to stand out. In retrospect, I was on my way to becoming a partner quickly and had my own clients when I was only two years out of law school, probably unheard of today.

Herbert Brownell, from time to time, gave me exclusive responsibility for some of his clients. We had an excellent relationship. He was the only lawyer who worked at Lord, Day & Lord behind a closed door. His office had a huge Attorney General flag which hung from a pole next to his desk to impress clients (and me, to tell the truth).

Its litigation group was small with only five partners. It had represented the *Times* in the famous libel case *Sullivan v. The New York Times*. When that case reached the Supreme Court, as noted earlier, the *Times* hired Herb Wechsler of Columbia University Law School to prepare a First Amendment argument. I had worked on this case as a young lawyer. In fact, I worked on all the *New York Times* cases ever to reach the Supreme Court (a total of four).

My career plan was to work for four years at Lord, Day & Lord and then go into public service. Since I was not necessarily a fan of Wall Street, I did not think I would like working at a Wall Street law firm. The fact of the matter is, I loved it. I had particularly enjoyed working with Ferdinand Eberstadt, who had an investment firm, F. Eberstadt & Co. He, as noted earlier, had been a partner of the law firm Cahill Gordon and the investment powerhouse of Dillon, Read.

One day all his partners, angry at him for allegedly taking more than his share, walked out of his firm. I represented him with respect to the firm's dissolution and Cahill Gordon represented the departing bankers. Eberstadt enjoyed my company, and the two of us would lunch together in his private dining room and watch the ticker tape listing the changing share prices.

In 1962–63, the *New York Times* endured a terrible strike by the International Typographers Union. The *Times'* president and publisher, Orvil Dryfoos, died and Punch Sulzberger replaced him. Amory Bradford, who had been running the company, resigned at Punch's behest and Harding Bancroft took Bradford's place. The *Times*, realizing it had no young blood coming through the ranks, asked

Lord, Day & Lord if they could suggest a young lawyer to take on legal and other responsibilities at the *Times*. That was me.

I set up their legal department. Since I had been apparently on a fast track at the firm, I did not want to be a "house" counsel. That is a pejorative term for a lawyer who takes responsibility for giving legal advice but relies on outside counsel to do the real legal work. I tried to do all the legal work myself that I possibly could so that I would be responsible for it.

I knew at some time I would have to ask Lord, Day & Lord for an opinion on the Pentagon Papers. This was because the fate of the newspaper could possibly rely on the outcome of a decision to publish. The newspaper needed an opinion from a major firm on which it could rely to justify any decision to publish. But I had not reached an appropriate point in my discussions with Abe Rosenthal to ask Lord, Day & Lord for an opinion. More to the point, I knew what Louis Loeb's reaction would be. A moderate Republican, he would be highly offended and angry if the *New York Times* published classified information.

While I was pondering my next move, Bancroft asked me late in the day whether I had heard anything about the secret newsroom project. Reston, in the afternoon, had called Punch about the meeting with Sheehan that morning. Punch, in turn, asked Bancroft to check into it.

I told Bancroft I had attended that meeting. I explained that the Pentagon Papers were a history of the Vietnam War and they were classified "top secret sensitive." Before I could explain my preliminary legal view, he became visibly upset and said the Pentagon Papers could be the most important event in the history of the *Times*. It was particularly "bothersome" (his words), if the *Times* published top secret documents or any "JCS" (Joint Chief of Staff) papers.[5]

In his State Department career, Harding had been cleared for access to classified documents. He was familiar with the material the Joint Chiefs looked at. There wasn't any such material in the Pentagon Papers, but Harding was concerned there might be.

I told him my view was that the objective of the *Times* should be to figure out how to publish the Pentagon Papers and I should lead the effort to do that. In fact, I had been working on the project for weeks. He disagreed. He did not think it was an appropriate objective. The future of the whole institution depended on whether the proper decision was made. He, therefore, was going to call Louis right away, in my presence. I was highly offended, since I was the general counsel in my eighth year in that position. He was supposed to be running the company; I, its legal affairs.

"If you put the question to Lord, Day & Lord that way," I said, "there is only one way they are going to answer. They are going to say 'don't publish' and you are going to polarize the whole issue and make things worse. I will never be able to work with the reporters and editors to structure the publication." Harding kept on insisting that we needed Lord, Day & Lord's advice. I then suggested we ask a constitutional lawyer such as Telford Taylor, a neighbor and a famous international lawyer who represented the United States at the Nuremburg trials for WWII crimes. Taylor taught Constitutional law at Columbia University and was a regular practicing lawyer (unlike Wechsler). Harding said "no."[6]

I said, "Okay, if we have to ask Lord, Day & Lord's views now, will you let me do it my way? I don't want to call Loeb." I wanted to call Art Hooker, a younger (age forty-five) partner and a friend of mine (who was a Democrat). I thought if I worked with him, perhaps Lord, Day & Lord and I could come up with a mutual opinion. Harding said, "I don't care how you do it, as long as you do it."

At 6:00 p.m. I called Hooker. I told him about the papers and suggested the two of us should work together, because I was sure there was a way to get them published. If it got into Louis' hands before we agreed on the law, we would all be finished. I then explained to Hooker what I thought was the law. I said I wanted Lord, Day & Lord to prepare a memorandum on all the legal issues, particularly the legislative history of the Espionage Act. I wanted to know what Congress had in mind when it passed 793(e). Did Congress intend it to apply to newspapers, or not? Perhaps he could find some long-haired guys to do the research.

I told him I had not seen a copy of the Papers yet, but I would the following day. If he wanted a copy he should call me. I had spent six weeks wondering what the *Times* had, and the next day I found out.

CHAPTER IX
A FIRST LOOK AT THE PENTAGON PAPERS

The next day, the Papers were wheeled into my office in several supermarket carts. They filled every nook and cranny. I reached for Volume One and I was surprised by what I read. Immediately, I began to focus on ways to publish the Papers without legal risk.

My philosophy as a publishing lawyer was that anything could be published. I had always found that if you took a word out here and there, shifted a paragraph here and there, anything was possible. I developed this point of view over eight years of representing reporters and editors who were principally concerned about libel.

In 1964, a year after I arrived at the *Times*, the Supreme Court decided the *Sullivan* case. Sullivan had won a half-million dollar verdict against the *Times*. The *Times* then was making little money and payment of this verdict, along with other million-dollar claims pending at the same time, would have bankrupted it. The *Times* appealed to the Supreme Court and won.

Reporters and editors were particularly eager to have me check what they wrote so that they wouldn't end up in another *Sullivan* case. I was very busy. I realized the easiest way to deal with troublesome articles was merely to say they couldn't be published and the problem would go away. Don't publish the Pentagon Papers, and everyone sleeps well at night. However, to me this seemed an inexcusable way to carry out my job. My natural inclination was to publish. This approach won me a large following in the newsroom with reporters and editors. In part, this was a reason I had been invited to the meeting with Sheehan the day before. Being a good lawyer for the press requires more than knowing libel law. It is equally important to have a great news sense, an understanding of context, and what I like to call the "anger factor."

If a story with borderline libel made someone angry, I would try to find a way to rephrase it to make it sound more diplomatic. Technically, the story as re-done may have been just as libelous, but in the real world, no one was going to sue. I had removed the anger from the equation. Most lawyers did not practice law this way, but I did. I always tried to use common sense and be practical. To be good at my job required the skills found in a good editor who placed a story in context and related it to current events.

I had to make a judgment on how publication of the Papers would be received by the public in the middle of the Vietnam War. I had to place the Papers in the context of the public debate about the war and I had to decide how newsworthy the Papers were and how the government and juries would react. All of these decisions contributed to my final judgment.

At the time, the war was highly controversial and the *Times'* coverage was sometimes equally controversial. In 1966 and '67, Harrison Salisbury had gone to North Vietnam to report on the impact of U.S. bombing of North Vietnam. The *Times* and Salisbury were criticized in statements by the State Department and Defense Department, which insinuated that Salisbury and the *Times* were traitors.[1] My own view of the war was anodyne.

While I was disturbed by the war, I would not have joined a protest against it. First, I would not have been permitted to do that as a *New York Times* employee. Secondly, I did not have a moment to breathe and with the heavy responsibilities of my job and a young family, I simply had not had the time to form an opinion. During the Iraq War, my passion was greater. I marched against that war.

I was not uninformed about the war, however. I watched President John F. Kennedy address the nation in 1961 to warn about the spread of communism in Southeast Asia. He told the nation he was considering sending non-combat troops to Laos to help that government fight its own communist rebels, who were being supported by the Soviets and North Vietnam.[2]

I had followed the escalation of the war. Under President Johnson, the number of combat troops in Vietnam had swollen to 500,000, even though the United States had never declared war against North Vietnam. Assistant Attorney General Nicholas deB. Katzenbach had fashioned a paper, the Tonkin Gulf Resolution, which he called "the functional equivalent of the declaration of war."[3]

The Johnson Administration reported to Congress that North Vietnamese vessels had attacked U.S. ships in the Gulf of Tonkin. He said U.S. ships had returned fire. Katzenbach asked Congress for authorization to respond militarily to North Vietnam's aggressive action. This, of course, was not the same as asking Congress to declare war on North Vietnam. President Johnson probably did not have the support of the country for that.[4]

Katzenbach was one of my professors in law school. I always thought his defense of the legality of war by relying on the Tonkin Gulf Resolution was slippery and wrong. This specific incident came into focus later when I reviewed Sheehan's articles before they were published. The war was sold to the American public on the back of George Kennan's domino theory. This posited that South Vietnam was merely one domino on the communist play board; if South Vietnam fell to the communists it would push over Cambodia, Thailand, and all of Southeast Asia. The North Vietnamese therefore had to be stopped at all costs.

The young men who were drafted to fight this war were never persuaded by this theory. There was huge unrest, and the 1960s was a decade of popular discontent. This unrest spilled over into the early 1970s. This was the context in which I had to evaluate the publication of the Papers.

I looked at the forty-seven volumes stacked in my office and plunged into Volume One. I was surprised to discover it read like the history I studied in college, where I specialized in American history. I had always assumed that North Vietnam had broken the relevant agreements that partitioned the country and was entirely at fault. I accepted this assumption without giving it much thought. It did not seem inconceivable to me that North Vietnam was part of the evil empire. If South Vietnam fell, so would the rest of Southeast Asia.

According to Volume One, North Vietnam had been promised twice there would be elections for all of Vietnam so it could determine its own future.[5] While Vietnam was a French colony, the French had made an agreement in 1946 for such elections and broken its agreement. Later, the 1954 Geneva Accords, which separated North and South Vietnam, also provided for such an election. The United States had used its best efforts to make sure such an election did not take place.[6] I simply did not know that.

I felt cheated. I had always believed the North Vietnamese had violated the 1954 Geneva Accords. Now, it turned out from this secret history, it was not true. Of all the volumes I read, this had the greatest impact on me. Strangely enough, Ellsberg had the same reaction when he read it.[7]

There were two parts to Volume One, as there were to each volume in the series. There was a narrative and then there were documents. In the case of each volume, the documents supported the narrative. The documents differed from the narrative, since they were verbatim reproductions of diplomatic cables, presidential memos and the like.

When I finished the first volume I looked at the sources cited: I couldn't believe what I found. They were generally articles from the *New York Times*. My face lit up. This report was almost identical to those I prepared for my Strategic Intelligence Research Analysis Unit. In those reports I stamped, with some guilt, statements from the *New York Times* "secret." In this report they were stamped "top secret."

Putting law aside for a moment, it just wasn't possible that the *Times* could be stopped permanently or indicted for republishing what it had already published. That was just plain ridiculous. I perused the other volumes. They were all written the same way. The arguments in the volumes were supported by the documents attached. Each volume had a myriad of quotes from and citations from the *Times*, the *Saturday Evening Post* and other open sources.

I thought this was a slam dunk. Stories on the Pentagon Papers could be published in some form without legal risk. The narrative could be easily summarized and published. It was just history. But if the documents were published, courts and even juries might find that offensive (the "anger" factor) and they might cause trouble for the *New York Times*.

The easiest solution was to publish articles based on the narratives all at once. If that happened, particularly without the documents, there would be nothing in the real world the government could do about it. It would not be able to ask for a prior restraint because if all the articles were published, there would be nothing to stop. Under this scenario, a grand jury would not be interested in indicting the *Times* even if the Espionage Act applied. The grand jury would merely be looking at another long article on Vietnam, albeit based on classified documents.

It might also be possible to thread the documents through this summary without attracting too much attention. At this point I could not reach a judgment on the particular risk the documents presented. It was impossible to read them all. There were too many. I would have to make a judgment on the publication of the documents when Rosenthal prepared the articles and documents for final approval. If there was one thing I was sure of, it was that if we did not publish the story all at once we would be enjoined at least temporarily.

My particular scenario was: if the *Times* published in installments, Secretary of Defense Melvin Laird would be pressured by the military to defend the classification system. He would then call Attorney General Mitchell or even the president to demand legal action, that is, a prior restraint.

I thought I knew President Nixon like a book. He hated the *New York Times* and he hated the liberal establishment. He thought they were his enemies. I had been battling him for three years. I had studied him since the Alger Hiss case, and I knew he had a particular sensitivity to the sanctity of classified documents. Alger Hiss, after all, had given Whittaker Chambers classified documents for delivery to the Russians. And Nixon made his reputation with that case. He would certainly agree with a recommendation to enjoin the *Times*.

If the government tried to enjoin the *New York Times*, assuming a publication in installments, I thought it would succeed, at first. The government would say the *Times* wanted to publish forty-seven volumes containing 7,000 pages of classified information, including highly sensitive documents. It would effectively say to the judge, "You don't know what's in those forty-seven volumes, you've got to stop it."

I didn't think there was any judge in the world who would let it proceed. Forget what the law was, forget what the First Amendment is, a judge was not going to let those documents out of his hands without at least knowing something about their contents. I wanted to have a discussion with Rosenthal about this scenario. Abe and I had developed a close relationship during the *Caldwell* case and talked about matters like this at great length. I knew that Rosenthal would not accept readily, or at all, the idea of publishing in one fell swoop. The editors and reporters thought they had a hot story, and they wanted to run it in installments to get all the attention they could out of that publication.

Accordingly, I knew my suggestion to publish all at once might, as a practical matter, kill the story. No one would read it because it would take up pages and pages of the *Times*. It would be hard to slog through. If no one read it, no one would realize the war was built on a tissue of lies—the whole purpose of publication in the first place.

At the very least, I wanted Rosenthal to understand the practical risks involved in not publishing all at once. During the injunction, the *Times* would lose the momentum of the story. More to the point, the *Times* would have to defend everything in the forty-seven volumes of the Pentagon Papers in the process—not just the articles. I never had an opportunity to have a full discussion with Abe Rosenthal and his peers on this subject. Harding Bancroft upended my strategy.

Several days after I had read the Papers, I received a call from Art Hooker. He told me Louis Loeb was furious about their possible publication. Despite my suggestion to Hooker that he and I should work out a common position before telling Loeb, he had told Loeb anyway. He said Loeb had set up a meeting with Punch a few days hence. At that time Loeb would give his firm's advice. There would be no discussion of my views of the law. There would be no legal memo provided, as I requested. There would be no legislative history of the Espionage Act. Nothing.

I, too, was furious. I had been chief counsel of the paper for eight years. I had fought one case on its way to the Supreme Court (*Caldwell*). I had almost single-handedly put together a financial transaction essential for the economic survival of the *Times*, but in the end, I was a zero.

The next day I visited my wife in the hospital with our newborn daughter, Ashley. I told her of my humiliation, and that I was going to resign. It was a thoughtless conversation to have with a young mother of twenty-nine who had an infant and a three year-old son. She thought I was crazy, and said so. After all, I had a family to support.

Many years later, Abe Rosenthal told me he had also decided to resign if the Papers were not published. When the *Washington Post* was faced with the same decision, its editors said they would resign if the Papers were not published.[8] Abe told me that he thought the fear of mass resignation of reporters and editors influenced Punch's ultimate decision to publish the Papers.

I was still hopping mad several days later when Bancroft's office called to invite me to the meeting with the publisher, Lord, Day & Lord, and top editors. In the interim, I had read more of the Papers, and I was even more convinced they could be published. Perhaps I would have a chance to explain my views at the meeting. I was dubious, however. It appeared to me the die had been cast.

CHAPTER X
LORD, DAY & LORD SINKS THE SHIP

I had no idea what exactly Lord, Day & Lord was going to say when they came to the *New York Times* on April 29 to give advice on the Pentagon Papers.[1] Their recommendations turned out to be astounding. In the end, it contributed to the demise of the firm, a 150-year-old New York City institution, which slipped below the waves just twenty years later.[2] Because of the huge risk of publishing the Pentagon Papers, I accepted the fact that the opinion of Lord, Day & Lord was necessary. It would be imprudent for the *Times* to publish solely on the basis of an opinion of one lawyer, me. Publication could jeopardize the *New York Times'* standing as an institution.

If, for example, a successful legal action were brought against the *Times* for such publication, it would not only threaten to destroy the paper's reputation for integrity and loyalty, but also threaten its economic base. If the publisher and others of the *New York Times* went to jail, readers and advertisers could be expected to flee.

The Sulzberger family could not take the possibility of the destruction of its enterprise lightly, merely because a group of reporters thought they had a hot story. Further, no one could be sure the Pentagon Papers themselves were not forged. And so it was important to get an opinion from a firm of lawyers, rather than just one lawyer.

When a firm of lawyers gives its opinion, it is from all the partners in the firm. By giving a firm opinion, it puts the credibility of that law firm behind that opinion. While the institution of the *New York Times* was on the hook, so too was the reputation of Lord, Day & Lord.

This was to be a unique meeting in the history of the *New York Times*. A group of editors rarely, if ever, met with a group of lawyers to decide what to publish. An editor typically met with one lawyer and, for eight years previously, that was me.

In the many years I had been giving advice to editors and reporters at the *Times*, I never turned to Lord, Day & Lord for advice. If a lawsuit was brought against the *Times* for what it published, I would ask Lord, Day & Lord to defend the suit. I was protective of my relationship with reporters and editors and I did not want to share it with anyone, including my old law firm.

The board room of the *New York Times* was an impressive place on the top floor of the *Times* building in Times Square. It commanded a full view of the Hudson River and many miles into New Jersey and upstate New York. It was beautifully paneled and frequently used for receptions for groups of over 100. A long polished mahogany table for meetings was in the middle of the room.

Punch Sulzberger was the fourth publisher to sit in the large office adjacent to the board room. It was originally occupied by his grandfather, Adolph Ochs. It was later occupied by Arthur Hays Sulzberger, Ochs' son-in-law; Orvil Dryfoos, Sulzberger's son-in-law; and then by Sulzberger's son, Punch. Most great statesman of the world had been to this office. On the wall hung a sword, a gift from Haile Selassie, the Emperor of Ethiopia.

Punch was a beloved figure at the *New York Times*. His cousin, John B. Oakes, the editorial page editor, said he could charm the birds off the trees. I never heard him raise his voice at anybody, or indeed even get slightly angry at them.

He had convinced himself he was not smart. He seemed to have an intellectual inferiority complex from his failures at school. He did not make it through St. Bernard's, a New York City grade school with high academic standards. Several other similar experiences followed before he joined the U.S. Marine Corps in World War II.

This background, coupled with his unpretentious manner, led some to conclude he was not very intelligent and could be taken advantage of. I never thought this to be the case. I would sit next to him at *Times* stockholder meetings with the responsibility of answering questions he could not. I would, therefore, have an answer ready for every question that was asked. Without exception, his answer was better than the one I was going to give.

He was able to use his humble view of his own intelligence to his advantage. If one of his projects went off the rails, as inevitably happens in any organization, he would effectively say, "What do you expect, you know me." He instinctively had the right answer for the big organizational issues he confronted. He could then, however, be talked out of what he instinctively thought was correct. The Pentagon Papers would test that instinct.

When the meeting with Lord, Day & Lord began, he sat at the head of the table. Others sat near him in order of importance. Herbert Brownell Jr., the former U.S. Attorney General, and Louis Loeb were at his elbow, as were Scotty Reston and Abe Rosenthal. Tom Wicker, the Washington columnist, sat near Rosenthal, as did Jim Greenfield, the foreign editor. Then followed Art Hooker and Jack Castles, Loeb's partners. Castles was an excellent litigator who would presumably represent the *Times* in court, should there be a lawsuit. At the very end of the table, so far below the salt that I was nearly invisible, was me.

Louis spoke for the assembled Lord, Day & Lord lawyers. He said not only would it be a crime to publish classified information, but it would be a crime even to look at the Pentagon Papers because they were classified. He said that the Espionage Act covered the publication of classified information. He recommended in the strongest terms that the *New York Times* not publish the Pentagon Papers. He added that Punch's father would never have considered publication.

Brownell confirmed Loeb's view of the law. He said that Classification Regulation 10501 controlled the *Times'* proposed publication. The Espionage Act effectively incorporated that classification regulation. Any publication of classified information was illegal.

He also said that as a former Attorney General of the United States, he was sure that if publication took place, criminal prosecution would inevitably follow. There was a risk, he said, that those responsible for the publication would end up in jail.

I couldn't believe my ears. This advice was directly contrary to the advice that I had given to the reporters and editors of the *Times*. I was chagrined. I would have thought Loeb's advice could have at least been run past me so that I would have had a chance to comment on it. But Louis was then seventy-three, I was thirty-seven. He had worked at the *Times* all his life. I had worked there for eight years. He was Lord, Day & Lord's senior lawyer. I was once a junior lawyer at his firm. He was president of the New York City Bar Association, I was a junior member. It was easy to bypass me.

More than that, I was flabbergasted by what had not been discussed. Where was the First Amendment in this analysis? Lord, Day & Lord focused on criminal risks of publication. I thought the principal risk was prior restraint. And where was the promised memorandum on the meaning of the Espionage Act and its legislative history?

Scotty Reston spoke for the editors. He said Loeb's views didn't make any sense to him. He had been publishing classified information for years. How in the world had he published a story on the Dumbarton Oaks Security Conference in 1944, or the Yalta Papers in 1955, both of which had been classified? Loeb and Brownell did not have a good answer for Reston. They implied he and the *Times* had "gotten away with it." Reston received the Pulitzer Prize for the publication of the Dumbarton Oaks story.[3]

Punch looked shaken by this advice. The editors around the table related their experience with classified information and expressed extremely polite disbelief of what Lord, Day & Lord told them. I knew it was time to speak up. I was outnumbered by four partners of a law firm where I had been a junior associate. Also, I did not want to get into a lawyer's wrangle in front of the editors. They would not know whom to believe.

I thought that Lord, Day & Lord's view of the real risk with respect to publication was wrong. The real risk was that a judge would enjoin the *New York Times* from publication. I did not think that their judgment about the likelihood of a criminal prosecution was correct. A lot would depend on what was in the documents the *Times* chose to publish.

I did not talk through my scenario that Laird would complain to Mitchell, who would tell Nixon to take action about the leak. I did not say that Nixon, who hated the press, would approve such an injunction to add another chapter to his war against the media.

I merely said that I believed the real risk with respect to publication was an injunction. I explained the reasons. No one in the room agreed with me. Tom Wicker said, as a Washington columnist, he knew the Nixon Administration well. It would never bring such an injunction. The others agreed that I did not understand Washington politics.

While Wicker's remark made me feel like two cents, I persisted. An injunction would raise First Amendment questions. We should rethink the form of our publication, e.g., installments. Again I was met with disbelief. I did not give up. I referred to an injunction as a prior restraint, but I sensed no one in the room was familiar with the term.

Reston then said that if there was an injunction against the *New York Times*, the *Times* should disobey it. Since I was the only one in the room who had caused the *Times* "to disobey" an injunction, I said that under no circumstance could the *New York Times* disobey such an injunction.

During the Baltimore runaway grand jury case the year before, Fred Graham and I had believed we were disobeying an injunction because the First Amendment permitted it. An injunction not to print thousands of classified pages raised a different First Amendment question. A judge would not easily dismiss such an injunction out of hand. He would want to be sure the thousands and thousands of pages in the Pentagon Papers did not contain an important national secret, such as how to make a hydrogen bomb.

Further, if the *Times* disobeyed a prior restraint order of this magnitude, it would be tied up in contempt proceedings at the same time it tried to print. It would be a holy mess. A judge might very well not only stop the publication, but fine or jail the *Times'* officers. It was out of the question.

Reston ended the meeting by saying that if the *New York Times* did not publish the Pentagon Papers, he would publish them himself in a paper he owned, *The Vineyard Gazette*. This, of course, was an absurd suggestion made to underline his belief the Papers should be published. *The Vineyard Gazette* was a small weekly paper published in Martha's Vineyard with roughly 48 pages an issue. The Pentagon Papers consisted of 3,000 pages of narrative and 4,000 pages of government documents. By the time Reston had published the Pentagon Papers, winter would have come and gone, perhaps several times.

After the meeting I had lunch with Art Hooker and Jack Castles. Hooker was a liberal Democrat and I thought I knew where his sympathies lay. Castles was a very conservative Yale graduate. The secretary of Yale at the time told me Castles, as an active alumnus, had been a real thorn in the side of Yale because of his ultraconservative views. Yale was going through revolutionary changes in its student body and was trying to adjust to the student protests relating to the Vietnam War. Castles opposed Yale's policies in dealing with those problems.

Castles, I thought, probably exacerbated Loeb's reaction to publishing classified information. Three of the Lord, Day & Lord lawyers were Republicans—Loeb, Brownell, and Castles—so in a sense, there was no chance they would be sympathetic to the publication of the Pentagon Papers.

Nonetheless, I respected Jack's legal judgment. I impressed on him and Hooker my view of why the government would successfully seek a prior restraint. It seemed to me that they really did not appreciate the significance of a prior restraint against a publisher. They had not, of course, been thinking about the possibility of prior restraints against the press over the last few years, as I had. They did not know that attempts to enjoin the press had been increasing. Nor did they know of the circumstances in which I had advised the *Times* to disobey a prior restraint one year earlier. They said I was just flat out wrong.

For the next five weeks, I tried mightily to persuade Harding Bancroft that my legal analysis was correct. I told him the *Times* was not committing espionage. The Espionage Act did not apply because it did not cover the publication of classified information. I told him the test would be what kind of information the *Times* published. This was a difficult conversation. Harding would not look at the section of the Espionage Act that Lord, Day & Lord thought applied.

He was a lawyer who was countering my well-researched legal arguments with his own opinions, but he still should have at least looked at what the law was. Many of these discussions took place as we drove home from the *New York Times* building on 43rd Street. We both lived on the Upper East Side. In exasperation one evening, I said in the cab, "Damn it Harding, read the goddamn law." He wouldn't.

After the meeting with Lord, Day & Lord, I heard little from Rosenthal and Frankel as to where the Pentagon Papers project stood. The reason for this, I later discovered, was that Punch had told Abe that he was not going to make a decision about whether to publish the Papers until he knew *what* he was going to publish. This was an eminently sensible decision.

All the editors had told him up to this point was that the Pentagon Papers existed and that they showed treacherous behavior by the government. The editors also did not know all of what they were going to publish. The sheer size of the Papers made it very difficult for anyone to get their arms around them. Additionally, Neil Sheehan was slow in producing articles for his editors and didn't start writing them until mid-May. He was also having problems with Ellsberg, which I didn't learn about until later.

In the ordinary world of publishing, this history was an oddity. First, the number of classified pages, 7,000 was unprecedented. Second, and more to the point, while there were huge arguments over whether to publish or not, no one knew at the time of those arguments what it was they wanted to publish. And none of the lawyers, including Bancroft, who opposed publication, had ever taken a look at the Papers, except me.

As we shall see, other lawyers (including judges) involved in the Pentagon Papers case had the same knee jerk reaction that it must be illegal to publish classified information. What accounts for this reaction? It certainly does not speak well of a legal education system that produces graduates who reach opinions without bothering to investigate the facts. But that may be too harsh. The better theory is that none of these lawyers, including some of the judges, had enough appreciation for the First Amendment.

In the month of May, a principal concern of the editors was that the documents might be forgeries. While Sheehan could rely on Ellsberg, no one else could. Jim Greenfield, the editor of the project, did not know Ellsberg personally. He had to assume that Ellsberg was totally unreliable and even a kook. He had to authenticate the documents and information in the Pentagon Papers through alternate sources. He, Abe Rosenthal, and their colleagues read over forty or fifty books on the Vietnam War to assist in determining the authenticity of what they had.

Because of Rosenthal and Frankel's silence during this period, I thought the project was dead. I took my newborn daughter and the rest of my family to Connecticut for a ten day vacation, starting Memorial Day weekend.

While I was on vacation, in a memo dated Tuesday, June 1, Rosenthal told Messrs. Sulzberger and Reston he was ready to go: "I believe we are now in a position to give the publisher sufficient information on which to base the decision."[4] The memorandum outlined six articles to be published in installments. Only four of these articles were "in hand" and ready for the publisher's review. This was the first time Punch saw what the editors had in mind, and he was disappointed. He sent them back for further work. Presumably, he and Sydney Gruson, formerly the foreign editor and now Punch's assistant, could not follow the storyline.

I thought the Pentagon Papers would never be published.

CHAPTER XI

WE WILL PUBLISH AFTER ALL

I walked back into the *New York Times* on Monday, June 7, ready to focus on new projects. I thought the Pentagon Papers project was dead. Obviously, I was wrong. What followed was one of the most tumultuous weeks in the history of journalism. In the morning I paid a visit to the fourteenth floor, the executive floor, where Bancroft and Sulzberger had their offices. Sydney Gruson, the newly minted assistant to Sulzberger, had a rather large office there. Sydney surprised me with a comment that publication was "foolish." He said the news people had lost their senses. Rosenthal was much too emotional about the publication of the Papers.

This comment indicated that the project was still alive. Apparently, Reston and Rosenthal still wanted to publish. Lord, Day & Lord had not sunk the ship after all. I dismissed Gruson's comment, thinking it was shallow and not worth heeding.

I did not know Sydney well. He had been a foreign correspondent most of the time I had been at the *Times*. I had been advising the top management group of the *Times*, including the principal editors, but he had not been part of that group. Sydney had been promoted to foreign editor for a short time before he became Punch's assistant. While he had attended the April meeting when Sheehan had presented the Pentagon Papers, I did not attach any particular significance to his presence.

He created a certain amount of political turmoil before and after he arrived on the fourteenth floor. When Abe Rosenthal became the managing editor of the *Times*, he had passed Gruson over as his assistant managing editor. Gruson, who had supported Abe's candidacy as managing editor, thought Abe would support him for assistant managing editor in return. Gruson was furious at Abe when he subsequently did not support him, and did not speak to Abe for a year. The two were still barely speaking to each other.

He became Punch's assistant on the fourteenth floor. Andy Fisher, who was one of the vice presidents of the company, also on the fourteenth floor, had learned that Sulzberger had promised Gruson a vice presidency as a consolation prize. Fisher wondered, "Vice president of what?" That meant unless Fisher became president, Gruson would dilute his power. As a result, Fisher went in to see Sulzberger and demanded to be president of the company, or else he would resign. Sulzberger refused him and he resigned. Gruson ultimately became the vice president of acquisitions, where he toiled endlessly knocking at doors of small newspaper companies so that the *Times* could buy them.

Clifton Daniel, one-time managing editor of the *New York Times*, married to Margaret Truman, the president's daughter, told me Sydney was the most charming person he had ever met. For Daniel, who, with his wife, consorted with kings, queens, presidents and senators, that was quite a compliment. Sydney was handsome, a ladies' man of sorts and went far with only an eighth grade education.

What I didn't know about Sydney then was that Punch Sulzberger considered him to be his best friend.[1] He played an important role in the publication of the Papers because Punch relied on Gruson for advice in publishing matters. Punch had little, if any, experience in reading articles before publication. Sydney, no doubt, had been instrumental in sending Sheehan's articles back to Abe for rewriting the week before, thereby achieving some manner of revenge against Rosenthal. Two days later, I received a call from Bancroft to review the articles slated for publication that had been rewritten after Punch's initial rejection. Despite Sydney's hints, I was still surprised to learn the project was indeed still alive.

Bancroft laid the articles for the first installments before me. I reviewed them the way I had been reviewing articles for eight years. My task was to approve them as submitted or to change them so they could be published. I expected that my advice would be followed. I believed that if my conclusion was that the Pentagon Papers could not be published legally, they would not be published. Conversely, if I said the reverse, they would be published in the form I suggested, subject to Sulzberger's final approval.

I asked Bancroft whether my assumption was correct, that my idea of a single publication had been rejected. He asserted it had. I wondered what role Lord, Day & Lord would play at this point. I assumed he may have been talking to Louis and not telling me. But as we began to read the articles, he said we shouldn't tell Louis. I did not know what that meant, and chose not to inquire. All I knew was that I had been asked to review the articles and to give my opinion on whether they were publishable.

I started making changes in them to minimize the risk of publication. When Bancroft asked me, "what are you doing," I said, "I'm reviewing the articles and making changes to them so they are publishable." It occurred to me then that in all the years Bancroft had been at the *Times*, he had never reviewed articles for publication. While he came to the *Times* as a lawyer and had overseen lawyers who worked for the *Times*, he never gave legal advice himself. He had not developed a relationship with the editors. In short, while he was an excellent business executive for the *Times*, he really didn't understand how the process of publishing worked.

I was stunned at what I read. The first article explained how the Johnson administration used deceit to get the Gulf of Tonkin Resolution through Congress.

As earlier noted, I did not pretend to be knowledgeable on the ins and outs of the Vietnam War, but I had focused on the legality of the war and the Gulf of Tonkin Resolution. The Johnson Administration had used this resolution as its justification for war.[2]

That administration had told Congress and the public that the North Vietnamese had fired upon U.S. navy destroyers in the Tonkin Gulf. The story was that it was an unprovoked attack and Congress should authorize the U.S. to retaliate against North Vietnam.

What the Pentagon Papers showed was that the U.S. had waged a secret war against North Vietnam to provoke them into attacking U.S. forces. Johnson ordered clandestine attacks against North Vietnam, to which the North Vietnamese had to respond as a matter of self-defense.[3] The Gulf of Tonkin Resolution was therefore built upon a tissue of lies and did not give the U.S. legal justification to attack North Vietnam.

I could not see how any court or jury could find this story offensive. It was embarrassing to President Johnson because it proved he lied. He was not in office any more, however. It was not helpful to the Nixon administration in quelling antiwar protests. The protestors had said all along they had been lied to, and here was the proof.

The publication didn't damage national security in any way. The North Vietnamese knew they had been provoked. All in all, it was just another hard-hitting story on the war published daily by the *Times*—albeit based on classified documents.

A second story described how Johnson deceived the American public during the 1964 campaign. He ran on a platform of restraint to differentiate himself from Republican nominee Barry Goldwater, who openly advocated bombing North Vietnam. But Johnson was secretly planning to bomb North Vietnam as well. In September, before the election, Johnson's advisors had reached a consensus and drawn up a secret plan to start bombing the North after the election. The *Times* said the fact "that such a consensus had been reached as early as September is a major disclosure in the Pentagon Study."[4]

These stories showed the U.S. government had lied about the Vietnam War from the start. My judgment therefore was, regardless of how the laws were written, no court was going to penalize a newspaper criminally for showing how the government had lied, particularly when the government's own papers proved it. In retrospect, perhaps I was naïve to think the government did not lie to the public, but I was truly astonished. I turned to Harding and said, "I can't believe this, they lied." He said, "What do you expect?"

I then read the documents Rosenthal wanted published, which were my greatest concern. Before reading them, I had considerable doubt whether they could be published. When I read them, however, I changed my mind. All the documents did was support or prove the assertions in the text. For example, the assertion that the U.S. was actively trying to provoke the North Vietnamese in the lead-up to the Tonkin Gulf incident was supported in a memo from Robert McNamara to President Johnson.[5]

If such assertions were publishable, it followed that the proof of such disclosure as set out in the documents was also publishable. Apart from that, the documents stunned me as much as the narratives did. They were heartless. They urged Johnson to escalate the war without regard to its consequences to the American public.

One document written by McGeorge Bundy advised Johnson to adopt "a sustained reprisal policy."[6] Bundy advised Johnson "to retaliate against any VC act of violence to persons or property."[7] Each reprisal would be announced tit for tat. After a while such announcements would not be necessary, because the public would not notice the war had escalated.

Bundy said, "we should execute our reprisal policy with as low a level of public noise as possible."[8] There was nothing in the memo as to its effect on the American public. The war would be escalated without letting the public know. It was hard, pragmatic and, I thought, somewhat cruel.

Bundy had been the Dean of Faculty of Arts and Sciences at Harvard. He was doing his job as National Security Advisor. Again, perhaps I was naïve, but I couldn't believe our government worked this way within its inner circles. I thought the American public would have the same reaction.

I concluded the documents had to be published to inform the public how presidential decisionmaking took place. With all its deceptions and lies, I was sure the general public, the courts, and juries, if any, would feel the same way. The documents might be provocative, but it was worth the risk to publish the information. If a criminal case developed, we would win.

I spent a day and a half reviewing the articles and selected documents with Bancroft. At the end of this review, I told him, it was my opinion that the publication was legal. We would win any legal challenge the government made. But when we finished this review Bancroft sent a memo to Punch, saying he opposed publication. He never told me about this memo, which I found only recently. I went through the whole Pentagon Papers case not knowing he was opposed to their publication. He said the story without the documents was a perfectly good story. "Publication of the documents may force Washington to take action which it does not want to take and which it would not take on the basis of the narrative alone. Thus it is my view, the risks to the institution of the *Times'* printing of the documents outweigh the benefits to be gained."[9]

In his defense, he did not tell Punch the Pentagon Papers could not be published legally, all he said was publication was not worth the legal risk. At least I had persuaded him that publication of the stories, without the documents, did not violate the Espionage Act. Despite the legal assurances I gave Bancroft about the documents, he was still concerned about their publication.

When Bancroft's memo arrived in Punch's office, Gruson decided to see if he could persuade Rosenthal not to publish the documents. He drove Rosenthal home with that end in mind. The next morning, Rosenthal told Gruson that either the Papers would run with the documents or not run at all.[10]

Shortly thereafter, Punch sent a memo to Abe approving publication but said, "in the unlikely event the government moves in court to force us to cease publication, we will honor any court injunction."[11] Punch noted in the memo he was going to Europe, and Bancroft would be in charge in his absence.

CHAPTER XII

NIXON THREATENS: LORD, DAY & LORD QUITS

Amid the excitement over Tricia Nixon's wedding, it took a while for the significance of the Pentagon Papers story to grab the political establishment's attention. But the next day, Monday June 14—Flag Day—turned out to be a dramatic day in the history of freedom of the press. By then, everyone in the White House and the Justice Department had read the second story in the Pentagon Paper series. It described Johnson's perfidy during the 1964 election. He had lied to the electorate about his plans for Vietnam.

Punch left on the morning of June 14 with Carol for his long-scheduled business trip to England. Punch, whose support for publication of the Papers was lukewarm at best, was happy to be out of town. I had time on my hands that morning, which permitted me to focus on another part of Nixon's war against the press—the *Caldwell* case. That is where Nixon's war began. Nixon's Justice Department had threatened Earl Caldwell with jail unless he disclosed his sources.

Caldwell had gone AWOL. After destroying his notes, unbeknownst to the *Times*, he had hired his own lawyer. Although the *Times* was not a party in Caldwell's case anymore, it nonetheless was supporting him with an amicus brief to the U.S. Supreme Court.

I had hired Alex Bickel to write this brief, hoping to persuade other media companies to sign on to it as amici. The brief set forth my position as to what the law should be to protect reporters. Alex, Floyd Abrams, myself, and others had worked on a draft of this brief for many weeks. The brief was due to be filed in five weeks, on July 21.

Alex and Floyd were coming to my office at 11:30. We were going to meet with Reuven Frank, the famed executive editor of NBC News, and other network lawyers at noon to discuss it. This was an important meeting. The three networks (ABC, NBC, and CBS) had not joined the brief and some of the lawyers and executives for the networks had not met Alex Bickel or me. They wanted to meet us, learn about our brief and educate us on how their networks gathered the news.

Cahill Gordon represented NBC and Floyd Abrams had set up the appointment with Frank. The lawyers were to have luncheon afterwards at the University Club.

On the way over to Rockefeller Center, NBC's headquarters, Bickel said to me, "The *Times* did a great job in publishing the Pentagon Papers." He said it was "very courageous." I tried to give him a response to show how cool I was and that I had no fear of the consequences of publication. That was not true, of course.

As we walked into Reuven Frank's office, the TV sets were on. NBC News was reporting that Secretary of Defense Melvin Laird had asked Attorney General John Mitchell to investigate what the *New York Times* had done. I said to myself, "This is just as I predicted. We are really going to be in for it now."

Frank explained to us how TV news worked and how it used sources. We listened, as a confidence-building measure. We then explained to Frank and the other journalists the general theory of our brief.

At lunch at the University Club we were joined by Gene Roberts, the national editor for the *New York Times*. Roberts was an investigative reporter for the *Times* and point person on the *Caldwell* case. He later won five Pulitzer Prizes for investigative reporting when he was editor of the *Philadelphia Inquirer*. Roberts kept notes of the meeting for Abe Rosenthal.

At the beginning of lunch, Bickel became effusive about the *Times'* publication of the Pentagon Papers. He said the *Times'* action was "magnificent" and "outstanding." He would "defend us all the way to hell."[1] If the government tried to get the *Times'* sources, "he would say no." He would resist any effort by the government to obtain the documents we worked on to get the names of the sources. If the government wanted to bring criminal charges against the *New York Times*, "let them do it, you have a damn good case." He would welcome handling such a case (little did he know). Alex then read parts of his brief to the assembled group. The brief was excellent. We had few comments.

In the middle of the afternoon, Laird issued another statement saying the *Times* had published "highly sensitive information that should not have been made public."[2] At the time Laird issued his statement, Nixon had a meeting with Haldeman. He told Haldeman, "I think that story in the *Times* should cause everybody here great concern …[it's a] bunch of crap…[it's] treasonable, due to the fact that it's aid to the enemy and it's a release of classified documents….Neil Sheehan of the *Times* is a bastard and…has been a bastard for years."[3]

Nixon clearly had read the articles by this time. Perhaps encouraged by Kissinger's call the previous day, he was the anti-press hawk he'd always been. The *New York Times* was his enemy. It always was. Yet Nixon didn't know what to do about the *New York Times*. While he instructed Kissinger the day before to call Mitchell, the Attorney General strangely had not yet called Nixon twenty-four hours later to discuss Nixon's legal options.

Nixon told Haldeman he wasn't sure "we can do much now." He said the Justice Department should "subpoena all these bastards [the *Times*] and bring the case."

He said, at the very least the White House should freeze out *New York Times* reporters; the *Times* was "irresponsible, goddamn—don't give 'em anything."

Nixon continued his tirade against the *Times*, "Henry [Kissinger] talked to that damn Jew Frankel all the time—he's bad, you know—don't give 'em anything!...I just want to cool it with those damn people, because of their disloyalty to the country."[4]

Mitchell had probably not called Nixon because he could not figure out what to do, nor could his lawyers. They didn't know what the law was. They had asked William Rehnquist, the future Chief Justice of the Supreme Court, then head of the Office of Legal Counsel, for his opinion.

The only law he could find was *Near v. Minnesota*. He did not volunteer that the Espionage Act applied. Later during the day, the Justice Department decided, nonetheless, the Espionage Act did apply. With this advice in hand, Mitchell called John Ehrlichman and told him he wanted to sue the *Times*. He hoped Ehrlichman would tell Nixon before Mitchell called. Mitchell did not reach Nixon until after seven. He had tried to reach Nixon through Ehrlichman several times before 7:00 p.m., but Nixon was on the phone.

In the meantime, Mitchell had sent a telegram to Sulzberger asking the *Times* to stop publication. Robert Mardian, an assistant attorney general under Mitchell, read this telegram to Bancroft at approximately 7:00. Mitchell called Nixon for approval at 7:13 p.m. to go forward with the case. He said the federal government had sued to stop a newspaper from publishing before. (It had not.) He said that it was customary to give a publication notice to stop publication. (It was not.)[5] He did not explicitly tell Nixon he'd already done this. The purpose of Mitchell's call was to get Nixon's approval to take the next step to go forward with the case.[6]

They sounded like two older lawyers who really didn't know what law they were talking about.[7] But there was no doubt they were going hellbent against their common enemy, the *New York Times*. Nixon concluded "as far as the *Times* is concerned, hell they're our enemies. I think we just oughta do it [sue]."[8]

At the time Mitchell was attempting to reach Nixon to stick it to the *Times*, I was on my way home. I had stayed later than usual waiting for the axe to fall. I knew from Laird's statements during the day that some action was certainly going to take place before the day was over. I got home shortly after seven.

When I opened the door to the apartment (my family was still in Connecticut), I heard the phone ring and then stop. I thought it might be Bancroft, but then again, it could have been someone else. I was expecting a call from the *Times* at some point. And for about twenty minutes I heard nothing. I began to fidget. "Something must be going on," I said to myself. I decided to call Bancroft. "Harding," I said, "is anything going on?"

He said, "We have received a phone call from the Justice Department to stop publishing." There was a pause. He did not say, "You'd better get over here in a hurry." I volunteered, "I'd better come over." I will never know how long he'd been sitting at the *Times* knowing what Mardian had told him without calling me, but it was at least half an hour. He did not extend an invitation to go to the *Times* and I had to invite myself. I had the distinct impression he was never going to call me. He was going to freeze me out.

I got to the *New York Times* at about 7:45 p.m. I went to the executive floor, the top floor of the *New York Times,* and headed to Harding's impressive office. Like the boardroom, it had a sweeping view for miles and miles across the Hudson and up the West Side of New York City. The first time I went there, several years earlier, I was overwhelmed. I pinched myself, wondering how in the world had I ever gotten here.

I heard a ruckus before I got to the office. Sydney Gruson and Abe Rosenthal were yelling at each other. They were arguing over the text of the telegram Mitchell had sent the *Times.* Mardian, Mitchell's colleague, had read it to Bancroft:

> "I have been advised by the Secretary of Defense that the material published in the *New York Times* on June 13, 14, 1971...bears a top secret classification.... As such, publication of this information is directly prohibited by the provisions of the Espionage Law, Title 18, United States Code, Section 793.... Accordingly, I respectfully request that you publish no further information of this character and advise me that you have made arrangements for the return of these documents to the Department of Defense."[9]

Mardian had also told Bancroft that if the *Times* did not stop, the government would sue. It would seek a temporary restraining order the next morning. Sydney was in favor of stopping publication. Bancroft agreed. Rosenthal was livid. With Punch in London, Sydney was acting for him, even though Punch had appointed Harding to be in charge of the *Times* when Punch was gone.

I thought Sydney was taking advantage of the situation by trying to lord it over Rosenthal. It was Rosenthal, after all, who had refused to support Sydney as his assistant managing editor. Now Sydney was acting like the publisher of the *New York Times* in Punch's absence.

They stopped yelling for a minute and asked me what I thought. I said, "You can't stop publishing if someone sends you a telegram. If there is a court order, that is something else. But this is not a court order. There is no penalty for disobeying a telegram." I remembered only a year before, I had been threatened with a court order to stop publishing and I refused to obey the order, but it turned out only to be a threat. If threats stopped the presses, there would be no newspapers. Everyone would threaten. Papers would never publish.

They listened to my reasons and Harding then said, "Let's call Louis [Loeb]." I had not talked to Louis since the last time he was at the *Times,* when he angrily advised the *Times* not to publish the Pentagon Papers. I suspected he'd been in touch with Bancroft in the interim, even though I had not been told of those conversations.

Louis was as angry as he had been earlier. He said "it was unpatriotic" to publish classified information. The *Times* had always been patriotic and should continue to be so. He was on the loudspeaker and spoke in complete sentences in stentorian tones for which he was famous as an after-dinner speaker.

He spoke, however, too long. He lost his audience. Every time he returned to the theme of patriotism, Rosenthal impatiently walked back and forth across the room. I became embarrassed for Louis and felt sorry for him. He had been the counsel for the *New York Times* for virtually all his adult life, but he never grasped the concept of "publish or perish."

Harding thanked Louis. There was no need for discussion. He had said what everyone expected him to say. "Let's call Punch." He was in London and it was early morning there. We reached him at the Savoy Hotel. Harding put Punch on the loudspeaker and recounted the night's events. His presentation was tilted heavily towards his own position that we should stop publishing. He made his presentation in a gentlemanly way, repeating Louis' arguments to Punch. Sydney and Abe made brief comments in a measured fashion. It was, however, largely Harding's call.

I said nothing, since I had not been asked to give my advice. It was not appropriate for me as a lawyer at that moment to be in the middle of an intramural debate about whether to publish or not. Abe, however, became impatient. He started jabbing me in the ribs, whispering, "say something, say something, say something." I finally said, "It would be a very great mistake to stop publishing. We don't have a court order telling us to stop. All we have is a telegram. I think it would be a bad precedent for the future of American journalism to stop publishing merely because someone sends you a telegram."

Punch asked: "Do we increase our risk by refusing to follow the government's request?" I thought for a moment about whether it might help the government's criminal case. The government could assert we had been told we were breaking the law, but went ahead anyway, and that might help its case. All things being equal, however, I did not think that would tip the balance in favor of the government if the case went to the jury in a criminal trial.

I did not say any of this to Punch. I said merely, "I think that our risk has increased by perhaps five percent." He then said, "Okay, let's continue to publish." I had won, at last. Abe said to me later, "Suppose we had stopped. Can you imagine the headlines the next day? It would have been the end of American journalism as we know it."

Harding and Sydney proposed the following answer to Mitchell's telegram:

> "We have received a telegram from the Attorney General asking the *Times* to cease further publication.... The *Times* must respectfully decline.... We have also been informed of the Attorney General's intention to seek an injunction to restrict further publication.... The *Times* will oppose any request for an injunction for the same reason

that led us to publish the articles in the first place. We will of course abide by the final decision of the court."[10]

I objected vehemently to the language, "We will of course abide by the final decision of the court." I thought this was a very unwise statement: it just invited the court to enjoin us. As I started to argue with Bancroft about this language, I got another jab in the ribs, this time from Gruson. He whispered in my ear, "You've won enough for one evening." I retreated.

Bancroft then called Scotty Reston and read him the draft telegram. I did not know it at the time, but we reached Reston at Robert McNamara's home—the very man who commissioned the classified study at the center of this controversy. He and Reston were having dinner. Reston said the telegram seemed very weak to him. Why did we have to put the language in about obeying the injunction? Bancroft gave his views. At this point I felt honorbound not to say anything, although I agreed wholeheartedly with Reston.

Reston finally gave in. He was the one, after all, who said back on April 29 that the *Times* should disobey the injunction. It was this history, no doubt, that led Punch to insert in his memorandum of approval sent to Messrs. Reston and Rosenthal the previous Friday, that "if there is an injunction the *Times* will obey it."

We called Mardian and Gruson read him our response. Our telegram was sent at 8:30 p.m., approximately forty-five minutes after I entered Bancroft's office. Abe and Sydney then left and Harding said, "Okay, what do we do next." I said, "We should call Louis and tell him to have his partners in court tomorrow." I called Louis and told him that we were going to continue to publish and we needed the support of his firm. He said, "You'd better call Herb." I did not normally call Herbert Brownell, the former attorney general of the United States, "Herb." But I said, "Yes, I will call Herb."

So I called Herb. I opened the conversation cordially by saying that he looked well on television on Saturday at Tricia Nixon's wedding. I then told him what had happened and I wanted Jack Castles—Lord, Day & Lord's litigation partner—in court the next morning. He said very politely, that Lord, Day & Lord could not do that. He said he had a conflict because when he was attorney general, he had drafted Executive Order 10501 which set up the nation's classification system. It established the categories "top secret," "secret" etc. He would be called as a witness against the *Times* and that would be a conflict of interest. Lord, Day & Lord therefore could not represent the *New York Times*.

I was stunned. We had not followed his advice. I respected him for advising us to take a course we obviously were not inclined to follow. But why had he not told us of his supposed conflict earlier? Because he did not have a conflict.

Only Lord, Day & Lord thought Executive Order 10501 had relevance to the case, but it did not. It controlled the activities of government employees, not the press. Additionally, it was hard to imagine someone who had been Attorney

General in the 1950s would be called as a witness as to what he had done twenty years before.[11]

Brownell was at the time a prominent member of the Republican Party. He knew virtually all the cabinet members on a first name basis. He did not want to take on his own party on behalf of a liberal newspaper. Later, I learned that shortly before I spoke to Brownell, Mitchell had called him. While Mitchell did not directly tell him not to represent the *Times*, he strongly suggested it.[12] Brownell and Mitchell knew full well they were backing the *Times* into a corner. It would be extremely difficult to find new lawyers that late at night.

Harding seemed absolutely unperturbed by the possibility we would have no lawyer at all. He was a donnish man with no sense of urgency. For some reason my highly energetic nervous system shut down. I was as cool as a cucumber. I knew we were right. It was only a question of time until that was proven.

And so I sat back in my chair and listened patiently to Harding's musings. He speculated about the type of lawyers we should have and whether they would represent the *Times*. The seconds ticked away before we were due in court. After more than an hour of chatting, Harding suggested we call Herb Wechsler, the First Amendment expert at Columbia Law School, whom he had engaged as the *Times'* counsel in the Sullivan case. Wechsler won the case and his victory was a credit not only to him and to Harding, but also to the First Amendment.

Harding got Wechsler on the phone. Wechsler said he couldn't do it because he was on vacation in Wellfleet. He recommended Rod Perkins of Debevoise & Plimpton, Telford Taylor (whom I had recommended earlier in April for advice), Paul Williams of Cahill Gordon, Larry Walsh of Davis & Polk, and Maurice Rosenberg of Kramer, Nessen. I knew most of the lawyers personally or by reputation. Rod Perkins was a future partner of mine at Debevoise & Plimpton. He was not, however, a litigator. I told Harding I didn't think any of the suggestions useful.

It was now getting near 11:00 p.m. In all probability, we would be in court in twelve hours or so. I told him that our best bet would be to see if I could get Alex Bickel to do the case. I told Harding I had lunch with Bickel that day. If Bickel would agree, perhaps we could get Cahill Gordon (Abrams' law firm) to back him up.

Harding agreed and I then sought to locate Bickel. I called Joanne Bickel, Alex's wife in New Haven, for clues. When she answered the phone I said, "Are you Mrs. Bickel?" Joanne, a former Miss Maryland, answered in an offended tone, "I am indeed." She seemed to think I thought Alex had women to whom he was not married living in his house. She said, "Try the Yale Club." I did, but no luck.

We were now getting close to midnight. I decided I would do the case myself. The David against Goliath image appealed to me. I knew the law better than the government. I had been working on the case for two or three months. The government lawyer would have had two or three hours to catch up with me. There was only one problem: I was not a litigator. My court experience consisted of two uncontested divorce cases.

Nonetheless, I was confident I could hold off the government long enough until the reserve troops arrived. I tucked the research I had done into my briefcase and I went to the third floor where the editors and reporters worked. They surrounded me and peppered me with questions. They asked what was going on and who was going to be the lawyer.

I told them it was Alex but I couldn't find him. I got home after midnight, and once again the phone was ringing. This time it was the *New York Times* night desk. They said triumphantly, "We found him. He's at his mother's house on the Upper West side. Here's the number."

I called Alex. "Would you do it?" I asked. I told him Lord, Day & Lord had quit. If we could back him up with Cahill Gordon, he should have enough support to do the case. He said, "Yes." I then called Floyd Abrams to engage his law firm. It was getting near 12:30 am. I knew Floyd would be dying to do the case. I was worried, however, that his firm might not share the same devotion to the First Amendment that he had. He might have partners who would think as Louis Loeb did, that it was unpatriotic or even traitorous to publish classified information.

He said he would let me know. He called back and said his firm would do it.[13] I put him in touch with Bickel, and gave Floyd my view of what the law was. The Espionage Act did not apply, the classification regulation did not apply. It was simply a First Amendment question and I had advised the *Times* to publish because it would win the case under the First Amendment. I offered to go down to Floyd's law firm with Bickel to share my views. He said he would prefer to do it separately with Bickel. I said to myself, "Fine by me. It's been a busy day. I'm going to bed."

CHAPTER XIII
NIXON STOPS THE PRESSES

I went to the office the next morning bleary-eyed, expecting to hear from the U.S. government as well as from Floyd and Alex. I knew the government would call to get us into court as quickly as possible. I also wanted to know from Alex and Floyd whether their view of the law, which they had researched all night, was the same as mine.

The call from the government came first. At about 10:00 a.m, Michael Hess, an Assistant U.S. Attorney for the Southern District, called to say I had to be in court in two hours, by 12:00 o'clock. I gave the news to Alex and Floyd when they arrived shortly thereafter, red-eyed from no sleep. They took it stoically. We had known we were going to be in court that day, but perhaps not that early.

I was curious to learn what they found out about the laws they had been researching all night. I had a fixed view of the law, but no one had double checked me since Lord, Day & Lord would not do it. Alex and Floyd had found nothing new. The Espionage Act was the only possible law that applied. But they thought it only applied to espionage, not to publishing a newspaper.

As to Executive Order 10501, which Brownell had used as an excuse to resign, they thought it was irrelevant because it did not apply to newspapers. It was meant to apply to those who where employed by the government as civil servants, members of the army, members of the navy, etc. That left the First Amendment, which prevented prior restraints. They further said that the fact we had published classified information was not, as such, legally significant. In other words, they read the law the same as I had. Or, to put it another way, Lord, Day & Lord was absolutely wrong.

We grabbed a cab to Foley Square, the downtown part of Manhattan. The *New York Times* was then on Times Square, in midtown Manhattan. We arrived there about one half hour before we were due in court and we went to a coffee shop for a cup of coffee to perk us up.

The night before I had felt like David against Goliath. Before finding Bickel and Abrams, I was one lawyer against all of the United States Government. Now the situation had changed. We were the Three Musketeers. Of course, Floyd's huge firm, with over sixty litigators, was in the wings, but not available to us at that early moment of the morning.

I can still remember the horrible taste of the coffee as we huddled to decide what Alex was going to say. Alex and I had bonded during the *Caldwell* case. He was dapper, brilliant, with a good sense of humor. He still wore the same tailored gabardine suit he wore at lunch the day before which seemed, miraculously, newly pressed. Given a boutonnière, there would have been a whiff of Fred Astaire about him.

I suggested politely what points Alex might make. He had to impress the judge that no prior restraint had ever been granted against a newspaper in a federal court in the history of the United States. There was a good reason why this had not happened—the First Amendment prevented it. Certainly, the judge did not want to go down in history as the first person to take such a significant step. Secondly, Alex had to tell the court classified information had been published before and he should refer to the Cuban missile crisis in the *Saturday Evening Post* as an example. And, of course, he should point out the Espionage Act did not apply.

We went over to the court at 12:00 and learnt two things. Murray Gurfein was our judge. He had just been appointed by Nixon that week to the federal court at age 63. This would be his first case as a federal judge. His clerk wouldn't let him hear the case until the government filed its papers appropriately, which it had not. Gurfein told us to come back after lunch at 2:00 o'clock.

I was happy to have Gurfein as a judge. He had tried to sue the *Times* on behalf of a client several years before. He and I had had extended correspondence. I found him then to be gentlemanly, curious, an admirer of the *New York Times* and easy to deal with.

The delay in the hearing gave us a chance to look at what the government claimed in order to obtain an injunction. I looked at its legal papers with particular interest. Since no one in over 150 years had tried to do what the government was doing, I wondered how they were going to do it. It is a monumental task to enjoin a newspaper. It should not be easily achieved.

The government, for example, should not be able to go and see a federal judge and say, "Enjoin that newspaper. I don't like what they're printing." It has to set out its case and give the newspaper a lengthy opportunity to respond. The government's briefs were flimsy at best. They said they were suing the *Times* because publication of the Pentagon Papers would "prejudice its defense interests."[1]

I thought, "this can hardly be a basis for stopping the presses." The *Times* publishes material that prejudices defense interests every day. Further, they offered no proof how the Pentagon Papers prejudiced national interests. There was only a statement, in the form of an affidavit, by one Fred J. Buzhardt, the general counsel for the Defense Department.[2]

An affidavit is a piece of paper on which statements are made and then sworn to be true before a notary public. They are used all the time in court cases. Lawyers like to use them because they're quick and once the court accepts them, there is no way to cross examine the person who made out the affidavit. We didn't know who Fred Buzhardt was, nor did anyone else. There was no way of knowing whether he was telling the truth. Certainly the First Amendment required more before stopping the presses.

Worse than all that, the memorandum of law submitted by the government, only four pages long, said that Section 793(d) was violated by the *New York Times*.[3] "For goodness sake," I thought, "the government cited the wrong Section. It's 793(e)." Section 793(d) only applied to government employees. I began to feel better for our band of three lawyers. We knew much more about the law than the government.

Alex, Floyd and I went over to the nearby Lawyers' Club for lunch. There I met for the first time two other lawyers from Cahill Gordon, Larry McKay and Bill Hegarty, who were going to be part of our team of five to take on the United States government.

McKay was a character straight out of *Guys and Dolls*. He was New York City born and clearly had learned a lot from the streets. He was a graduate of night school at Fordham Law. He had an overwhelming reputation at Cahill. He had once represented a manufacturer of a detergent whose contents were said to be poisonous to children. The detergent was also packaged in a way that resembled an orange juice container. At the end of his argument, he reached for a glass of the detergent, drank three swigs, and returned to the counsel's bench (he lost the case anyway).[4]

McKay sat in a corner office at Cahill as a surrogate judge for each case the office had. He listened to proposed arguments and would dismiss them as being "ridiculous" or whatever, even though the law may have been on Cahill's side. Bill Hegarty was a Princeton and Yale graduate, as tough as nails. As a young associate representing Ferdinand Eberstadt, I had encountered Hegarty as the lawyer for the other side. He was very impressive.

Cahill Gordon had a reputation of being a back alley Irish litigating firm. There were many who asked me later why I picked a firm of that reputation for the *New York Times*. It did not seem a logical combination. Truthfully, when I thought of Cahill Gordon as a large firm to back up Bickel, I had a different impression.

My impression had been formed of Cahill largely through my work with Ferdinand Eberstadt, who had been a Cahill partner. He was the funniest and classiest guy I had met in my youthful days on Wall Street. He was an advisor to presidents and had been in a partnership with his close friend, James Forrestal (later Secretary of Defense) at Dillon Read, a famous investment bank. I thought of Cahill as a major New York City firm.

I was extraordinarily pleased with our team. And I think we were all pleased with one another. At lunch we gossiped more than we talked about strategy. We did that so as not to burden Alex with too many instructions. We wondered where Mike Seymour (Whitney North Seymour, Jr.) was.[5] He was the United States Attorney for the Southern District, i.e., New York City. This was a national case, but the only person representing his office was a junior lawyer, Mike Hess.

As we lunched, the waiter brought a phone to the table and said it was for me. It was from Punch, in London. There was no way I could take the call privately. Punch sounded very worried, even scared. He asked whether I thought he should come back to New York. I said, "Yes, I think so." He said, "Do I have to?" I then said (perhaps more sternly than I should have), "You have to come back. This is the greatest First Amendment case in the history of the United States. The publisher of the *New York Times* has to be seen in New York showing the flag. If you are not here, it will be noted. Your absence will be taken as a sign you do not believe in our case. This will hurt us with the judges and the public."

I got a begrudging answer from him that he would come back. When I put down the phone, Bickel, Abrams, McKay, and Hegarty broke out into loud applause. They seemed surprised I would talk to one of the most powerful men in the country that way. I was even a little surprised myself.

Alex, Floyd, and I went back to court at 2:00 p.m. Before we could get started, the ACLU, through its general counsel Norman Dorsen, asked the court to participate (intervene) in the case. This was totally unacceptable to me because of the differences I had had with the ACLU in the *Caldwell* case. Dorsen's request was effectively that he be co-counsel with Bickel, Cahill Gordon, and me. I knew Gurfein would not agree to this request, and he did not.

Mike Hess began his argument by saying the Espionage Act applied.[6] He again said the relevant section was 793(d) not 793(e), the section I thought, if any, was applicable. Again, I smiled to myself. The government was bringing an historic case but it didn't even know what law applied. When it caught up with the knowledge I had gained over the last three months, it would realize how wrong it was, and we would win.

Gurfein politely asked, "Don't you mean 793(e)?" which covers "unauthorized possession of information relating to national defense" and not "authorized possession" as set out in 793(d). I thought this question would unnerve Hess, and I felt embarrassed for him because it showed he did not know what he was doing.

Without blinking an eye, Hess agreed with Gurfein. It was 793(e). Hess was very impressive, quick on his feet, with an honest and fair manner. He later became a partner in a prominent New York law firm, corporation counsel of New York City under Mayor Rudy Giuliani and, after that, a founding partner of Giuliani Partners LLC.

Hess said the *Times* had published exact reproductions of classified documents which were marked "top secret." His emphasis on documents did not surprise me. I had been worried about the documents since the first time I had heard of the Pentagon Papers. He pointed out the *Times* had invited an injunction by saying it would obey an injunction if issued. I grimaced, thinking of the argument the night before with Bancroft in which he insisted on saying the *Times* would obey an order, and I objected. Hess said a few days of "slight delay" would not harm the *Times*, but if the injunction were not granted it would cause irreparable damage to the United States. This was because serious injury was being inflicted on U.S. relations with other nations. Without an injunction, the case would be moot, since the *Times* would publish its whole series before the government could do anything about it. He had already heard from Secretary of State Rogers that friendly nations had complained about the damage the security breach was causing.[7]

Bickel followed the path I suggested. He said the case was a classic one of censorship forbidden by the First Amendment. This was the "first time in the history of the Republic that the government had sought to enjoin a newspaper." He said the government cannot enjoin a crime, which was what the government was attempting to do, since the Espionage Act was a criminal law.

Bickel said the Espionage Act was not intended to cover situations such as publishing. Under Section 794, the government might be able to enjoin battle plans, but the publication of a history was clearly not a battle plan. The First Amendment guaranteed that the court could not enjoin a newspaper. He said, further, that the government needed a statute to bring the case, which it did not have.

As will be explained later, this was a hint of an argument about separation of powers, which I did not consider, but with which Alex became unrealistically enamored during the case. He pointed out it was not unusual to print classified information, including, for example, in the memoirs of presidents. To cement this point, he described the article in the *Saturday Evening Post* about the Cuban missile crisis.

Gurfein perceptibly winced when he heard Bickel say that the government's request to stop the presses was the first in U.S. history. Gurfein, however, countered by saying, "But there has never been a publication like this in the history of the country." That effectively squelched, at least for the time being, the major point I had urged on Bickel in the coffee shop.

Gurfein then invited Bickel, Hess, and Robert Mardian of the Justice Department for a private conversation in his chambers. Mardian, the assistant attorney general, was Mitchell's representative, and was easily characterized as a right-wing zealot. He was known in the Justice Department as "Crazy Bob." He was the head of its Internal Security Division.[8] Bickel told me, "He was from a different planet with eyes that glowed like coals."

In chambers, Gurfein asked Bickel if the *New York Times* would voluntarily stop publication. This would give Gurfein more time to look at the Pentagon Papers. Gurfein asked why a few days would make any difference. He thought it was a patriotic thing to do. Bickel said he was not authorized to agree to Gurfein's suggestion. When Gurfein was through, Bickel sought me out and told me of Gurfein's request. I said I would check.

By this time a huge crowd had gathered inside the courtroom and in its anteroom. It was filled with anti-Vietnam protestors who hissed every time the government lawyers walked by. With a pocket full of quarters, I rushed for the phone booth in the anteroom and finally got inside. It was very hot and there was no air conditioning. I told Bancroft, "The judge wants us to stop publication voluntarily—please tell me what to do." He said, "I'll check and call you back."

This was not an encouraging response. First of all, with whom was he going to check? Sulzberger was presumably unreachable in London and had left instructions that in his absence Bancroft was in charge. The night before at the *Times*, we had an all-out argument about whether we were going to obey Mitchell's telegram and stop publication. An oral request from a judge should not be any different than a telegram. The decision I was asking Bancroft to make had already been made the night before.

I waited and waited inside the booth, and waited some more. If I gave up the booth, there was no way I would get back in to take Bancroft's call. In the meantime, Gurfein was waiting, presumably impatiently, for an answer. There was no response. The anti-war protesters started banging on the telephone booth to get to the phone. My shirt was drenched with perspiration. I did not know how long I could hold off the protesters.

After about twenty minutes I gave up on hearing from Harding and called him back. I said, "Harding, we can't stop publication, it would be terrible." He said, "I agree." I went back to tell Bickel and Gurfein, who promptly issued a temporary restraining order or, to put it another way, a temporary prior restraint, and entered it at 4:30 p.m.

Alex, Floyd, and I went back to the *New York Times* in the early evening to report to Bancroft and to meet and have a drink with Reston, Rosenthal, Frankel, Sheehan, Smith and the others involved with the Pentagon Papers project. We met them in the backroom of the newsroom floor. As we entered, Reston said to Bickel, "The future of this institution is in your hands."

This was the first time the editors would have a chance to meet Alex Bickel. I was concerned about their reaction. They had total confidence in me, but who was this new guy? Alex was wonderful with the editors, even though he had lost the case for the time being and had not had any sleep. He was confident and ebullient. The editors went one-on-one and three-on-one with him to see if he was a "true believer" in the First Amendment. He persuaded them he was. But to put them on, he said, "You are always going to hate me." The reason they were always going to hate him was because he did not believe the First Amendment was absolute, that is, without any exceptions. I thought this was somewhat amusing, because neither did I, nor did any of the others at the *Times*.

CHAPTER XIV

NIXON HAS THE PRESS WHERE HE WANTS IT

Nixon had the *New York Times* right where he wanted it. He had finally gotten even. He had its presses stopped, at least as far as printing the Pentagon Papers. The California gubernatorial candidate of 1962 who said to the press, "You won't have Nixon to kick around any more," was triumphant for the moment.[1] What would his next move be? Nixon told Haldeman he wanted to "destroy the *Times*."[2] He was going to do this the same way he destroyed Alger Hiss.

Nixon told Haldeman that he had destroyed Hiss in the press. He had made Hiss a part of his attack on the Eastern establishment, and he was going to do the same to the *Times*. He asked Haldeman to round up public figures on both sides of the aisle to attack the *Times*. Maxwell Taylor, a respected five star general, said the *Times* showed "a practice of betrayal." John Tower, the influential senator from Texas, wondered whether the *Times* had lived up to its motto "All the News that's Fit to Print." W. Averell Harriman, Roosevelt's former Ambassador to Russia, said, "the *Times* had misled the public."[3]

Harding Bancroft had disqualified himself from being a leader of our team. He had taken the wrong side when he was against publication of the Pentagon Papers. Therefore, the task of leading our team fell to me. I knew more than anyone else where each piece of the case was. Even so, it was difficult to keep up with the fast-moving events. I was so busy that I had my fellow lawyers at the *Times* taking care of my laundry.

We had two days to get ready for a trial which promised to be a candidate for the trial of the century. It was set for Friday, so that left Wednesday and Thursday to get ready. Theoretically, we could use Tuesday night for strategy sessions. But Alex and Floyd had had not slept for thirty-six hours. And I had been up half the previous night.

The purpose of the trial was to decide whether the injunction Gurfein had granted should be made permanent. The issue was whether the Espionage Act, the First Amendment, or Executive Order 10501 permitted the injunction. These were the same questions I had been looking at for three months. Alex had added another issue: separation of powers.

Since the government had brought the case to begin with, it had the burden to prove it. It would attempt to do so by having witnesses testify. They would, no doubt, say the publication damaged national security. We had no idea who these witnesses would be. In an ordinary trial, you would have a chance to find out the identity of potential witnesses through a process known as "pretrial discovery." Lawyers can use this process to question prospective witnesses under oath in a conference room before the trial begins. We did not have time to do that.

With a case of this magnitude, a reasonable time frame from beginning to end would be two or three years. We were trying to do all of that in two days, or two and a half days if one wanted to count the research the young lawyers would have to do Tuesday night. We had no research readily available to us. In garden variety cases, lawyers prepare reams of research. All we had were the materials I gave to Bickel and Abrams Monday night, and whatever else they had been able to find in the early hours of Tuesday.

Our strategy was to break our team down into two groups. Bill and I would look at the facts and Alex and Floyd would do the "law." This meant the huge resources of Cahill Gordon would check out the nuances of the Espionage Act and whatever else they could find. Based on that research and his knowledge of Constitutional Law, Alex would write a major brief defending the *Times,* which would be delivered the next afternoon, Thursday, the day before the trial began.

Floyd would assist Alex with that brief. Ordinarily, such a brief would take months to finish. For example, the brief Alex was writing on the *Caldwell* case was still not finished, and he begun that two months earlier. This brief would guide Gurfein when the government made its cases through its witnesses.

To counter what the witnesses said was left to Hegarty and me. When the government witness testified, Hegarty would have to use his wits to contradict what they said. This was because we decided to use affidavits, not our own witnesses, to discredit the government. Affidavits were what the government had used to obtain an injunction against the *New York Times.* All of us at the *Times* believed that the classification system the government used was nonsensical, generally speaking. Over-classification by the government was notorious, as proven by my own example of stamping articles from the *New York Times* "secret."

We thought it would be easy to find former government officials to agree with us. All we had to do was call them on the phone, work out a statement, and get them to sign it. I was in charge of this process, since Hegarty did not know any of the *Times* personnel who could make calls. Nor was he sufficiently familiar with the names of those who had been in government who could provide us with such statements.

We were surprised at the turn-downs we received. I called Cy Vance, who had been a Secretary of the Army under Presidents Kennedy and Johnson. He said, "I'd better not do that." As I talked to him, it became clear it was not in his self interest to become involved in the case. It was generally thought he wanted to be Secretary of State, which he eventually became under Jimmy Carter, and participating in this case could well have jeopardized that ambition.

Cy's reputation was that he liked to tread lightly and not leave footprints. The *New York Times* later said in a story on him by Leslie Gelb, "Wherever he has gone he has left no footprints."[4] When he resigned from the board of directors of the *New York Times* Company to become Secretary of State, he stopped by Punch's office to say goodbye. Punch asked me to join them. After some pleasantries, Punch said to Cy, "I have a present for you." He unwrapped a huge plaster of paris foot, obviously one which would leave no footprints, and gave it to Cy with a big smile. Cy was not amused.

I suggested to Scotty Reston that he call McGeorge Bundy, who was national security advisor to Kennedy and Johnson. He turned Reston down quite coldly, saying "Your problems are not mine." Max Frankel called Nicholas Katzenbach, Assistant Attorney General who drafted the Tonkin Gulf Resolution—another rebuff. Bancroft called George Ball, former Under Secretary of State, and General Matthew Ridgeway, former Joint Chief of Staff. They both declined. I called Ted Sorensen, who was JFK's assistant and he said "yes."

This was a courageous thing for Sorensen to do. Years later, when President Jimmy Carter proposed he become head of the CIA, he had to withdraw because of that affidavit. Congress made it clear it was not going to confirm anyone in Carter's cabinet who submitted an affidavit in the Pentagon Papers case.

Sorenson's affidavit was similar to others we submitted from James McGregor Burns, the Roosevelt historian; Barbara Tuchman, the European historian; and Francis Plimpton, president of the New York City Bar Association.[5] In addition, six *New York Times* reporters submitted affidavits swearing that they regularly used classified information in their reporting. They were Neil Sheehan, Hedrick Smith, Tad Szulc, Robert Smith, Walter Rugaber, and John Finney.[6]

These affidavits said that classified information was commonly leaked and the leaks in the Pentagon Papers did not damage national security. The historians stated that it was important for the historical record that the history of decision making in the Vietnam War be available for study.

None of these affidavits, however, was as significant as the one Max Frankel submitted. It described in detail how classified information was leaked all the time in Washington, D.C. for political purposes. Max had been working closely with Bill Hegarty in order to help him with his cross examinations. This was a difficult job, since Bill did not know who the witnesses for the government would be. Bill was an extraordinarily talented trial lawyer, who specialized in withering cross examinations. He was not, however, a true believer in the First Amendment. When Bickel had met *Times* editors and reporters Monday night, he had convinced them he was a true believer, or at least enough to gain their confidence (privately he told Floyd and me he was not a "First Amendment voluptuary").

Hegarty infuriated Frankel by indicating his disbelief in the manner in which classified information was leaked. He was ready to accept that some classified information was classified without merit. But he was far more protective of the system than Frankel thought he should be. The *Washington Post* had the same problem with its lawyers, when the government sought to enjoin it. None of them were apparently true believers. They had to be convinced.

Frankel, frustrated by his conversation with Hegarty, decided he had to convince Hegarty. He wrote a long memorandum telling Hegarty how leaking classified information in Washington really worked, and how wrong he was. Frankel wrote: "For the vast majority of secrets, there has developed between the government and the press (and Congress) a rather simple rule of thumb: the government hides what it can, pleading necessity as long as it can, and the press pries out what it can, pleading a need and right to know."[7] He said, "A small and specialized corps of reporters and a few hundred American officials regularly make use of so-called classified secret and top secret information and documentation."[8]

"I know how strange all this must sound. We have been taught, particularly in the past generation of spy scares and the Cold War, to think of secrets as *secrets*— varying in their 'sensitivity' but uniformly essential to the private conduct of diplomatic and military affairs and somehow detrimental to the national interest if prematurely disclosed. .... For practically everything that our government does, plans, thinks, hears, and contemplates in the realms of foreign policy is stamped and treated as secret—and then unraveled by that same government, by the Congress and by the press, in one continuing round of professional and social contacts and cooperative and competitive exchanges of information."[9]

Hegarty, now persuaded, turned this memo into an affidavit. It was clearly one of the best legal papers filed in the case. It showed that the fears generated by the government about publishing secrets in the Pentagon Papers were simply not valid.

As Bill and I were preparing these affidavits, we did not know that Alex had taken a trip to the Second Circuit Court of Appeals in New York on Wednesday morning. Nor did we know that Sulzberger had landed in New York that morning from London and given a press conference. Neither event particularly helped us.

Alex had unwisely decided to pay a call on Judge Henry Friendly, the chief judge of the Second Circuit, where our case was pending before Judge Gurfein. He and Friendly were working on an academic project of mutual interest. Bickel went to see him about it, which he should not have done, because of the pending Pentagon Papers case. After discussing the project, Bickel told Friendly he thought he should have considered, and might still consider, appealing the restraining order granted by Gurfein the day before that had stopped the presses.

Friendly was rude to Bickel. He said, according to Bickel, "Everyone knows you can't appeal a TRO." Alex, for whom the Pentagon Papers case was his first case ever, didn't know that and was somewhat mortified. A TRO is only a temporary decision or temporary order by a court, and can't be appealed: when the final order is entered, one can appeal.

We were going to start our case at the trial level before Judge Gurfein on Friday morning, two days hence. It was inevitable, no matter who won the trial before Judge Gurfein, that it would be appealed to the next court. There were eight judges on that court, and Friendly was the chief judge.

He had an excellent reputation. He reportedly had the highest grades ever at Harvard Law School, other than the great Supreme Court Justice Louis Brandeis (for whom he clerked on the Supreme Court). To be the second smartest law student to ever go to Harvard was impressive. I had first heard of him when I was in law school. I had sat next to Judge David Bazelon, who was the Chief Judge in the Washington, D.C. Circuit Court of Appeals, at a law school dinner. His position on his court was comparable to Friendly's.

Bazelon complained to me about the quality of representation for the poor and civil rights in his court. He said the only good lawyer to appear before him arguing such cases was Henry Friendly. He appeared in those cases free of charge, pro bono. Bazelon's statement stayed with me through the years. It inspired me in part to be energetic and enthusiastic about First Amendment cases. Curiously enough, Bazelon and Friendly, as we shall see, played major roles in the Pentagon Papers case.

Friendly had been an partner at a major New York City law firm called Root, Clark, Buckner & Ballantine. He had led an acrimonious break-off from that firm and formed his own firm, Cleary, Gottlieb and Friendly. He then left to join the Second Circuit Court of Appeals. It was thought he did not like the *Times*. No one was sure of the reason, but there was a rumor that the *Times* had written something unflattering about his wife. As time developed, it turned out he didn't like me and I didn't like him. After the Pentagon Papers case, I said that the *New York Times* would disobey prior restraint orders. He told colleagues he would never sit down to dinner with me.

Punch came back from London sometime around noon. He was mobbed by the press when he got off the plane. Punch was a private person who did not enjoy making public appearances. At the press conference he said all the right things but appeared despondent, depressed, and dejected. He said the Pentagon Papers consisted of history and there should be no problem in publishing history.[10] Plainly, however, Louis Loeb and Herb Brownell had scared him to death.

In a sense, then, the Pentagon Papers case was not Punch's finest hour. He never came to any of the court hearings and was not particularly communicative during the case. (His finest hour, arguably, in cases of this sort, was when *New York Times* reporter Myron Farber was jailed for not disclosing his sources; but more about that later.)

Nonetheless, he had bet the ranch on a story which he did not find as exciting as the editors did. It took enormous courage for him to do that. From his point of view there was much to be despondent about. Rosenthal had sent him drafts of the stories to be published on June 1. He did not think the stories were important enough to risk going to jail and destroying his enterprise. He was joined in this view by Sydney Gruson and Harding Bancroft, whose offices were virtually next to his.

He sent the stories back several times before a final version was delivered nine days later, on June 10, when I read them with Bancroft. It turns out Punch was probably right about the stories, inasmuch as they did not make a splash. I thought the stories were extremely important to run, but I was a pushover in that regard. I had been trained as an undergraduate to be an historian. The Pentagon Papers were grist for my mill. They set out an important history of deceit as the country was led into a war it could not win.

The Pentagon Papers themselves have to be distinguished from the Pentagon Papers case. The case was historic and held the nation's attention for several weeks. The public was more interested in the case than the Papers. The case was about censorship, whereas the Papers were about history.

It is hard to say, however, the Pentagon Papers were hot news. They recounted events that had taken place no more recently than three years before, and in some cases, decades before. History of that sort had never been hot news. Punch's view was that if it was not highly readable, with overwhelming disclosures easily accessible to the reader, he should not take the risk of destroying the *Times*.

Since hardly anyone focused on what the Pentagon Papers said until they became the subject of an historic lawsuit, Punch's instinct may have been right. Several years later, in an amusing speech before the Committee to Protect Journalists at their annual dinner in 1996, he said:

> The more I listened the more certain I became that the entire operation smelled of twenty years to life. I quickly called the *Times*' longtime outside lawyers. Lord, Day & Lord was a well-established firm numbering among its clients the Cunard Line. Whether they were traumatized by the loss of the *Titanic* I really can't say, but they certainly were cautious. So cautious, indeed, that their senior partner [said] if the *Times* chose to publish the documents his firm would refuse to defend us.

> With all that cheerful advice, I called Abe Rosenthal and told him that if I were going to go to jail for publishing something, I thought it made sense to read it.... It wasn't too long before there was a knock at the door and in comes Abe, pushing a large shopping cart overflowing with papers. With a beatific smile, he announced, 'Here you are. Happy reading.' He loved it. Right then, I vowed to get even—when I got out.... He did not know it was possible to read and sleep at the same time. They were long—very long.

But one thing was undeniable. If I had been in charge of that mess, I'd have tried to keep it secret also...I have never understood why President Nixon fought so hard to squelch these papers. I would have thought that he would bemoan their publication, joyfully blame the mess on Lyndon Johnson, and move on to Watergate. But then I have never understood Washington.... I was convinced that one of two things would occur: Either they'd come and take me to jail or readers of the *Times* would fall back to bed exhausted by the weight of our coverage.

Monday morning came and, as I was still a free man, I assumed our readers to be asleep, so I went to Europe. It was a fine visit, lasting about three hours. But, ever confident, I told my wife to keep my suitcases and I'd be right back. My clothes had a wonderful holiday.... The rest is history. It was a fascinating time, but, like this speech, I'm glad it's over.[11]

The case for us, however, had just begun. We were pushing to prepare our briefs and affidavits for delivery the next day, when Nixon's lawyers dropped a bombshell—they wanted the name of our source.

CHAPTER XV

NIXON'S LAWYERS WANT OUR SOURCE

On Wednesday afternoon, Nixon's lawyers made a request that would have forced the *Times* to disclose its source. They wanted to copy our copies of the Pentagon Papers. Our documents, however, contained Ellsberg's handwriting, which could be traced to him. We had no alternative but to resist forcefully.

Mike Hess called Floyd Abrams to make this request on behalf of his boss, Mike Seymour. We had not anticipated that Nixon's lawyers would want our sources in addition to stopping our presses. The *Times* had already resisted Nixon's subpoena to Earl Caldwell, and that case was in the Supreme Court. We wanted Caldwell's case to be decided there, not in the middle of what we thought was going to be an historic case against censorship. If Nixon's lawyers wanted to pursue the issue of disclosure of sources they could, but it would be an all-out fight. Perhaps, we thought, our forceful resistance would persuade Judge Gurfein it was not in his interest to hold us in contempt, any more than it was in ours. He was already presiding over a high profile case and he did not need a second case going on at the same time.

The reason Seymour wanted a copy of the Pentagon Papers was that, incredibly, he did not know which copy we had. When the *Times* first published, it took two days for the Justice Department in Washington to come up with a copy, which it found in a desk in the State Department that had once belonged to "Bill" Bundy, the brother of Mac Bundy.[1]

No one in the government had kept a precise inventory of what each of the fifteen copies of the Pentagon Papers contained. Some copies had documents missing. The *Times'* did not have four chapters on the secret negotiations for ending the war in Vietnam. And so Seymour, in a sense, was playing blind man's bluff. He was seeking an injunction against the publication of the Pentagon Papers but he didn't know exactly what he was seeking to enjoin. On the other hand, if the Pentagon Papers had been so secret and confidential, one would have thought the government would have taken more care to protect them.

Seymour wanted the *Times* to photocopy its 7,000 pages of the Papers, which we would then deliver for his use at the trial, set a few days hence. When Floyd called us for instructions, we told him to tell Hess we were not going to comply. When Hess heard this, he immediately obtained an order at 5:15 p.m. for the *Times* to be in court the next morning at 10:00 to explain why it would not comply with Seymour's request.

Since we had told Hess we were not going to comply, this order did not come as surprise but, nonetheless, it was very much unwelcome. We were trying to get ourselves ready for a trial a little more than forty-eight hours away, which required extensive preparation. We had no time to prepare for another case. The *Times* was expected to deliver an authoritative brief on the Pentagon Papers case the next day, Thursday, answering the charges made on Tuesday, when the government had obtained a temporary restraining order.

While the demand for our sources was unwelcome, we knew exactly what we were going to say. After all, Floyd, Alex, and I had started off the week by working on our "Caldwell brief" to the Supreme Court. We would make the very same argument again before Gurfein. The government had to show 1) a compelling (overriding) interest why it needed to reveal sources; 2) that such information was "essential" to its case; and 3) it had made every effort to obtain the information sought from other sources.[2] This is what the courts had decided in the *Caldwell* case. We wanted Gurfein to follow that case.

As we said in our brief: "There is no 'overriding national interest' here such as could possibly justify forcing a reporter to breach his confidence. There is indeed, in a case such as this, if there ever is, an overriding national interest in *protecting* the confidence and thus making this sort of reporting possible. Government officials here are trying by injunctive process and disguised subpoenas to shield other government officials, past and present, from searching scrutiny."[3]

I took more than a little pride in our defense. The *Times* had been fighting Nixon for eighteen months. In that time, we had come up with a new defense, the reporter's privilege, and we were prepared to throw it at him. But where would we be if we had not decided to fight Nixon eighteen months ago? We would not have had this defense and Nixon would have run all over us. We would have had to fight the government without any arrows in our quiver. Now we had the *Caldwell* precedent, and we would use it to stop Nixon from getting our source.

There was an additional benefit from having stood up and fought. During the *Caldwell* case, New York State had passed an absolute shield law. This law stated that under no circumstance could a reporter be required to disclose his source. It gave a reporter absolute protection to "shield" him from testifying, hence the name, "shield law."

I had been active in the passage of this bill along with my friend, Al Hruska of Cravath Swaine & Moore, who worked closely with Robert Douglas, counsel to then-Governor Nelson Rockefeller. Douglas got the bill through the State Legislature. Since the shield law was a state law, it was not clear that it protected the *New York Times* in a federal court. Nonetheless, we could use it to persuade

Gurfein our position was reasonable. After all, if the New York State Legislature thought sources should be protected, he should too.

Alex called me to say he could not present our argument Thursday morning. The *Times*, of course, had hired Alex to be its voice, backed up by Cahill. But he could not do everything. He was in the middle of his brief and had to finish it. He said Floyd had to do the argument in his place. There was no time to consider options for who could do this or that. Events were transpiring so quickly that we had to react almost without thinking.

Floyd's argument was his first appearance on the national stage. He has since become an authority on the First Amendment. Then, however, he was the youngest man on our team. He was a very junior partner. In ordinary conversation, his speech would occasionally break up into an imperceptible stutter. But that didn't happen when he stood up in court on Thursday to make our argument. He did an excellent job. He was appropriately antagonistic to the idea the government would even dare to want any information in our possession including copies of the Pentagon Papers.

Gurfein cut Floyd off before he could get to his main point about protecting sources. Gurfein wanted to be "practical," he said. Instead of turning over a copy of all the Pentagon Papers to the government, why not just turn over a list of the volumes the *Times* had. Floyd said the *Times* would turn over a list of what they had published. Gurfein said that he wasn't interested in that. He wanted a list of everything the *New York Times* had, and asked Floyd to relay his request to the *Times*. He wanted an answer before 5:00 p.m. The trial, of course, began at 10:00 the next morning.

Floyd then launched into his main argument. It was a dress rehearsal for the argument to be made in the Supreme Court by Earl Caldwell's counsel. Floyd finished by saying, "The Caldwell case and its progeny pose the most serious, the most significant and some of the most difficult judicial issues for resolution… we submit…that nothing should be done in this case which could compromise the confidential source."[4] In a sense, he made his reputation with his argument, which appeared substantially verbatim in the *New York Times* the next day.[5] There are few, if any, lawyers who have had their entire argument printed word-for-word in a national newspaper.

After the argument, Bill Hegarty and I hurried back to the *Times*. I had to convene a group of editors responsible for the Pentagon Papers to decide how they would respond to Gurfein's request to deliver a list to him. I rounded up Jim Greenfield, Tom Wicker, Abe, and Harding. Since I had led the conversations with Abe and other editors in developing the *Times'* position on the reporter's privilege over the last eighteen months, I ran the meeting.

In the past, meetings with the *Times'* editors and reporters on sources had been incendiary. Reporters would rather go to jail than turn over information on sources, no matter what the circumstances. For whatever reason, probably because we were under so much pressure, this one turned out to be calm and reflective.

My position was that generally speaking, the *Times* should not give a list of news material in its possession to anybody, particularly to the government, without a demonstration of compelling need. But in this case, if you believed the government, it did have a compelling need for at least a list of what we had. Furthermore, that information was not available from other sources. The question was whether never letting the government know what we had was a principle we should defend under the First Amendment under all circumstances, particularly the present one. I thought not.

It would have been counterproductive, however, to tell the editors and reporters sitting around the table my position. They had to reach their own conclusion. A principal issue for them was whether as a matter of fact, the list, as requested by Gurfein, would identify their source. Jim Greenfield's concern was that if the *Times* gave the government its list, the list itself could be used to trace the source.

The volumes the *Times* had might be the only ones the source had. I didn't know who the source was, although it was generally believed to be Daniel Ellsberg. No one around the room was going to confirm or deny that. As a matter of principle, reporters and editors never disclose their source to anyone, including me, regardless of the circumstances.

After two hours of deliberation, the editors concluded there was no risk in giving the government the list that Gurfein had demanded, and that no First Amendment principle was violated. Bill and I then called Whitney North Seymour, Jr., to set up a meeting to see if he would agree with this approach. While Gurfein had suggested the *Times* deliver a list, he had not ordered it. The *Times* and the government had to agree.

In the afternoon Bill and I met with Seymour and Hess. This was my first opportunity to meet Seymour. As U.S. Attorney for the Southern District, he held what most thought was the best prosecutor job in the country. His predecessors were nationally known. It was the tradition of the office that the holder would be independent of the Attorney General and not bring political cases or other cases which he thought were inappropriate. Seymour was a Republican, it being customary for a Republican president to appoint one of his own party as prosecutor for the Southern District.

According to his memoirs, Seymour did not have an easy time at the Justice Department. He and Mardian did not get along, and he thought many of Mardian's positions on national security were nonsensical.[6] It seemed, however, he was perfectly comfortable bringing a suit against the *New York Times*.

He was tall, aristocratic and the son of Whitney North Seymour, a noted lawyer who had argued, at that time, more antitrust cases in the Supreme Court than any other lawyer. He was the presiding partner at Simpson, Thatcher, where his son had been a partner before he left to become the prosecutor for the Southern District of New York.

Seymour had gone to Yale Law School with Bill Hegarty. There was some jawing at the beginning of the meeting. Seymour wanted a copy of the Papers, no matter what. Bill and I finally talked him out of it and we made a deal to give him only a list.

Many years later, Judge Murray Gurfein told me he had never intended to enforce the government's request which would have disclosed our sources. He said he knew the *Times* would never turn over the Papers and disclose its source. He did not want to be in the position of holding the *Times* in contempt.

In fighting for the press, I remembered what he said. It was a lesson. In such a fight, one should never give an inch and always be prepared to go into contempt. Judges do not want to send reporters to jail any more than reporters want to go there. A seemingly tough, unyielding position will persuade courts to come up with a reasonable solution as Gurfein did. The question before us at the end of Thursday was, however, not how reasonable Gurfein had been, but how reasonable he would be the next day when the trial began.

CHAPTER XVI
THE REPUBLIC STILL STANDS

Friday, June 18 was a historic day. It was the first trial involving a prior restraint on a newspaper in a federal court in the nation's history. The courtroom was packed. There were hundreds of anti-Vietnam War protestors on the courthouse steps. Again, they hissed at the government lawyers as they went by. Inside, the packed room overwhelmed the air conditioning. Perspiration streamed down the faces of the lawyers.

The case had become the number one story in the country. There was far greater interest in the trial of the Pentagon Papers than in the Papers themselves. Every time I walked with the other lawyers up the courthouse steps, the press would shout "here they come," and run over for an interview. Jerry Rubin, the famed antiwar protestor, peered over my shoulder as I talked to the press in front of a gaggle of microphones.

There were actually two separate hearings scheduled for the day. First, Gurfein was to hold a public hearing in the regular courtroom. Then later in the afternoon, a classified hearing was to take place in the basement of the courthouse, where only the judge, the lawyers for both sides, and the government witnesses would be allowed to attend. Earlier that morning, there had been a major break in the case. The *Washington Post* had published part of the Pentagon Papers. The series was entitled "Documents Revealed, U.S. Effort in '54 to Delay Viet Election."[1] Further, it distributed the story to the 345 members of its news syndicate, including the *New York Post*.

We were elated. We thought our case was over, as a practical matter. How could the government stop us and not the *Washington Post*? And if it stopped the *Post*, how about the others that were sure to follow? The government was chasing a swarm of bees.

The *Washington Post* and the *New York Times* were fierce rivals and remain so today. There was some arrogance on the behalf of *Times* editors toward the *Post*. They thought it was, in a sense, an upstart. Abe Rosenthal was quite vocal about it. He did not think the *Post* was on the same intellectual level as the *New York Times*.

In fact, it may not have been at the time of the Pentagon Papers, but it was clearly on the rise. Kay Graham, the owner, and Ben Bradlee, the editor, brought the *Post* along quickly. Later, after its sensational reporting on Watergate, which began the next year, 1972, most press observers thought the *Post* had reached the level of the *Times*.

Even though the *Washington Post* was our arch-competitor and had stolen our story, we were all quite happy the *Post* had published. We welcomed its support. It helped our argument that publishing classified information was not traitorous, as the Nixon Administration was portraying it.

Ellsberg had given a little more than half of the Pentagon Papers (4,000 pages) to Ben Bagdikian, the *Post*'s assistant managing editor for national affairs. They were read at Bradlee's home by reporters Chalmer Roberts, Murrey Marder, and Don Oberdorfer, the *Post*'s Vietnam specialists.

The *Post* lawyers, Roger Clark and Anthony Essaye of Royall, Koegel & Wells, were also at Bradlee's home and were advising against publication. They sounded a lot like Lord, Day & Lord. One of them allegedly said: "I am convinced the government can make a substantial criminal case against you if something damaging slips into the newspaper. They already waved the espionage flag at the *Times*."[2]

Fritz Beebe, the chairman of the *Post*, also advised Kay Graham not to publish. He held the same position at the *Post* as Harding Bancroft held at the *Times*. He had the same background as Bancroft. He'd been a lawyer at Cravath Swaine & Moore. Neither had newspaper experience. Each had represented the corporate side of his respective paper.

To complicate matters, the *Post* had just made a public offering of limited voting stock to the public. Beebe was worried about the impact of the publication of the Pentagon Papers on the offering. The terms of the offering were substantially similar to the ones I had drafted for the *New York Times* four years earlier.

The reporters, however, were astounded by the government lies the Papers revealed. After hearing the lawyers argue against publication, some said they would quit unless the *Post* published. In the end, Graham ignored the advice of Beebe as well as that of her lawyers. She published. It was a courageous decision. She was, however, able to rely on what the *Times* had done, which made the decision easier for her. Similarly, *Post* editors could rely on the work the *Times*' editors had done.

Bradlee knew that the *Times* had spent months verifying the documents. He did not have to worry whether the Papers were fake or not. Years later, I asked him on my TV program, "How did you have time…to check it all out?" Bradlee answered, "The *New York Times* had those documents for three months…I should have had more than twelve hours, but I didn't. So you have to do what you have to do."[3]

At the beginning of the public hearing, based on the publication by the *Post*, we asked Gurfein to dismiss the case. Bickel stood up and said, "the Republic still stands and it stood the first three days [we published.]"[4] There was laughter in the courtroom. Gurfein was not happy with the remark "the Republic still stands." He said, "apparently the remark that elicited the laughter is your statement that the Republic still stands. I don't see anything funny about that." Bickel said, "I'm surprised that it's a laughing matter." Gurfein said, "So am I."[5]

Gurfein said that he was troubled by two matters in connection with the Pentagon Papers. First, he was worried that the Pentagon Papers disclosed codes. Secondly, he was concerned about the impact of messages from government to government. "I am concerned about…the lack of perhaps paraphrase of code messages…[and] materials sent by foreign governments which do not belong to the United States under the rules of international law…and a few other limited categories of that type or perhaps the revelation of methods of intelligence gathering."[6]

As someone who had general intelligence training, but certainly not at the level of Judge Gurfein, I recognized his approach. The sources and methods of intelligence are considered by the intelligence agencies to be sacrosanct, not subject to disclosure under any circumstances. Similarly, the first thing you learn as an intelligence analyst is that classified material contains codes, but only a trained eye can see them. Gurfein was sitting in this hearing as much as an intelligence officer as a judge. He was not going to be satisfied that the *Times* could publish until he had satisfied himself on those two points.

In a sense, Gurfein took over the hearing. He asked nearly as many questions of the witnesses as did the lawyers. His polite and courteous disagreement with witnesses was as effective as the cross examination of those witnesses by Hegarty. Knowing the mindset of intelligence officers, I felt certain the question of codes would be raised in the case. I thought the government would raise the issue (which it did); I did not anticipate the court would raise it.

In this connection, I spent much of the previous afternoon lining up witnesses who were code experts. I engaged Andrew Gleason, a professor of mathematics at Harvard University, and David Kahn, perhaps the most famous code expert in the US, to be our witnesses. I had spent some time with David going over what his testimony might be. He subsequently wrote the book *The Code Breakers*, one of the classic works on code making and breaking.

I was correct to anticipate that the government would attempt to make the case into a code case. Nixon later said that a principal reason he brought the case was his fear publication would disclose intelligence about codes.[7]

And so the issue of codes was a dominant theme in the Pentagon Papers case. It was present in our case before Gurfein and Friendly, it was part of the *Washington Post* case, and it surfaced again at the Supreme Court. Apparently, the government reasoned that no one would challenge its unsupported allegation that the publication of the Pentagon Papers broke codes. The courts would just accept that allegation.

The government, however, never came out and flatly said "the Pentagon Papers case is a code case." To have done that it would have had to have sued the *Times* under Section 798 of the Espionage Act, which specifically prohibits the publication of codes. Nonetheless, the government kept references to codes in the case to suit its own purposes: to scare the court.

The first witness the government called was Dennis J. Doolin, deputy assistant secretary of defense for Internal Security Affairs. He was on leave from Stanford University. Doolin was a mild-mannered academic. He was totally ineffective as a witness but he had an interesting story to tell. He had been asked three times by Senator J. William Fulbright (D-Ark), Chairman of the Senate Foreign Relations Committee, to declassify the Pentagon Papers. He refused the request every time.

He did not know, nor did we at the time, that Daniel Ellsberg had asked Senator Fulbright to read the Pentagon Papers into the Congressional Record. Fulbright did not think he could do this without going through proper channels. This meant making a request to the Secretary of Defense Melvin Laird. Laird then asked Doolin, who said "no" each time.

Doolin could not explain satisfactorily to Judge Gurfein why he had turned Fulbright's request down. He tried again at the secret hearing which took place at the end of the day, and again failed. It turned out he had only read six volumes of the forty-seven.

It also turned out he had been assisted by another analyst named Kathryn Truex. Who was Truex? He said she was "deputy director of the Office of Special Concerns in Health, Education and Welfare." "Is she on loan to the Department of Defense?" asked Seymour. Doolin's reply: "This is a permanent position. She transferred, Miss Truex is now my wife."[8]

The fact that an engaged couple was in charge of declassifying the Pentagon Papers did not increase confidence that the decision had been made objectively. Doolin could not explain the general rules of declassification. Documents are stamped, One, Two, Three or Four in addition to being stamped "top secret," "secret," "classified." Documents in the lower group were declassified faster than those with the numbers One and Two.

Apparently, the Pentagon Papers were never stamped with numerals. They were not subject to declassification unless Doolin or his fiancee approved. Doolin became so confused about how the system worked that the government had to call another witness, George MacClain, director of the Security Classification Management Division in the office of the Assistant Secretary of Defense for Administration. He testified later in the afternoon and explained the system to Gurfein's satisfaction. It was clear Gurfein had concluded that in the ordinary course of things, there would have been no way the Pentagon Papers would be declassified, perhaps ever.

The government's case had gotten off to a terrible start. Doolin used up most of the morning trying to explain the classification system. He couldn't. He typified the government bureaucrat who stamps everything in sight "secret." He underscored our argument that stamping a document "Secret" was not the final word on the subject. The other two witnesses the government called after Doolin, Vice Adm. Francis J. Blouin, vice chief of Naval Operations, and William B. Macomber, deputy undersecretary of State in charge of administration, were better, but left a lot to be desired.

Macomber stated generally that publication of the Pentagon Papers made relationships between the United States and other governments difficult to maintain. Such governments, he claimed, would not have confidence in the ability of the United States to keep its secrets. Blouin made short, vague statements like "it would have been a disaster to publish all of these other documents," and "any intelligence organization will derive a great deal of benefit from the articles that have already been published."[9]

Blouin's statements, on the surface, were excellent ones for the government. The government wanted to prove the publication was "a disaster." But could Blouin prove it? What secrets had the Pentagon Papers revealed? Why was it a disaster? We would have to wait for the secret hearings. We thought, however, generally the government's case thus far was incompetent. It would have to do a lot better to win in the secret hearing.

We had now spent two hours in the morning listening to Doolin and Blouin and about the same time after lunch at the public hearing, listening mostly to MacClain describe how the classification system worked. At 4:30 we left for the secret hearing room with visions of the Spanish Inquisition.

CHAPTER XVII
WHAT SECRETS DOES THE GOVERNMENT HAVE?

Judge Gurfein led a procession of participants in the trial to the secret hearing room—Messrs. Seymour, Hess, Mardian, Bickel, Hegarty, Abrams, Bancroft, Max Frankel, and me. Messrs. Doolin, Blouin, Macomber, MacClain, and Buzhardt— witnesses for the government—also followed him. There the government was going to reveal its secrets.

This room was at the bottom of the U.S. courthouse in Foley Square. It was a deep, dark, dank room—suitable for secret trials. It was indeed a place where the Spanish Inquisition could have been held—appropriate for the first national security case against a newspaper.

Strict rules of security were followed. All notes were marked "secret." They were torn up at the end of the hearing and deposited in a safe place and then the government took them away. Alex Bickel was expected to destroy the notes he made in preparation for his closing argument before he left the secret hearing room.

Judge Gurfein sat at the end of the hearing room. Floyd and I sat at a counsel's table, as did Hegarty, Bickel, and Frankel. Frankel was there to provide Hegarty with input for cross examination. In a sense, we were going to do the trial all over again, but this time with all the government's secrets laid out. We were expectant, waiting to hear what the government had.

On came Doolin again, and he wasn't any better than he was the first time. The more specific the questions became as to the national security secrets disclosed in the Papers, the less convincing he was. He refused to name any particular document or any particular information in the Pentagon Papers which he thought damaged national security. His basic point was that in the international arena, if you can't keep secrets, you can't have effective relationships with other nations.

He told Gurfein he did not have to identify particular damage to national security. "The point here is not an individual document; the point is the study and the point, in my opinion, sir, is the fact, as Mr. Macomber said this morning, you can't do business if you can't keep secrets, either in a military or a political sense. That is the basic point."[1] He used as examples the reactions of Australia and Thailand to the Pentagon Papers.

The Australian Prime Minister William McMahon was furious at the publication of the Pentagon Papers. The official position of the Australians was that they contributed troops to Vietnam because of SEATO (South Eastern Asia Treaty Organization). In fact, they had been muscled by the U.S. to provide those troops. If the Australian public found out about this, the Prime Minister would be forced to pull his troops out of Vietnam. And if Australia left, then New Zealand would not be far behind.

The U.S. was flying most of its jets out of a Thai Air Force base under secret cover and the Thai government was embarrassed at this disclosure. If the Thai government was forced to publicly admit such base existed, Doolin argued, the U.S. would not be able to use the base anymore.

Doolin also said the publication of the SEATO contingency plan damaged national security. Judge Gurfein noted "that could only be so if the plan was current." It was not. It was three years old. SEATO was thought to be moribund at the time of the publication of the Pentagon Papers. Doolin said third party countries would not act for the United States. This would make negotiations for peace and the release of POWs difficult. It would also "threaten" the phased withdrawal of U.S. troops.

Doolin frustrated Gurfein with these answers. They were too general. He would not point to specific secrets in the Pentagon Papers. Gurfein became a scolding mother. "I will give you one more chance…to add to your testimony…with more specificity those dangers to security you mentioned."[2] He couldn't.

Doolin also said publication of the Pentagon Papers would reveal codes. "I do know…from reviewing the study…that it gets into the area of communications intelligence…. This material as used in the study, is not so identified and can only be picked up, your honor, by a trained eye."[3]

Gurfein asked, "You are talking about intercepts?" Doolin replied, "Signal intelligence, electronics intelligence, communication intelligence, the whole range of that intelligence and this can only be picked up in the study by a trained eye and the only way you could acquire that particular item of information is by this channel."[4]

As I noted earlier, I always thought codes would be part of the case. Gurfein's answer to this assertion seemed to be conclusive, "there must come a time that wouldn't be true anymore?"[5] In other words, even if Doolin were correct, although there was no evidence that he was, the codes were three years old. They would have been changed.

"It is difficult for me to take a statement that is so general that communications intelligence, I think you said, can be picked up in a study by a trained eye," Gurfein said.

Doolin: "It can, sir."

Gurfein: "The question is…are we to believe our codes are so inflexible that we don't change enough to fool an enemy?"

Doolin responded: "I'm not talking about ours, Your Honor, I'm talking about theirs."

Gurfein: "You are talking about interception?"

Doolin: "Yes sir."

Gurfein: "In that field doesn't the enemy normally intercept? Everybody intercepts everybody else."[6]

Clearly, Gurfein was tiring of hearing generalized claims about codes. His attitude was "They read us, we read them, so what?" I wanted to applaud, but of course I could not.

Doolin's statement was typical of the government's case. He and the government were using scare tactics they could not prove. Doolin was saying, effectively, "there is communications intelligence in the Pentagon Papers. Only a trained eye can see it. I do not have a trained eye so I can't see it, and the *New York Times* can't see it either. But trust me, it's there." It is very difficult to respond to that type of assertion.

Before the secret hearings started, Hegarty and Seymour agreed in Gurfein's robing room that "codes were out of the case."[7] The reason for this agreement was the government had not sued for breaching codes under Section 798 of the Espionage Act. It was unfair to bring codes in the case tangentially without giving the *Times* a fair chance to respond. It was a lack of "due process," which is a lawyer's term for fairness.

Over the course of the next two weeks, however, we learned to our dismay there is no such thing as "fair play" or "due process" in a national security case. References to codes by Doolin, and later by others, continued. Finally, at the end of the hearing Hegarty complained to the court. The government was not living up to its promise to keep codes out of the case.

Seymour disagreed with Hegarty's characterization. He said, "I do want to make it clear that having gone to some extremes to try to be perfectly fair on the question of codes, that our position has been turned unfairly against us."[8] Seymour went on to say that he would agree not to "hint" at the existence of codes, but that agreement did not foreclose the question of whether codes were still a question in the case. "I think it is disingenuous of the counsel for the defendants to argue that there is no such question in existence. There is certainly a question in existence."[9]

This was a very peculiar answer. He would not "hint" at codes, but nonetheless, the "question" of codes was still in the case. Either codes were in or out of the case, they can't be both. As will be seen, this "question" of codes continued to appear in this case and in the *Washington Post* case.

As in the morning's trial, Vice Admiral Blouin followed Doolin. Blouin had said in the morning the Pentagon Papers would materially damage national security. We were waiting for him to tell us exactly how. He couldn't. All he could give was general answers.

After the trial, Seymour said he was instructed not to ask witnesses specific questions. This was because Mardian was concerned that such questions would elicit answers that would damage national security.[10] If so, this would explain Blouin's inability to pinpoint damage.

Blouin was also handicapped since he only had started reading the Papers on Wednesday night. Naturally, with 7,000 pages to read, he didn't get very far. Doolin, it will be recalled, only read six of the forty-seven volumes. Blouin's principal point was that the Tonkin Gulf Control Study should not be published. This was a study, not technically a part of the Pentagon Papers, that analyzed the "Tonkin Gulf incident." The Johnson Administration had used the incident to justify the Vietnam War.

Blouin went into great detail why publication of the study damaged national security. Hegarty interrupted the testimony to say that the *Times* didn't have the Tonkin Gulf Control Study. All they had was a three page summary. Ellsberg had apparently kept the full study out of the material given to the *Times*. This deflated Blouin. He based a major part of his testimony on the assumption the *Times* had a highly secret document. He was wrong. They didn't have it.

Blouin also testified on codes. "On the matter of codes which has come up several times...I felt there were reference to codes and traffic on V, B, pages 451 through 474 which seem to contain old messages. There again, it isn't so much maybe the fact that these are old messages—that would let anyone who has kept the tapes of that old traffic, if they can get translation and go back into their files and break them—we grant there have been changes made since those days."[11]

Hegarty objected, "Your honor, before the witness testifies, I would like to move to strike the testimony with respect to the effect on codes.... The United States Attorney in your robing room said codes were out of the case."[12] Gurfein did not strike the testimony. The government once again got away with using codes as a scare tactic.

Blouin also objected to the description of withdrawal plans, strategic strike capacity and the military command structure. He said he did not like to "read in such great detail"[13] about our strategic strike capacity. As to military command structure, he said, "I don't see any purpose in publicizing it in detail."[14]

Gurfein said, "Every day on television I can find out almost the entire order of battle of the United States Army and Marines, isn't that true? 'I am here with the First Division at so and so and we are doing this.' Warfare today is different from what it was in the days when there was really security. Everybody and his brother knows what everybody is doing today. The question I am asking you is can you relate, and [whether there are] instances of serious impact.... I wonder in the times we live in whether you don't have to adjust...."[15]

Blouin could not cite one example "of serious impact."[16] A few days after this unconvincing testimony, Blouin was fired as a witness by Robert Mardian.

His place was taken at the *Washington Post* trial by Lieutenant General Melvin Zais, who was an operations director for the Joint Chiefs of Staff.

William B. Macomber, deputy undersecretary of State in charge of administration, testified next. He was known to his friends as "Butts," his middle name. He had gone to Yale and Harvard Law School, where he was a classmate of Alex Bickel.

Macomber was what you would expect of a Yale man who had become a diplomat. He was well-dressed, well-groomed, well-spoken, and well-educated. When he left the State Department he became the president of the Metropolitan Museum of Art, an important post in the social and cultural world of New York City, and one at which Macomber excelled.

His point was the same as it had been in open court: Publication of the Pentagon Papers made it very difficult for the United States to conduct diplomacy. He said that such publication had "embarrassed" the governments of Australia and Canada. The government had asked a Canadian diplomat, Blair Seaborn, to act for it in secret negotiations with the North Vietnamese. Seaborn was a member of the International Control Commission (ICC), a supposedly neutral body.

The North Vietnamese were led to believe that Seaborn was acting on behalf of the Canadian government. He was not. "The fact that we've gone and talked about it is a source of embarrassment to them. It has raised questions in parliament and with the opposition that apparently Canadians just go to the beck and call of us."[17]

In Australia, as Doolin previously testified, publication of Australia's role in Vietnam had made Prime Minister William McMahon furious. His predecessor, Robert Menzies, had told his parliament that Australian troops were going to Vietnam because of his SEATO obligations. Macomber said, however, "the documents imply they went there through United States maneuvering." He said further, "this is the kind of revelation that undermines our relations with an extremely important ally."[18]

Gurfein did not seem impressed with his testimony. Even if Macomber was correct that publication caused "embarrassment" to the Canadians or created a "political storm" in Australia, could that be said to damage national security sufficiently (if at all) to justify a prior restraint?

Gurfein seemed more interested in Macomber's third point, that the Papers contained an "eyes only" telegram from U.S. Ambassador to Russia Llewellyn Thompson. He said the Russians would know how we thought, and would restrict the candor of future ambassadors to Russia. Macomber was followed by Messrs. MacClain and Buzhardt, but their testimony was inconsequential.

It was now 8:30 p.m. We had been going since 10:00 am, with an hour and a half break for lunch. We were in a tiny room in the basement of the court. It was a case of immense national interest, but no one except us knew what was going on. And no one would find out until 1977, when the transcript of the secret hearing was finally released by the Federal District Court. Even then, however, parts of the transcript remained classified.

The government had presented no case at all. There were no secrets in the Pentagon Papers. None of the testimony constituted a clear and present danger to our national security. "A clear and present danger" may or may not have been the appropriate test to apply in this case. But it was one way to think of it.

Macomber complained about political embarrassment. Blouin complained about command structure, battle plans, and similar items, which were already public. He just didn't want to give them more publicity. Doolin's complaint was that publication inhibited the nation's ability "to do business."

They did not complain about the publication of secrets. They complained about the kind of information the *Times* published daily. And so, as a common sense matter, putting the law aside, we should win. I wanted the court to say not only that we won, but that in the future something like clear and present danger, or better, would have to be shown. It certainly wasn't shown in what we heard.

Whatever test the court adopted, it should require some demonstration of immediacy, i.e., that there would be an immediate danger to the country. The Pentagon Papers were history. It is virtually impossible to show the publication of history can cause immediate damage. Everything the *Times* published was three to twenty-five years old.

I did not know exactly what was the applicable articulation of the test. It was a case of first impression. No case had ever been decided like this before. It was like the *Caldwell* case, where we had to invent a First Amendment test.

The only case that came close to this one was *Near v. Minnesota* (the newspaper libel case). The court there said—but did not decide—that an injunction could be granted if a newspaper published the sailing date of troop ships. I never thought the example of troop ships was cataclysmic enough. My own example of what should not be published was the secret of the hydrogen bomb. That seemed to me a far more cataclysmic situation than the dates of sailings of troop ships.

As Alex got up to speak, these were the thoughts that went through my head. I wanted him to parallel my thinking. Because of the pressure of events, we had not had time to thrash out a particular test as we had during the *Caldwell* case. I knew instinctively that his views were the same as mine from the discussions we had had over the last months on the *Caldwell* case, but I did not know precisely what they were in this context.

While quite fatigued, Alex didn't show it. His argument in the secret hearing room was the best of his arguments, save for the one he would make in the Supreme Court. He made a convincing case and the government's argument did not measure up.

He started by saying that the government "has a burden of proving for purposes of the First Amendment...the grave consequence, serious dangers, enormous impending events which will befall us if your Honor lifts the temporary restraining order and this publication goes on."[1]

He made it clear the government had not met its burden. He said he was "not talking about the case coming to the attention of the President that somebody's possession of the ultimate atomic weapon secret or sailing dates of ship and troops—I am not talking about that. I am talking about a case in which...all that is alleged essentially is that these are classified documents in the judgment of officers of the government who classify documents...and the *Times* has them and it is inconvenient and otherwise disagreeable to the government that the *Times* has them."[2]

It was clear that the *Times* was proposing an extremely difficult test to meet, although, in my mind, the troop ship example muddied it up. Seymour, from his perspective, said that all the government had to prove was irreparable harm. It should be apparent there is a huge difference between proving irreparable harm or a superior test, such as clear and immediate danger.

Bickel repeated the argument made in his brief that the Espionage Act did not apply. He relied heavily on the legislative history of the passage of the Espionage Act. Cahill Gordon had discovered that Congress, in 1917, had not intended to include the publication of newspapers in Section 793(e) of the Espionage Act, just as I had initially suspected. I had asked Lord, Day & Lord to research this point for me. It had never delivered a memorandum on this subject. In fact, it never delivered a memorandum of law to me at all. I found their memorandum after the case; they apparently delivered it to Bancroft, who did not show it to me. In any event, the memo did not cover legislative history. I had interpreted Section 793(e) appropriately.

This history of the Espionage Act was quite compelling. In 1917 Congress had proposed an amendment to a predecessor version of the Espionage Act that would permit censorship of the press during wartime. There was testimony in the House explicitly saying what this amendment intended to do. This amendment was vigorously opposed.

In the Senate, Senator Henry F. Ashurst made a rousing speech to defeat this provision. He was quite clear that, as originally drafted, it would allow censorship of the press—prior restraint. He was against the provision because it violated the First Amendment.

He said, "What does 'freedom of the press' mean?…'Freedom of the press' means simply, solely, and only the right to be free from a pre-censorship, the right to be free from the restraints of a censor. In other words, under the Constitution as amended by Amendment No. 1, 'freedom of the press' means nothing except that the citizen is guaranteed that he may publish whatever he sees fit and not be subject to pains and penalties because he did not consult the censor before doing so."[3]

In 1957, Congress again considered amending Section 793(e). Senator Humphrey of Minnesota noted the amendment contained "new criminal penalties against disclosure of secret information by newsmen."[4] The sponsor of this amendment, Senator Norris H. Cotton of New Hampshire, agreed with Humphrey that his proposed amendment should be changed. Cotton said that in any amendment to 793(e) it "should be made crystal clear that at the present time penalties for the disclosure of secret information can only be applied against those employed by the government [and not the press]."[5]

It was not by chance that 793(e) penalized "communication" but didn't use the word "publication." Congress never intended to cover "publication" in 793(e). When I read this history, I thought it would ultimately eliminate the Espionage Act from consideration in our case. The Nixon administration had brought the case against the *New York Times* under a law that absolutely did not apply to the *Times*.

Bickel also argued that Executive Order 10501 did not apply. This was the regulation that governed classification in the Executive Branch—those who work directly or indirectly for the president. That would, of course, include government agencies and the like. He said the president had no inherent power to make the Executive Order binding on those not working in the executive part of the government.

In other words, it couldn't apply to newspapers because newspapers are obviously not part of government. The only time the president could possibly impose these regulations on newspapers would be in a national emergency. But even then, it would be arguable whether they would be applicable, because of First Amendment considerations.

Bickel then courteously ridiculed the testimony of Doolin, Blouin, and Macomber. Blouin had essentially talked about disclosure of the rules of engagement. But

Bickel pointed out that these rules were already public. Macomber talked about the chilling effect disclosures had on diplomatic relations with Australia and Canada. Bickel said it was not enough to complain about "chilling effect."[6]

As for Macomber's concern about the disclosure of Ambassador Thompson's cable in Moscow, he said that was no different than what popular syndicated newspaper columnist Walter Lippmann wrote all the time. Why shouldn't the public know?[7] Bickel also critiqued the government's lax security surrounding the forty-seven volumes of the Pentagon Papers. Doolin had testified to the whereabouts of the fifteen copies of those forty-seven volumes. They were scattered throughout the government and elsewhere. One copy, for example, was in the safe of former presidential advisor Clark Clifford in his law office.

Bickel said to Judge Gurfein: "Well, how grave a danger can there be in the case of documents which are in peoples' law offices, which are obviously there for use by memoirists who have written on the subject with great frequency, like Townsend Hoopes, Roger Hillsman, and others; what great dangers to the national security can there be in that?"[8]

Gurfein had said at the beginning of the open hearing he had concerns about two types of documents: 1) communications between governments, and 2) communications intelligence. After listening to testimony all day long he repeated his problem, "what concerns me is the government-to-government business a good deal, and what also concerns me is if there is any breach of communications intelligence; those two things bother me."[9] Gurfein ended where he started. Apparently, all the government's testimony, except as to those two points, had not impressed him. We assuaged some, if not all, of his concerns about communications intelligence shortly before he adjourned the secret hearing.

Gurfein asked whether the cables that appeared in the history parts of the Pentagon Papers were paraphrased before they were given to the Pentagon Papers authors. Apparently, Gurfein had been trained to write such paraphrases when he was an intelligence officer in World War II. The answer was that there were no such paraphrases. Codes change, so generally the paraphrases were not done anymore. Vice Admiral Blouin said, "Your Honor, you and I are the only two who remember those days."[10]

This exchange apparently satisfied some of Gurfein's concerns about communications intelligence. There was, of course, more to communications intelligence than how it was transcribed. As Seymour said, communications intelligence was still a "question" in the case.

The government knew full well it could not bring a code case unless it used another section of the statute. More to the point, the government had not shown that the *Times* had released any codes. The government had smeared the *Times,* in a sense, by continuing to refer to communications intelligence in the trial. We would have to wait until Gurfein's opinion to find out how he would deal with this issue, if at all.

I thought that Gurfein's comments were very good for us. He seemed to be worried about the Thompson telegram. But I did not think he would enjoin the publication of the telegram. It hardly presented a clear and immediate danger (or even a present danger) to the country's national security. Communications intelligence continued to be a wild card. Hopefully, Blouin's testimony had satisfied him.

After a short break for dinner, we reconvened in Judge Gurfein's courtroom in open session. Bickel returned to the point that a very high standard must be adopted by the court for this case. He said, "The standards in a prior restraint case are the highest. I don't know how to define it except as your Honor and I and Mr. Seymour are narrowing it down by picking one and other example. We have the troop ship example and we now have the design of the atomic bombs example."[11]

He also pointed out, as did our brief, there was no intent by the *Times* to damage national security and aid foreign powers. That distinguished the *Times'* publication from ordinary espionage. With ordinary espionage a spy intends to damage national security by communication with the enemy. The *Times*, with its publication, did not intend to commit espionage, it intended to inform the public.

The hearing ended at 11:00 p.m. Gurfein said he would deliver an opinion to us at 1:00 p.m. the next day. But there were more dramatic events to come. Although we didn't know it at the time, when we started our closed hearings, the government also sought to enjoin the *Washington Post* from publishing its Saturday edition in a District of Columbia federal court.

When Alex Bickel told Judge Gurfein on Friday morning the *Washington Post* had published the Pentagon Papers, it came as a surprise to the government attorneys. They did not know the *Post* had published a new installment, and so they had no idea how to respond to Bickel's question about whether the government intended to enjoin the *Post*.

A hurried conference between Hess and Mardian followed. Mardian called Washington and was instructed to proceed against the *Post*. Hess subsequently informed Gurfein that the government would attempt to enjoin the *Washington Post*.

The government had to move quickly, otherwise the *Post* would publish another installment. This was not easy. All the government's witnesses were in New York testifying in the *New York Times'* case. Its knowledgeable lawyers (Hess, Seymour, and Mardian) were there, too.

The government therefore had to turn to its B team and start from scratch.[1] It selected Kevin Maroney, a career prosecutor in the Justice Department. The government's legal documents were just as flimsy as they were in New York. Kevin Maroney stated he wanted the *Washington Post*'s presses stopped on the say-so of the affidavits of two State Department employees.

Judge Gerhard A. Gesell of the Federal District Court in D.C. started the proceedings at 6:00 p.m., while our case in New York was going on. Gesell was the son of the famous baby doctor Arnold Gesell who, like pediatrician Dr. Benjamin Spock, told mothers how to bring up their kids. Gesell had a superior educational background.

He was a graduate of Yale University and Yale Law School.[2] He had also been a partner at the blue chip firm of Covington & Burling. The firm was thought to be among the best in Washington, D.C. It was reasonable to expect that with that background, his work would be of the highest quality.

The atmosphere was different in Gesell's courtroom than it had been three days before in Gurfein's. That day was historic. It was the first time the United States had attempted to enjoin the press in a federal court. The *dramatis personae* were colorful: a famed Yale constitutional law professor, a young lawyer from a U.S. attorney's office and a Judge sitting on his first case. Anti-Vietnam War protestors had hissed at the government's lawyers.

In Washington, the request for an injunction against a newspaper was no longer the first in history. The issue had now become whether the government could catch all the thieves. The Pentagon Papers case had become a game. When the government's back was turned, the *Washington Post* published. Perhaps when its back was turned again, someone else would publish.

Gesell knew what to expect because he knew what had happened before Judge Gurfein earlier that week. Maroney told him the Espionage Act gave him the basis for an injunction. He said that the *Post*'s publication came within the 793(e) of the statute, as Hess had argued in New York. Gesell wondered whether an injunction could be issued at all under the First Amendment. Would the "clear and present danger" test apply?

This was the first and last time the clear and present danger test was mentioned in the Pentagon Papers case. Gesell did not know that at roughly the same time he raised the question of what test the First Amendment required, the same issue was being discussed in New York before Judge Gurfein in the closed session.

Roger Clark, counsel to the *Post*, answered Maroney's arguments. According to accounts of discussions at the *Post* before publication of the Papers, he had vehemently opposed publication.[3] The *Post* had the same type of argument as we had at the *Times*.

But Clark made an excellent argument that the Espionage Act did not apply. He pointed out the Internal Security Act of 1950, which reenacted Section 793 of the Espionage Act, specifically said it should not be "construed to authorize, require or establish military or civilian censorship or in any way to limit or to infringe upon freedom of the press or of speech as guaranteed by the Constitution of the United States."[4] Clark had taken advantage of the time that had passed between the date of Bickel's initial argument and his. He was able to say that the legislative history of the Espionage Act proved the Act was irrelevant.

Alex did not have that information available to him when he first appeared before Gurfein. Clark was not a First Amendment lawyer or a constitutional scholar like Bickel. He did not say, for example, that Executive Order 10501 did not apply to newspapers. Nor did he say, for better or worse, that the government needed to cite a statute as an authority to enjoin newspapers (Alex's separation of powers argument).

He said the issuance of a prior restraint order violated the First Amendment. He did not say, "which First Amendment," nor did he respond to Gesell's question of whether the "clear and present danger" test applied. This was the principal weakness of the *Post* lawyers throughout the case. They did not seem knowledgeable about the First Amendment.

Unlike Bickel, Clark did not give the court specific examples of previous leaks, such as during the Cuban missile crisis. But he was able to say, as Bickel could not, that all the information in the Pentagon Papers "is going to get out some way…and if we restrain the *Post*…it is going to be the *Star* or somebody else bringing it the next day."[5] He was unable to say that the requested injunction would be the first in "the history of the Republic" as Bickel had, because it wouldn't have been. Judge Gurfein had granted the first injunction earlier in the week against the *Times*.

Judge Gesell went into his chambers and came out forty-five minutes later with an opinion in which he refused to enjoin the *Washington Post*.[6] This, of course, was markedly different than what Gurfein did the first time around when he had enjoined the *New York Times*.

Why did Gurfein enjoin the publication of a newspaper while Gesell did not? The answer is probably that Gesell had all week to think about the question, and Gurfein had only had a few hours. Gesell expressed skepticism of the sanctity of the classification system. He had been in Washington all of his working life and it seemed to him instinctively that unsupported allegations of damage to national security were just that, unsupported allegations. Gurfein, a New Yorker, took some time before he came to that position.

Gesell was persuaded by Clark that the legislative history made the Act inapplicable to injunctions. In his opinion, Gesell said, "Congress appears to have condemned any pre-existing restraint or censorship of the press by the language of the Internal Security Act of 1950."[7] Gesell also concluded that under the First Amendment no prior restraint could be entered against the *Washington Post* under any circumstances.

The government immediately (at 8:00 that night) appealed this decision to the Court of Appeals in Washington. This appeal, however, was not fast enough to stop the publication by the *Post* of the second of its series of the Papers.

At 2:15 a.m. on Saturday, the Court of Appeals reversed Gesell. The court said Gesell had to start all over again on Monday morning and have a full trial. A majority of the court concluded the First Amendment was not absolute and therefore Gesell had been wrong to say that there was "total freedom of the press."[8] It said that the government deserved a chance to prove its claim that the Pentagon Papers "has prejudiced and will prejudice the conduct of the Nation's military efforts and diplomatic relations and will result in irreparable harm to the national defense."[9]

Judge James Skelly Wright, one of the three judges on the appeal and a noted First Amendment scholar, dissented, saying, "This is a sad day for America. Today, for the first time in 200 years of our history, the Executive Department has succeeded in stopping the presses."[10]

Indeed, it was a sad day. But as we awoke on Saturday morning to read Gesell's opinion and Wright's dissent, we thought we saw some silver lining in those opinions. Gesell, based on what he had learned during the week about the *Times* case, had decided no restraint was in order at all against publication. Skelly Wright had agreed with Gesell that prior restraints were inappropriate. Lastly, while the Court of Appeals reversed Judge Gesell, it did not disagree the Espionage Act was inappropriate in the case because of the legislative history. Could it be that Judge Gurfein, when he issued his opinion on Saturday afternoon at 1:00 p.m., could rule the same way?

Judge Murray Gurfein arrived at his office at 8:00 on Saturday morning, ready to write his opinion. The two opinions in the *Washington Post* case had been published in the morning papers. He knew that Judges Gesell and Wright would not grant an injunction under any circumstances.

They did not think the government even deserved a hearing. Gurfein had given the government all day Friday and part of that night to make its case. Yet Judges Wright and Gesell didn't believe the First Amendment afforded the government even that opportunity.

Gesell had, of course, been overturned by the three-judge Court of Appeals, with Wright dissenting. The two Judges who had overturned Gesell, however, only said that Gesell should have a hearing, as Gurfein had allowed. They were not necessarily votes for the government. And so, if you added it up, two of the four judges who had looked at the government's case in D.C. thought it should be thrown out of court immediately. The other two merely said, "give the government a chance."

Certainly, these decisions must have influenced Gurfein. But, of course, he had to write his own opinion. What was he going to do with the government's argument about the Espionage Act? The government had brought its case under this Act, which had never been used for their purpose before. Was the *New York Times* correct in saying the law didn't apply?

If it didn't apply, what *did* apply? Would Executive Order 10501, which set up the classification system, provide the answer? And what about Bickel's argument that the government had no business being in court in the first place? Congress had never passed a law permitting the government to enjoin newspapers. And, finally, did the First Amendment trump everything else?

Gurfein's answered that the First Amendment was paramount, and so he set the *Times* free. He started the opinion by saying the government had brought the case "in good faith." That was highly debatable. Doubtlessly, Secretary of Defense Melvin Laird had complained in good faith to the Justice Department that there had been a massive leak of classified information. But there wasn't any doubt in my mind that Nixon had approved the lawsuit because of his animosity towards the *New York Times*.

Gurfein then turned to the *Times'* argument that the government had "no inherent power" to bring the case because Congress had never specifically given it the power to do so. Bickel had attempted to make this point when he first appeared before Gurfein on Tuesday. He insisted the government needed to point to a specific statute that authorized injunctions, to bring the case. But Gurfein said Bickel was wrong. He said the government had an inherent right to protect itself from breaches of security.

He then moved to the Espionage Act and focused on Section 793(e), the section I had first focused on when advising the *Times*. Gurfein said it did not apply because 793(e) only used the word "communicate," it did not use the word "publish." It was different than other sections of the Espionage Act. While those sections talked about "publishing," 793(e) did not.

Gurfein agreed with the argument in Bickel's brief that the legislative history of the Espionage Act showed Congress had never intended it to cover the act of publication. Gurfein said, "It would appear therefore that Congress recognizing the constitutional problems of the First Amendment with respect to free press refused to include a form of pre-censorship even in war time."[1] The legislative history that Cahill Gordon had dug up turned out to be highly persuasive. For me, it was the high point of the brief Bickel submitted before our trial.

As indicated above, even without this history, Gurfein did not think the Espionage Act applied. Its language did not fit. This, of course, is what I had initially thought as well. I also thought the statute was vague. Bickel had said in his brief it was vague and therefore unconstitutional. Gurfein found no need to comment on this point.

Gurfein also did not think it was even worth mentioning Executive Order 10501 that authorized the classification of documents. Herbert Brownell had refused to represent the *New York Times* because of his connection to this Executive Order, but Gurfein effectively didn't think it had anything to do with the case even though the government had urged Gurfein to consider it in its brief.

So if the Espionage Act and Executive Order 10501 did not apply, what did? Gurfein's answer was the First Amendment. He started with the proposition that "prior restraint on publication is unconstitutional" under the First Amendment.[2] He went on to say (unlike Judges Gesell and Wright) that the First Amendment is not absolute. He pointed out that the *Near* case referred to the possibility of enjoining the press if they published the dates of sailing ships.

Gurfein did not go further in his First Amendment analysis. He did not say, for example, that he was adopting the "clear and present danger" test. He did not pick up on Bickel's suggestion the previous night that a prior restraint could be granted only under extraordinary circumstances involving danger to the country.

On the other hand, Bickel had admitted the previous night that he didn't know how to articulate what the standard should be. We had not suggested a standard as such in our brief. This was a work in progress. Our position would have to evolve.

Gurfein's words about the First Amendment, however, were ringing. He noted that since the beginning of the country the "founding fathers" thought "that pre-censorship was the primary evil to be dealt with in the First Amendment."[3]

He went on to say, "If there be some embarrassment to the Government in security aspects as remote as the general embarrassment that flows from any security breach, we must learn to live with it. The security of the Nation is not at the ramparts alone. Security also lies in the value of our free institutions. A cantankerous press, an obstinate press, an ubiquitous press must be suffered by those in authority in order to preserve the even greater values of freedom of expression and the right of the people to know."[4]

At 1:15 p.m., Gurfein called Bickel, Bill Hegarty, Floyd Abrams, and me into his chambers to hand us the opinion and tell us we had won. He would, however, keep the restraining order in effect until the Court of Appeals—to which the government would obviously appeal—decided whether his decision to deny the injunction would stand.

According to David Rudenstine in his book *The Day The Presses Stopped*, when Judge Gurfein handed us his opinion, he asked if the *Times* would agree to not publish a particular document. Rudenstine does not say what the document is. He describes it only as a document that, if disclosed, "would make it unlikely that an unidentified third country would act as an intermediary between the United States and North Vietnam."[5] Rudenstine goes on: "Gurfein said that if the newspaper did not accede to his condition he would issue the appropriate order."[6] Rudenstine attributes this statement to Gurfein's clerk, Mel Barkan.

As far as I'm concerned, this event never took place. I was the only one present who could have committed the *Times* not to publish an item. I would never have agreed on behalf of the *Times* so to do. My general view of such orders was that they were unconstitutional and should be disobeyed. Further, the *Times* would never agree to an oral order. Barkan's recollection is that Gurfein orally ordered the *Times* not to publish.[7] No *Times* employee, or former employee, alive today remembers such an order.

It is possible that Gurfein suggested the *Times* not publish a particular document, such as the Llewellyn Thompson telegram, about which he expressed concern during the trial. There were many such suggestions to the *Times* about items in the Pentagon Papers which the *Times* did not publish. For example, the *Times*, from the beginning, respected suggestions made internally not to publish the names of CIA agents. But adhering to a suggestion is far different than following an order not to print. Particularly if such an order is only made orally.

I was elated that we had won. It confirmed the view I had held for some time: that prior restraints against the press were unthinkable. Because the government's case was so weak, I did not think that any other court would issue a prior restraint. There had never been one before in the federal courts, and I thought there would never be another.

This led me to commit the only mistake I think we made in this case. I called Abe Rosenthal, who was then sitting at the *New York Times* waiting to hear what happened. I told him about Gurfein's decision, and then told him to roll the presses since no court would enjoin us again. In retrospect, I wonder what I was smoking. But in my mind, prior restraints were so outrageous that there would never be another one.

This was a mistake, of course, since the government immediately tried and succeeded in getting a new prior restraint from the Court of Appeals. In New York City, the offices of the Court of Appeals are in the same building as the chambers and courtroom of Judge Gurfein. And so U.S. Attorney Seymour pressed the elevator button and went up to see the duty judge.

A duty judge is a judge who acts for the court over the weekend. The duty judge that day was Irving R. Kaufman, one of eight members of the Court of Appeals. He was a champion of press freedom and a great friend of Punch Sulzberger. However, when put to the test, he granted another prior restraint, which would last until his fellow members of the court could hear the case on Monday.

And so while we won a big victory, we had to see what the Court of Appeals had to say about it at 10:00 in the morning on Monday. Meanwhile, in Washington, Gesell had been ordered by the D.C. Appeals Court to start his trial at 8:00 a.m. on Monday, two hours before we started our appellate argument in New York City.

Assistant Attorney General Robert C. Mardian threatened that if the Times *did not stop publication the government would seek a TRO the next morning. Associated Press.*

Arthur Ochs Sulzberger was mobbed by the press when he came back to New York from London during the Pentagon Papers case. New York Times *photo, Barton Silverman.*

Alexander Bickel leaving Foley Square following the evening oral argument on Friday June 18, 1971 at the conclusion of the trial before Judge Gurfein. New York Times *photo, Donal F. Holway.*

The Pentagon Papers case led to Watergate. White House attorneys James D. St. Clair and J. Fred Buzhardt met with the press following a conference with Watergate Judge Sirica. Buzhardt also represented the government in the Pentagon Papers case. AP Photo, Bob Daugherty.

Times *lawyers Lawrence J. McKay, Floyd Abrams, Alexander Bickel, James Goodale and William Hegarty leaving the Supreme Court following argument of the case. Immediately before that argument, Solicitor General Irwin Griswold surprised the* Times *by claiming new violations of national security in the Pentagon Papers.* New York Times *photo, Mike Lien.*

Moments following the announcement the Times *had won the Pentagon Papers case, top* New York Times *executives celebrated. (L-R) Harding Bancroft, Arthur Ochs Sulzberger, A.M Rosenthal, Sydney Gruson and James Goodale.* New York Times *photo, Jack Manning.*

Daniel Ellsberg at a press conference in Cambridge, Mass., immediately following the Supreme Court decision in the Pentagon Papers case. A subsequent case against Ellsberg faltered after Nixon's "Plumbers," broke into Ellsberg's psychiatrist's office illegally. Bettman/Corbis.

CHAPTER XXI

GESELL SAYS "ABSOLUTELY NO" TO NIXON

At 8:00 Monday morning, the government's case against the *Washington Post* began again. Its case against the *Post* was, in theory, the same as its case against the *Times*. In each, the government attempted to stop publication of the Pentagon Papers. The two trials were very different, however.

The principal reason for the difference was that Judge Gesell was unimpressed by the government's arguments from the outset. He had, after all, already decided the previous Friday in favor of the *Post* before he was overturned by the Appeals Court. Furthermore, he knew the *Times* had won its case before Judge Gurfein on the previous Saturday.

We did not talk with the *Post* lawyers. We were too busy. Our appeal in New York City to the Second Circuit was going to be heard two hours after the *Post* trial began. We had spent all of Sunday getting ready for that appeal, while the *Post* spent it getting ready for its trial.

The government got off to a terrible start in the *Post* trial. Under constant probing from Judge Gesell, the government took a ridiculous position. The *Post*, it argued, could not publish material previously published, including speeches of Presidents Kennedy and Johnson. Those speeches were in separate volumes of the Pentagon Papers and, as such, were not classified. But since the speeches were part of a total study, they *were* classified.

If this sounds like *Alice in Wonderland*, it is. How can the government possibly come into court and ask it to enjoin publication of speeches Johnson and Kennedy made, that are in the public domain? This takes a little explaining.

George MacClain, the government's first witness, tried his best. He said once a study such as the Pentagon Papers was classified "top secret," everything in the volume became classified "top secret." Theoretically, an article from the *New York Times*, or a speech by Kennedy, could be pulled out of the study and published. But as long as such article was part of the study, the study could not be republished, nor could the article as part of the study be republished.

Gesell listened respectfully, but noted that the government was asking him "to enjoin the use of any documents in this study whether classified or not." He went on to say, "It makes no difference from the point of view of the United States, as I understand it, whether they are classified or not classified. They are all to be enjoined."[1]

MacClain and the government's counsel, Kevin Maroney, tried to wriggle out of this ridiculous position. They could not. They maintained if the government could point to one dangerous document, it could enjoin the whole study, including the speeches of Kennedy and Johnson. This position made no sense.

The government's next witness, Dennis Doolin, tried to clarify what MacClain said, but made matters worse. He had testified in the New York proceedings that a newspaper article could be classified "top secret."[2] When he was cross-examined on this point at the *Washington Post* case, he recanted. He said what he had meant to say was that when a *New York Times* article appeared in the study, it became classified because the whole study was classified.

Doolin offered this confusing explanation as to how public domain material can become classified: "The document itself, the whole thing, has the highest classification that is used in the sources. So therefore if [it] is unclassified material in a classified document [the] document is classified, but the unclassified items are not. If a newspaper was attached to a "top secret" document then the newspaper clipping would also be marked 'top secret.'"[3]

The answer, of course, made no sense. Doolin tried again, but to no avail: "Some of the best studies done of the early years of our Vietnam involvement are in the public domain. So these are cited in the study. But, they are not classified, and they are classified only insofar as they are not classified. The study is classified because there are classified data in it."[4]

Doolin could have said the material in the public domain could be pulled out from the study and published separately. His position, however, was that the public material was intertwined with the non-public material. It was all subject to classification as "top secret," and so none of it could be published.

Doolin, in some part, was anticipating what has become known as the "mosaic" theory of intelligence. The government used this theory in court following the Pentagon Papers case. The theory is that innocuous individual pieces of information can be combined as part of a mosaic and then become classified. Such a piece of information may mean nothing to the public. To a trained eye, when pieced within the mosaic, it becomes meaningful.

Even the Supreme Court has decided that "superficially innocuous information" can be withheld by government agencies.[5] This is because, if disclosed, it might lead an observer to discover intelligence sources. Essentially, Doolin was trying to say that the combination of classified and unclassified information in the Pentagon Papers was all part of a mosaic. The combination of the pieces would lead a trained eye to reach conclusions about the United States that were otherwise not obtainable.

Public interest groups have correctly attacked the mosaic theory because any information, however harmless, including previously published material, can be classified.[6] In other words, anything can be classified if the government believes it has an interest in doing so, whether it is relevant to national security or not.

When I first read the Pentagon Papers I noted that they were based in some part on articles the *New York Times* had published. I anticipated the government would seek to effectively enjoin the re-publication of those articles. I thought this would be a fatal flaw in its case, and it was.

The government's approach leads to an anomalous result. Suppose a harmless *New York Times* article becomes "top secret" because it is part of a top secret study. "Top secret" is defined in government regulations as information that, when released, leads to "armed attack[s] against the United States" and a "break in diplomatic relations."

But how can a harmless article suddenly become so volatile that it leads to an "armed attack" once it is covered by a "top secret" stamp? The government claims it becomes toxic because it is connected to other information that may not be so innocent. Preposterous though it seems, the government can transform an innocent *Times* article into a "top secret" document.

The government can internally use any classification system it wants, as weird as it may sound to an outsider, and so they are perfectly free to classify a *New York Times* article as "top secret." But it cannot come into court and impose that theory on the general public in a censorship case. Once Gesell had reached the conclusion that the government's reasoning was flawed, it became a foregone conclusion that the rest of the government's case before him would fall on deaf ears.

Nonetheless, he permitted the government to point to particular examples that damaged national security. Doolin had obviously been thinking about such examples over the weekend after he testified in New York on Friday. He was excoriated then for his inability to point to such examples.

This time he pointed to the LaPira peace process, which involved the use of Blair Seaborn, the Canadian ICC member, by the US, and the impact on peace negotiations of publication of the Pentagon Papers. Doolin, however, again undermined his own argument. Several of his examples had already been published. The information was in the public domain and the *Post*'s lawyers knew it.

The LaPira peace process had been described in detail in the book *The Secret Search for Peace in Vietnam* by David Kraslow and Stuart H. Loory. The use of Canadian diplomat Seaborn by the United States to explore peace negotiations with North Vietnam was described in *The Last Crusade* by Chester L. Cooper. Regarding this publication, Doolin and Gesell had the following exchange in court:

> Gesell: But you feel you are competent to express an opinion on matters [related to the Canadian diplomat]?
>
> Doolin: Very definitely in terms of guarantee of secrecy, yes, sir.
>
> Gesell: But you made that statement unaware that there had been

publication of the Seaborn mission, and, therefore, there was no secrecy about the matter?

Doolin: That is correct.[7]

Gesell asked the government lawyers, "What has that got to do with what is before me, if the protest here is a protest against disclosure of matters already in the public domain?"[8]

Gesell also dismissed Doolin's claim that the ability of the U.S. to use third countries to convey messages to Hanoi could well dry up because of publication of the Pentagon Papers. Gesell said he'd read about the use of third countries to send out peace feelers for years "as a mere casual reader of the newspapers."[9] What he read in the Pentagon Papers was no different than what he read in the daily paper.

Macomber testified next. His testimony tracked what he had said in New York three days before on Friday. The State Department could not conduct diplomacy in a "fish bowl," and he submitted a new affidavit to that effect. He again complained about the embarrassment to the Australians and Canadians about disclosures in the Papers. Glendon, on cross-examination, brought to Macomber's attention—as he had to Doolin's—that the Seaborn information was in the public domain.

This led to Gesell pointing out to Macomber: "here the 'top secret' stamp is not selectively used...[it] was used on volumes which now admittedly contain unclassified material, even public statements of the President...I am [supposed] to suppress all of it no matter what the degree of confidentiality or seriousness or ancient condition is. That is a difficult problem for me."[10]

Unlike in New York, no witness testified to codes in the Washington hearing. Gesell did, however, permit the government to introduce an affidavit from Admiral Noel Gayler, director of the National Security Agency (NSA). At first, Gesell would not accept the Gayler affidavit. The NSA insisted that the affidavit was for Gesell's eyes alone. This condition was unacceptable to Gesell because it meant that the *Washington Post* lawyers would not see it.

The NSA then changed its mind. It would submit the affidavit if the *Post* agreed not to tell anyone about it. The affidavit remained totally secret until 1994, when John C. Sims of the McGeorge School of Law filed a Freedom of Information Act (FOIA) request and succeeded in having parts of it declassified.

Some of the affidavit still remains classified. The part that was released had another bombshell in it. The government was suggesting that Section 798 of the Espionage Act, which covers codes, was part of the case.

It will be remembered that in New York the previous Friday, Messrs. Seymour and Hegarty had agreed that codes were out of the case. As explained by Hegarty, codes could only be brought into the case if Section 798 applied. Since the government had not used 798 in bringing a suit against the *Times*, it was not fair to slip it into the case. The *Times* would have no way to defend itself against these claims. But as noted earlier, Seymour slipped codes into the case anyway and Judge Gurfein never stopped him from doing it.

Gayler's affidavit explains how signal intelligence (Sigint) is important to the United States since it derives intelligence from "the intercept of foreign electro-magnetic signals."[11] Once a foreign power learns "that specific communication channels are being intercepted and explained" it's easy for the enemy to close off this intelligence, even when U.S. cyphers are secure from being read. "Valuable inferences may be drawn from an understanding of U.S. communications netting." Then comes the bombshell: "Protection of Sigint/Comsec is recognized as a special responsibility under federal law (18 USC 798)." A full explanation of these responsibilities is then blanked out for security reasons.

The affidavit does not say flatly the *Washington Post* is violating 798 and therefore there should be an injunction against it. For all practical purposes, though, the suggestions made in the affidavit amount to the same thing, that the government has special responsibilities under Section 798, and it can't carry out those responsibilities if the *Post* publishes the Pentagon Papers. "Publication of Sigint or Sigint related materials degrades the system and will directly and indirectly encourage by example further violations of trust."

While the affidavit did not seem to have that much effect on Gesell, it did apparently affect the *Washington Post*. Surprisingly, the *Post* agreed with the government not to publish a particular message pinpointed by the affidavit in the Pentagon Papers. It also agreed not to print the dates on which messages were sent that appeared in the Pentagon Papers. While newspapers in the past have decided on their own not to publish classified information (as in the Cuban missile crisis), few have agreed to do so. The court noted this agreement while referring to this particular message.

Gesell said this message might possibly have "some special significance in terms of compromising the signal intelligence system."[12] He then noted the *Post* had agreed not to use it "if it is in their possession." The court also noted that "the *Post* does not intend…to publish precise times of messages."[13]

There was no affidavit comparable to Gayler's in the *New York Times* case, although references to signal intelligence were multitudinous. Yet, almost at the very moment Gesell discussed Admiral Gayler's affidavit, an NSA representative, Milton Zaslow, met with the *New York Times* to discuss communications intelligence (Comint, which is similar to Sigint).

Zaslow had oversight of the NSA's operations in Vietnam. He had asked Seymour to set up a meeting with the *New York Times*. It was decided that Bancroft and Hagerty would meet him at the New York City Bar Association. At the meeting, Zaslow requested that the *Times* not publish any North Vietnamese communications intelligence intercepted by the U.S. government.

According to Bancroft's notes, Zaslow said specifically not to publish any item that "disabused" a foreign nation in "their belief in the secrecy of their communications," that disclosed any "sources we might have in that regard," that indicated the "manner" of obtaining information from such sources, or "the time" of such interception. Furthermore, there should be no references to "communications intelligence."

Bancroft read his notes back to Zaslow, who approved them. He then called Greenfield, the project editor of the Pentagon Papers and a former Assistant Secretary of State. Greenfield told Bancroft that because of his prior experience in government, he knew what Comint was, he hadn't found any, and if he did, he had no intention of publishing it. Bancroft called Zaslow back and said the *Times* would use its best efforts not to use Comint, but that if Zaslow were to grade the *Times* effort he should not expect to give it an "A."[14]

The government had sued both the *Times* and the *Post* for violation of the Espionage Act. But there was no discussion of the Espionage Act at all in the trial before Gesell. Amazingly enough, the Espionage Act seemed to have disappeared from the *Washington Post* case.

It would disappear from the *New York Times* case too, but not until later in the week. The government had brought historic prior restraint cases against the two greatest papers in the country. It based these cases on a law that the government effectively conceded does not exist. In retrospect, the law was a cover for the Nixon administration's true intent to disable if not destroy the *New York Times* and, now, the *Washington Post*.

It would not be reasonable to expect that either Maroney or Glendon would make closing arguments at the level that Bickel did. He was, after all, a constitutional scholar and expert in the First Amendment. Messrs. Maroney and Glendon were fine trial lawyers, but it is fair to say knew little, if anything, about the First Amendment.

The *Post*'s First Amendment argument was set out in an eleven page brief for the court's perusal. This was compared with the sixty page brief Bickel wrote on the eve of the *New York Times* trial. The *Post* proposed that the government had to show "serious, immediate and substantial threat to its ability to wage war, imminent risk of death to American military personnel or a grave breach of the national security."[15]

This was a good First Amendment test. It was not that dissimilar to the definition of "top secret." Glendon, however, did not use it in his closing argument. He said merely that "I think, Your Honor, against the standard which the Court of Appeals has set up and weighing the familiar principles of equity, that this preliminary injunction should be denied."[16]

The Court of Appeals, as previously noted, had set up a relatively weak standard. It was "to determine whether publication of material from this document would so prejudice the defense interests of the United States or result in such irreparable injury to the United States as would justify restraining the publication thereof."[17] Maroney had used this standard in his closing argument, saying that the evidence had met that standard.

Gesell again took only about an hour to write his opinion. As expected, he was influenced by the fact that some of the material of the Pentagon Papers was in the public domain. "The Court finds that the documents in question include material in the public domain and other material that was 'top secret' when written long ago, but not clearly shown to be such at the present time."[18]

He then reached two conclusions: 1) that the documents in question did not meet the definition of "top secret" as used in classification regulations; and 2) there is no "showing of an immediate grave threat to the national security."

This was an excellent result for the *Washington Post*. Gesell's opinion was a sliver, at eight pages compared to Gurfein's sixteen page opus. But then again, Gesell only had one hour to write it; Gurfein had twelve. Had a better First Amendment standard been argued orally to the D.C. trial court, it might have adopted a better standard. On the other hand, Gurfein did not adopt a very good First Amendment standard, either.

Meanwhile, back in New York, the news for the First Amendment was not good. The appeal from Judge Gurfein's decision began at 10:00 a.m. in the New York Court of Appeals. At this hearing, the government did not play fair. It decided to twist the rules applicable to appeals and followed by courts for centuries. Its tactics at this hearing made the *Times* lawyers and Max Frankel furious, and radicalized them for the rest of the case, and longer.

Whitney North "Mike" Seymour was a respected member of the New York Bar. He was a worthy opponent, and we all liked him. We could not believe, however, what the government and he did at the Court of Appeals hearing Monday morning in New York.

We had showed up there at 10:30 a.m., after working all Sunday to deliver briefs to the court opposing the government's appeal of Judge Gurfein's ruling. Such appeals are typically heard by a three-man court; in this case, Chief Judge Henry J. Friendly, and Judges J. Joseph Smith and Paul R. Hays.

But Judge Friendly told us our appeal had been postponed until the next day, Tuesday, at 2:00 p.m. It would be heard then by the full panel of the court. This consisted of eight judges in all, the three that were there Monday, plus judges Walter R. Mansfield, James L. Oakes, J. Edward Lumbard, Irving R. Kaufman, and Wilfred Feinberg.

We did not know then that the D.C. Court of Appeals had been talking about the case with the Court of Appeals in New York. The two courts had agreed they would hear appeals at the same time, which meant the *Post*'s case would also be heard on Tuesday at 2:00. The government was asking the Court of Appeals to send our case back to Gurfein for a new trial. Gurfein would have to do it all over again, and in the meantime, the prior restraint would remain in effect and the *New York Times* would not be able to publish. The government maintained Gurfein was wrong because he had decided the Espionage Act did not apply. He was also wrong because he had decided the First Amendment permitted publication.

Appellate courts decide only whether trial courts make mistakes in applying the law. Appellate courts do not hear new evidence. Once a trial is over, it is over. The only exception to this rule is when newly discovered evidence is uncovered after a criminal trial. Then the trial court (or an appellate court) can consider new evidence. Otherwise, it cannot.

Seymour then made a suggestion that was totally out of order. He stood up and said, "Your Honor, I have an application purely of a housekeeping nature."[1] He had prepared a Special Appendix pointing to particular portions of the Pentagon Papers which had damaged national security. He could not point to any part at our secret hearing, but now he was trying to get another bite out of the apple.[2] He had consulted some of the defense agencies over the weekend to review the secret transcripts and "their guidance is actually in affidavit form pointing out the particular portions."[3]

As soon as I heard the word "affidavit" I whispered to Bickel to object. I had read in the morning paper that the testimony in the *Washington Post* case, which was going on at the same time, was to be "in affidavit form." I said to Alex, "Those are the same affidavits they are using in Washington. They can't do that. They can't bring in new evidence into the appeals court." Bickel stood up and objected. He said the government could not have "two bites out of the apple." What Bickel meant was that the government had already had its chance in front of Gurfein to point to instances of damages to the national security not protected by the First Amendment. The government had failed.

Now the government wanted to do it again, and if it succeeded, it could prevent the *Times* from publishing for an indefinite amount of time. It would scare the judges into thinking it had found something really damaging when, in fact, it had not. Nonetheless, concerned by the government's unsupported allegations, the court would then send the case back to Gurfein. The government's allegations would once again prove baseless. The government would lose. It would then appeal back to the Court of Appeals with different references to the Pentagon Papers. The process would go on forever. Meanwhile, the *Times* would not be able to publish. Its story would be lost.

We waited to see how the court would react. Judge Friendly asked: "Is the affidavit anything more really than a pointer?" Seymour replied: "That's just what it is."[4] "As I understand it," said Judge Hays, "you are not adding anything to the testimony in the *in camera* proceeding. Is that right?" Seymour said, "I shade that a little bit your Honor, because the fellows who prepared these affidavits, these officials, have explained why they point to these pages so that technically it is an affidavit and can be construed as testimony…it could perfectly well be put in as a brief argument, and we will put it in that form if it will be more acceptable."[5]

Seymour's suggestion was extraordinary. He was more than "shading" his answer. He was asking the court to permit him to try his case all over again. We had won the case before Gurfein, fair and square. Seymour had tried to prove the Pentagon Papers damaged national security and the *New York Times* was not protected by the First Amendment. He had lost.

His suggestion that he put his new evidence in a brief rather than an affidavit was laughable. New evidence is new evidence, whether in a brief or an affidavit. The only difference is that if you slip it into a brief it is less noticeable that you have violated the rules.

Seymour later wrote in his memoirs that he had been told by Defense Department Counsel J. Fred Buzhardt he could not have government witnesses point to particular parts of the Pentagon Papers that damaged national security. Buzhardt said that if witnesses pointed to such parts, the disclosure in the secret hearing would in and of itself damage national security because everyone who was there (including me) would know the secrets of the United States.[6]

Having lost badly with this strategy before Judge Gurfein, Seymour sought a reversal of Buzhardt's position, and he got it. He had talked to defense officials who pointed out parts of the Pentagon Papers that damaged national security. Seymour now had the evidence he needed for the trial. There was only one problem: the trial was over. His only recourse was to go to the Court of Appeals and ask if he could do the trial again.

He knew very well that the ordinary rules applying to this situation would not permit him another trial. He was not allowed to bring new evidence on appeal and ask for a new trial. If the rule were otherwise, trials would go on forever. As soon as a lawyer thought of something he forgot to bring to the trial court's attention, he would bring it up on appeal and the trial would begin again.

In national security trials, this rule was particularly appropriate. The rule prevented the government from making unsupported allegations of damage to national security in order to frighten appellate judges. It protected defendants such as the *New York Times*, which had no way to challenge these assertions. We could not cross-examine the government in an appellate argument, we could only do that at the trial court.

We were all steaming mad that Seymour would try such a tactic. It was in violation of the law. We were also astounded at the court's mild reaction to what we viewed to be a highly illegal act. Friendly merely asked Bickel and Seymour to "work this out."

*   *   *

When we arrived in court the next day at 2:00 in the afternoon, we were very unhappy. The government had delivered its Special Appendix, all of which was secret. It pointed out seventeen items contained in 400 pages of the Pentagon Papers that the government asserted harmed national security. It asked the Court of Appeals to have Judge Gurfein hear this evidence.

We planned again to object to the government's use of the Special Appendix as unfair and a violation of our due process rights. We could not do this, however, until our secret hearing later in the afternoon. The early part of the afternoon was to be devoted to an open hearing, with Seymour and Bickel arguing.

Early that morning, *The Boston Globe* had started publishing the Pentagon Papers. It became clear Ellsberg would continue to give other newspapers parts of the Pentagon Papers after the *Times*, and now the *Post*, were enjoined. Later in the day, the government sought and obtained an injunction against the *Globe* in Boston. The Appellate Court knew *The Boston Globe* had published, and one of the judges made reference to it, but it was not a factor in our appeal.

Mike Seymour made an excellent argument about why the case should be returned to Judge Gurfein for further consideration. He did not, and could not, mention the Special Appendix, because it was secret and could only be discussed in the secret hearing to follow.

Seymour said the *Times* had been irresponsible in publishing the Pentagon Papers. What it should have done was have the Papers declassified under the Freedom of Information Act (FOIA). He did not point out to the court that it is virtually impossible to have documents de-classified under FOIA. It would take years and years for the government to consider de-classification of the 7,000 page study. And in the end, only parts, if any, of the Pentagon Papers would be declassified. It was impractical for a daily publication such as the *Times* to use the FOIA.

Seymour said the government was entitled to protect its secrets. The *Times* could not usurp the government's role and decide itself to de-classify the Pentagon Papers. He did not argue for the application of the Espionage Act. His reference to the standard the court should apply was vague. He pointed generally to the troop ship example used in *Near v. Minnesota.*

Seymour parried every question from the Judges. It was an impressive performance. It was one of the best arguments anyone made in the course of the Pentagon Papers case litigation.

Alex, on the other hand, had a terrible day. Just as his appearance before Judge Gurfein had been his first trial, this was his first appeal. He thought he was before a Judge sympathetic to him, Judge Henry Friendly. But Friendly was not friendly.

The first mistake Bickel made was to object to the characterization of the Pentagon Papers made by the Judge as "stolen documents."[7] This set off an acerbic exchange between Friendly and Bickel. Bickel said as far as he knew the *Times* could have gotten the documents from Clark Clifford or Robert McNamara.

Friendly: You aren't serious. Why don't you face the facts?

Bickel: I'm not a bit serious about that, Of course. But I don't know where they were gotten and I am simply resisting the word stolen.

Friendly: Let's say they received the goods in the process of embezzlement, then, if you prefer.

Bickel: Without dwelling further on the point, may I say I resist that as well.[8]

Bickel couldn't recover from this beginning. He should never have engaged in a petty exchange with Friendly. He couldn't get his argument out. It was convoluted. After winning a stirring First Amendment victory before Judge Gurfein, he all but ignored the First Amendment. He submitted an 83-page brief, of which only three pages were devoted to the First Amendment, and he did not provide the court with a First Amendment standard to guide its actions.

Bickel's argument went like this: first, the Espionage Act did not apply because of the legislative history and the fact the *Times* did not intend to commit espionage.

The Espionage Act was also unconstitutionally vague. Furthermore, since the Espionage Act didn't authorize injunctions, the government was without a relevant statute, and couldn't even ask for an injunction unless there was a national emergency. There was no emergency, and so the government should lose.

But where was the First Amendment in all of this? Bickel said briefly that it provided context for his argument, but he spent a great deal of time explaining how the Espionage Act didn't apply. This explanation took up far too much time, and worse, he was very unclear.

Further, he only confused the court when he said that the government had no power to bring the case at all. Bickel would not give up on this separation of powers argument, which was his favorite one. He insisted the executive had no power to enjoin the *Times*, because the legislature had not given it power to do so.

The government's brief, which was considerably shorter, only thirty-three pages, argued the Espionage Act applied, regardless of the legislative history the *Times* had uncovered. The "top secret" classification was appropriate, and therefore Gurfein should be reversed.

Judge Irving R. Kaufman, a friend of the *Times* and of Punch Sulzberger, called the *New York Times* newsroom after the argument, and said that he wanted Bickel to make more of the First Amendment. It was too late to do that in the Court of Appeals, but there always was the Supreme Court. All in all, it was a very bad day for Alex Bickel.

Floyd and I were not happy with his argument either. With the extraordinary pressure we were all under, however, we did not want to confront Alex. If we had, it would have thrown him off balance for the rest of the case.

Judge Friendly began the secret hearing as soon as Bickel finished his argument. Bickel, Hegarty, Abrams, Bancroft, and I attended on behalf of the *Times*. Seymour and his team were there for the government. This hearing was devoted substantially to whether the government should be allowed to use the Special Appendix. The day before, the court had left this matter to be worked out between Bickel and Seymour. Needless to say, they didn't work it out. The government had submitted the Special Appendix at 5:00 the afternoon before. The *Times* moved to strike it from the proceedings, and Bill Hegarty handled the argument.

The Special Appendix was horrendous for our case. As noted, it contained seventeen items which Judge Gurfein was to consider, and it took up 400 pages of the Pentagon Papers. It also contained nearly four pages of new allegations. It alleged, for example, that publication of the Papers would inhibit the governments of Thailand, South Korea, Philippines, and Japan from assisting in the withdrawal of troops. Hegarty objected strenuously to the use of the Appendix. Since the *Times* had just received the Special Appendix the night before, it had no way of responding to the specific allegations on the spot.

Seymour freely admitted that he had used the affidavits prepared for the *Washington Post* case. He had cut them up and put them in the Appendix. Most of the material Seymour used came from affidavits submitted by General Zais and Macomber in D.C. The affidavit he was most dependent on was submitted by Zais, although we did not know at the time that Zais was the author. Seymour used almost four pages verbatim from this affidavit. This conduct, unheard of in a normal case, for some reason did not shock the judges. They denied the *Times'* motion to strike the Appendix.

Seymour also did not mention to the court that Judge Gesell had been unmoved by the Zais affidavit. Gesell thought that it, along with the other government affidavits, did not damage national security or even justify being classified "top secret." Seymour knew Gesell had reached this decision since the *Post* case had taken place the day before. We did not know that Zais was the author of the affidavit until years after the case. It was secret.

Seymour did not want just two bites out of the apple; he wanted three. He wanted Gurfein to consider the items in the Appendix on a retrial of the case—that was bite two. And he wanted Gurfein to consider the items in the Zais and Macomber affidavits, which Gesell had already considered. That was bite three.

The Special Appendix was kept secret for many years. When it was finally released, public interest groups and others analyzed it. They concluded, and I agreed, that it was specious. A year later, after the case, when the government published its own edition of the Pentagon Papers, it only struck two or three sentences from the Special Appendix.[9]

The Special Appendix contained two parts. The first dealt largely with military matters, the second mostly with political matters. Two of the items in the military section once again dealt with codes, despite the fact that Seymour had told Judge Gurfein that codes were out of the case—that he would not even "hint" at mentioning codes.

One was a message from Henry Cabot Lodge and another was from a Vietnamese official.[10] The Appendix asserted that plain text versions of these messages breached national security. Admiral Blouin, however, had told Judge Gurfein that no one worried about plain text messages anymore. Governments changed their codes in a matter of minutes. There were several references to old SEATO contingency plans—one from 1961,[11] two covering 1964 and 1965,[12] and another from 1967[13]—as well as a 1961 national intelligence estimate for Vietnam.[14] The latter two were, in fact, taken straight out of the Zais affidavit. Judge Gurfein found that these SEATO plans were not current, and Judge Gesell had essentially ignored the Zais affidavit.

There were references to two chronologies of decision-making.[15] One of these also came directly from the Zais affidavit, ignored by Gesell. These chronologies could have been assembled from the public domain.[16]

There were five references to the Pentagon Papers that discussed our relationship with our Vietnamese partners. These passages were not complimentary, and were critical of that relationship. The Appendix said the references could not be published because in one instance, "it would make all facets of relations with the South Vietnamese more complicated,"[17] in another "it would promote communist propaganda,"[18] in a third, "it would hold Vietnamese officials up to ridicule," in yet another, it would show "our over participation" in Vietnamese activities,[19] and lastly because it would inform Vietnamese officials about our "domestic pressures."[20]

Holding top South Vietnamese officials "up to ridicule;" making relationships with them "more complicated;" letting people know how the U.S. "thinks," and enhancing "communist propaganda" hardly damages national security. The North Vietnamese would know about "domestic pressures" against the war by picking up any newspaper; they did not need classified documents to tell them that. And the idea that the U.S. wasn't exactly a hundred percent happy with the South Vietnamese commitment was no secret, either. The press reported information of this sort regularly.

The penultimate items covered two assertions which Gurfein had already decided did not damage national security. The first was the publication of Ambassador to the USSR Llewellyn Thompson's telegram[21] and the second were examples of third party negotiations to help bring peace.[22]

The last item referred to the fact that the Pentagon Papers detailed how the Kennedy administration had engineered the assassination of Diem. But this was public knowledge. In any event, even if it were not, it's hard to see how its publication would have damaged national security.[23]

In pejorative terms, the Special Appendix was, indeed, a "cut-and-paste job." Seymour had collected references to the Pentagon Papers from here and there, including directly from an affidavit used in another case, which the government had lost. When one took time to analyze it, there was nothing threatening there. But the judges of the Second Circuit in New York didn't know that.

In his book *The Day the Presses Stopped*, David Rudenstine wrote that the Special Appendix caused him "to begin re-thinking the meaning of the litigation over the Pentagon Papers."[24] Before he began writing his book, Rudenstine thought the government had a weak case. After reading the Special Appendix, he noted, "It alleged that further publication of classified material would injure current troop movements, disclose current and important intelligence matters, and harm current diplomatic efforts aimed at ending the war and gaining the release of American prisoners. In support of these allegations, it provided numerous specific page references to the Pentagon Papers."[25]

His conclusion was, in short, that the publication of the materials in the Special Appendix could very well have damaged national security. He said that just because material of this sort could be published under the First Amendment "does not mean the government's overall case was so weak that further disclosures did not threaten national security."[26]

The problem with Rudenstine's argument is that it requires that one believes the government's allegations. Just because it alleges that there may be damage to national security does not mean that, in fact, there will be damage to national security. It has been forty years plus since the publication of the Pentagon Papers, and to the best of my knowledge, not one allegation in the Special Appendix has turned out to have damaged national security. In order for Rudenstine to prove his point, he would have had to show that national security was damaged upon publication of the Pentagon Papers.

Unless we can do that, we are left with unsupported government allegations. These were the vice of the Special Appendix. The government could assert whatever it wanted, and there was no way to disprove it. Seymour, either wittingly or not, had fallen into Nixon's smear trap. He made allegations of damage to national security which the court had no way to evaluate without extending the prior restraint against the *Times*. It was just like Nixon's claims against Voorhees, Douglas, and the libel claim against the *Times*. The claims of damage to national security in the Appendix would turn out to be as baseless as his other charges. Meanwhile, as a practical matter, the delay would cause the *Times* to lose its case.

As the *New York Times* appeal took place in New York, the *Post*'s appeal was taking place in D.C. While the government had used its "B team" before Gesell, it was not going to do that in its appeal. It had its own scholar waiting in the wings, ready to enter the case.

Much to the surprise of everyone, Solicitor General of the United States Erwin Griswold stepped in to argue the government's case in the D.C. Court of Appeals. Usually, the solicitor general only argues cases in the Supreme Court, not in the appeals courts. Griswold had an excellent reputation not only as solicitor general for the Nixon administration, but also for the Johnson administration.[1] But Nixon's Attorney General, John Mitchell, put him in a terrible spot. At 11:00 that morning, Mitchell asked him to take over the government's appeal. The argument in the *Post* appeal was set for 2:00 that afternoon, to coincide with the *New York Times* case in New York. He only had three hours to prepare.

Lawyers need time to prepare for their arguments. Alex, Floyd, and I had spent several months working together on the *Caldwell* case, an important First Amendment case. Alex Bickel was a constitutional scholar, well versed with the First Amendment. In New York, we had three days to prepare for the trial, and two days to prepare for the appeal. By lawyers' standards that was a very short time, but nothing compared to what was demanded of Griswold.

Erwin Griswold had spent several years arguing constitutional cases as solicitor general and therefore had credentials as a constitutional lawyer. He was, however, a professor of tax law at Harvard, where he had also been the dean.[2] He was not a popular teacher at Harvard. As a young man living in Cambridge, I had heard tales that he was unfair and not particularly pleasant. Once, he was alleged to have given a tax exam, which required students to fill out a tax form. His students were livid, having prepared only to answer hypothetical questions.

We had great respect for him as the former dean of Harvard Law School and as solicitor general. When we ended up face-to-face with him at the Supreme Court later, our opinion changed. We became very angry with him because of what we viewed to be his unfair and unethical tactics.

With respect to his designation as counsel in the appeal of the *Washington Post* case, however, we only had sympathy for him as a fellow professional. He was put in an impossible position. He had to risk his whole reputation in a historic case without being able to get ready for it.

Mitchell had apparently chosen Griswold because he did not want Seymour to argue the government's case, should it reach the Supreme Court. Mitchell and Assistant Attorney General Mardian did not like Seymour, and did not think he could win. They were so desperate to win at least one of the appeals that they took the almost unprecedented step of asking the government's top lawyer to argue its case, starting at the appellate level.[3]

Griswold's argument in the D.C. Court of Appeals was rather pathetic. Apparently not knowing what else to say, he somewhat unbelievably argued that the Pentagon Papers case was one of intellectual property. He said the government had a copyright interest. When one owns a copyright, such ownership permits the owner to stop others from copying the papers.[4]

The government, however, cannot and does not own a copyright in its papers. It had no copyright in the Pentagon Papers. Only individuals or non-government entities can copyright their papers.

The government, therefore, cannot stop others from copying their papers, or ask courts to do so. That is why it used national security laws to stop the *Times* from publishing. Had the government argued it had a copyright in the Pentagon Papers when it brought its case against the *Times* instead of referencing the Espionage Act, it would have been laughed out of court.

Griswold used one third of the time of his argument pointing out to the court that authors like Hemingway could get injunctions against those who copied their material.[5] He said the purpose of the argument was to show that courts do grant injunctions against publication sometimes. There actually *were* exceptions to the general rule that injunctions can never be granted against newspapers with respect to what they publish.

The court, predictably, found this argument hard to believe. Griswold was asked whether his case depended on this argument, and he said it did not. But if it didn't, why was he spending so much time on it? The answer, presumably, was that he couldn't think of what else to say.

Griswold may have decided to use up some of his time to talk about copyright, irrelevant as it was to the case, because the brief the government gave him did not make much sense either. Rather than continuing to argue that the Espionage Act prevented publication, the government, for all practical purposes, had jettisoned that argument. Gesell, in his initial opinion, noted that publication of the Pentagon Papers would "interfere" with the government's foreign relations. Nonetheless, Gesell had decided that such interference was not sufficient to enjoin publication.

The government, in its brief, said that Gesell was wrong. The reason the government classified papers in the first place was to protect the disruption of foreign relations. And since this was so, Gesell's only option was to stop publication unless he thought the government had abused its discretion in classifying the Pentagon Papers "top secret."[6]

This argument, however, seemed hard to swallow for both Griswold and the Court of Appeals for the District of Columbia. It meant that once the government stamped its documents "top secret," that was that, unless it had abused its discretion when it stamped the documents. Our view, of course, was the Pentagon Papers was a First Amendment case that demanded a very high test.

But the government was proposing an abuse of discretion test. If the government had committed no abuse of its discretion, it could stop the *New York Times* from publishing. It's hard to believe that Griswold could convince anyone of this position. He must have realized that, because when Griswold reached the Supreme Court later on, he dropped it.

When the *Post* lawyer, Glendon, stood up to argue in the Appellate Court, the first thing he noted was the government had changed its position that publication of Pentagon Papers damaged national security. Now it was arguing it had not abused its discretion. Glendon said the government's new argument did not cut the mustard. He said the government had not met its burden to justify the injunction against the *Post*. Still, he did not say what that burden was.[7]

The Griswold-Glendon argument was an off-Broadway version of what took place in New York. The New York version featured a well-known constitutional law scholar, Alex Bickel, pitted against a well-prepared U.S. Attorney, Whitney North Seymour Jr. Bickel had written two scholarly first rate briefs totaling 120 pages for the *New York Times*. While his aim in one of the briefs was somewhat off the mark, the quality of his work was far superior to that in the Washington case. Whitney North Seymour, additionally, had become an overnight star, coming up with an ingenious, although inappropriate, way to pin the *Times* in a corner.

When the two courts announced their opinion, would the two cases be decided the same way? We would find out the next day.

CHAPTER XXIV
ALEX BICKEL QUITS

The next day, Wednesday morning, June 23, Alex Bickel left the *New York Times* case. Judge Friendly had humiliated him. His argument before Friendly's court had failed; he knew that his emphasis on separation of powers rather than on the First Amendment had been off the mark.

When Larry McKay, Bill Hegarty, Floyd Abrams, Alex Bickel, and I had dinner the night before, Alex was depressed. We did not talk about his argument. The less said, the better. I sat next to him, and in the course of the conversation he said sullenly, "You don't want me to finish the brief on the *Caldwell* case, do you?" It was due in a few weeks on July 17.

I said, "of course we do." We did not discuss it further. I realized then what a terrible day he thought he had had in court. Seymour had beaten him quite badly, even though Alex, in theory, had a better argument. I did not give a moment's consideration to replacing him. Everyone has a bad day in court now and then; the next day would be better.

This was Alex's first case, however. He was not accustomed to the ups and downs of litigation. He was not a practicing lawyer—he was a professor. The strain of the case had taken its toll, as indeed it might have. He was called late Monday night. He made an excellent argument the next day without any sleep. The next two days, Wednesday and Thursday, he produced an extraordinary sixty-three page brief. Virtually every word in it was his own. It was a beautiful brief. In large firms, briefs of this sort are usually written initially by associates and then re-written. This was not the case with Alex.

He had to make the opening and closing arguments Friday. The trial ended at 11:00 on Saturday night, and Sunday he had to write yet another brief for the Appellate Court. This brief was eighty-three pages long. Again, virtually every word was his own. The brief, while off the mark, was brilliantly done. The next day he had to deal, in some part, with Seymour's tactic of bringing in new evidence. And on the following day, Tuesday, he was beaten up by Judge Friendly.

Alex was exhausted as well as depressed. On Wednesday, he called to say "he was very battered." He said there was something on his mind: "whether we would want him to do the Supreme Court argument." We were not thinking of the Supreme Court at that moment. Our case was awaiting decision by Judge Friendly and the rest of his full court. We wanted to win that case, but if we went to the Supreme Court, we wanted Alex there. We told him we wanted him and to get some rest.

Bickel then told Floyd he was leaving for Stanford for rest. I had understood that Alex was going to a friend's house that had a pool. I had reached Alex earlier in March when he was in Palo Alto, and perhaps this was the same place. He told Floyd that he was going to come back Saturday or Monday. But he told Floyd that if he didn't come back in time for the argument in the Supreme Court, Floyd should do it himself.[1]

I did not know about this latter conversation. I knew Alex had gone off despondently, perhaps, in his own mind, never to return. In my mind, however, I always thought that if I told him to come back, he would.

Floyd had done a great job arguing for the protection of our sources the week before. It was, however, an unreasonable expectation that he would argue the case in the Supreme Court, largely because he was a newly-minted junior partner at Cahill Gordon and the most junior member of our team. He was regarded, rightly or wrongly, as too young and inexperienced, despite the superb argument he had made several days earlier—an argument that became one of the foundations for the reputation he built as a foremost First Amendment expert.

The most pressing question on my mind that morning was what to do about Seymour's Special Appendix. I was still very angry that the court had permitted Seymour to present the Special Appendix before the Appellate Court in order to get a second bite of the apple.

We had to come up with a strategy to deal with the Special Appendix. It would be a disaster if we had to go back and have Judge Gurfein try the case all over again. I was particularly curious as to what affidavits the government had introduced into the *Washington Post* trial. I thought if we knew exactly what Seymour had done, it would undermine the usefulness of the Special Appendix for the government. The government should *not* get two or three bites out of the apple.

With this in mind, I called Bill Glendon, the *Post*'s lawyer. We had not had any time to talk to the *Post* lawyers as the newspapers' cases went forward. Both cases had come to a stop the day before, and we were awaiting the decision from our respective Appellate Courts.

I reached Glendon on the phone. He was very uncooperative; he would not answer my question about what affidavits the government had introduced in the *Post* trial. He may have thought I was asking for top secret information—but in any event, Glendon would not help me at all.

I asked Bancroft to call Kay Graham, publisher of the *Washington Post,* to get Glendon's cooperation. Graham told him that Glendon "did not know what he [Goodale] was talking about."[2] They weren't going to tell us anything to help us out. So much for trying to cooperate with the *Washington Post*. We were glad the

Post was in the case, but the *Post* apparently was not glad we were. There was more than an undercurrent of competition between the two sets of lawyers.

It turned out the *Post* had its hands full later that morning. While the government in New York continued at length to assert that codes were broken, it made that assertion only in the highly secret Gayler affidavit filed with Gesell—which was bad enough. Then one of the more exciting, intriguing, and ridiculous events in the whole Pentagon Papers case took place.

On late Wednesday morning the government called Judge Bazelon. He was the chief judge of the District of Columbia Court of Appeals. It wanted to discuss a "housekeeping matter" that involved an affidavit.[3] These were the very same words Seymour had used with the New York Court to introduce the affidavits he had cut-and-pasted from the *Washington Post* trial.

Seymour had gotten away with this nefarious tactic, and the government knew a good thing when it saw it. Bazelon told the government to meet him in his chambers. The government team consisted of a representative of the National Security Agency (NSA) and federal prosecutors. Griswold was not there. The NSA representative was a deputy to Admiral Gayler, then head of the NSA. The *Washington Post* team consisted of Bill Glendon, Fritz Beebe, and *Washington Post* reporter George Wilson. They all had received a security clearance.

Gayler's deputy had a double-locked briefcase with him. He told Judge Bazelon that what he was about to learn would jeopardize the American effort in Vietnam if it was disclosed. The deputy undid the double locks and took out a large manila envelope. Bazelon opened it. Inside it there was another envelope. Bazelon opened that too. Inside, there was yet a third envelope. This envelope was sealed with a great big red wax seal with dangling red ribbons. Bazelon, with a half-smile, broke the seal.[4]

It was a radio intercept from a North Vietnamese radio transmitter off the coast of Vietnam. The document was shown to the *Post* lawyers. Glendon looked impressed and handed the transmission to Wilson. Wilson whispered to Glendon that he thought he'd seen the transmission before. Glendon said something to Wilson like, "You'd better be right about this one," and gave him a quizzical look.[5]

Wilson had a bag full of previously published material about Vietnam. He had used material from it at the *Washington Post* trial to contradict information in Doolin's affidavit. He fished out a report he thought was relevant.

Wilson later said the crisis of the moment sharpened his memory, and so he could remember the page number in a report where the information had previously been published.[6] It had been published in a public report by the Senate Committee on Foreign Relations. He went to the page he remembered, and there it was. It was not a government secret: it had already been published. Wilson had single-handedly destroyed the government's most significant point in all of the Pentagon Papers case.

The actions by the government in asking Bazelon to hold the hearing were highly improper. Its chance to appear before Bazelon's court had expired. It had asked for a re-hearing, and it was denied. Yet, undaunted, it was asking for another hearing. In this request for a re-hearing, it did not want the full court there, it wanted just Bazelon.

It then took the affidavit signed by Admiral Gayler, the head of the NSA, put it in three different envelopes and submitted it to Bazelon with great fanfare. Why the government needed all this fanfare is hard to understand. Upon inspection, the affidavit Gayler used in the trial court, declassified many years later, seems to be nearly the same as the one he submitted in Bazelon's chambers. It does not appear much different than the one shown to Gesell—without any fanfare.

The only difference seems to be that the message in the Bazelon affidavit is slightly longer. Each affidavit contained a message from North Vietnam alleging we had broken the North Vietnamese code. The Gayler affidavit given to Gesell said, "At 1940 hours…'received information indicating attack by PGM P4 imminent.'"[7]

The affidavit given to Bazelon said, "In the message sent by CTU72.1.2. to AIG-181 dated [deleted] the following sentence is included: 'RCVD info indicating attack by PGM/P-4 imminent. My position 19–10.7 N 107–003 proceeding southeast at best speed.'"[8] It is hard to see much difference between these two messages.[9] The government made a big production out of the apparent difference in order to scare Bazelon, without telling him it had already been rejected by Gesell. This gambit failed, and the result was highly embarrassing for the government.

While Griswold did not accompany the other prosecutors to Bazelon's chambers, he certainly knew what the NSA had requested. He should not have agreed to this procedure. Judge Bazelon should not have agreed to it either. But since Seymour had talked the Second Circuit Court of Appeals into permitting a second bite of the apple, perhaps Bazelon was persuaded by that court's decision.

*   *   *

At 5:00 p.m. the Appeals Court for the Second Circuit issued its opinion. We lost five to three. Judge Friendly, writing for the majority (Mansfield, Smith, Lumbard, Hays) said there had to be a new trial for the items listed in the Special Appendix. Judges Kaufman, Feinberg, and Oakes dissented.[10] The court did decide we could publish those items not in the Special Appendix. However, we were not about to publish anything unless we had the right to publish all of the Pentagon Papers.

The court also decided the standard that Judge Gurfein should use in re-trying the case was that the government had to show "immediate and grave danger" to national security. Its basis, in some part, was the definition of "top secret" in the Executive Order 10501. That regulation talked about "grave" danger.

Not only had the government won, but Whitney North Seymour's tactics had won, too. He had persuaded the court to accept a Special Appendix, which meant the presses would be stopped until Judge Gurfein had re-tried the case to determine whether the items in the Special Appendix damaged national security. Since we were all aggravated by Seymour's unethical tactics to begin with, we were even more aggravated that he won using them. The question for us was what to do about Judge Friendly's decision.

I wanted to immediately take the case to the Supreme Court. This technically meant we would apply for a writ of *certiorari*. I was met, however, with resistance from my colleagues at Cahill Gordon. They all thought we should agree to have the case re-tried as Judge Friendly had directed.

This view was totally unacceptable to me. For the first time, I lost confidence in Cahill Gordon's judgment. Regardless of what their view of the law was, our case was not merely a legal case: it was a political case. It was the press against the government. We had to battle all the way and never show the other side that we were weak or ready to submit to their will. I thought Cahill Gordon had lost sight of this political context.

Cahill Gordon had two arguments why we should not appeal to the Supreme Court. The first, advanced by Ray Falls, a partner who had been a Supreme Court Clerk, was that the Supreme Court would not take our case. His reasoning was that since there were items still to be tried before Judge Gurfein, the case was not in a final posture appropriate for Supreme Court review. He told me the Supreme Court "didn't like to take cases" in this posture. Since Falls had clerked for the Supreme Court and I had not, I was quite respectful of his views.

Floyd Abrams had another view. He did not think that trying the items in Seymour's Special Appendix under the standard "grave and immediate danger" would be all that bad. He thought we could probably win under that standard.[11] Bill Hegarty concurred.

I was not happy with "grave and immediate danger" as a First Amendment standard. "Clear and present danger" was better, but I was not that happy with that, either. For me, "clear and immediate danger" would be best. I wanted a standard that came closer to a global disaster that inextricably would result from publication of the secrets of the hydrogen bomb. I wanted to set an extraordinarily high standard so that it would be almost impossible to censor the press. A free press is the backbone of a democracy.

Our discussions were not complete when I was told there was a call from Fred Graham of the *New York Times*. Fred was the principal correspondent covering the Pentagon Papers case for the *Times*. He was the same Fred Graham who I advised to disobey a prior restraint order a year before. He was reluctant to do so, in part, I always thought, because he was a lawyer—a graduate of Harvard Law School. He followed my instructions, although it turned out the judge in question had not technically ordered the *Times* not to print.

For some reason Graham's call had come into the stenographer's pool, away from the offices of Abrams and Falls. There was a huge round clock on the wall ticking off the minutes as we neared the *Times'* deadline for publication of the next day's paper. Graham got me on the phone; "What are you going to do?" he said.

I didn't answer immediately because I was trying to decide what to do. Graham then said, "They'll only nickel and dime you to death." What he meant by that was if we went back and had a retrial before Gurfein, the government would think of endless ways to make that trial go on forever. If the government lost, it would appeal. When it got to the Court of Appeals, who knows, it would discover additional new evidence to prevent publication. The case would be sent back. The process would repeat itself and the case would go on forever.

I looked at the clock. The deadline was getting closer. If I told Graham we couldn't make up our minds, that would be the headline and it would be a bad one; it would show we were weak. That weakness would be influential with everyone who heard our case, that is to say, Gurfein or the Supreme Court. Further, it would show our weakness to the public.

In light of the deadline, I really could not call Bancroft and Sulzberger to get their marching orders. By the time I reached them, the deadline would have passed. It was early evening and this was before cell phones. I would never find them. And so, I told Graham we were appealing to the Supreme Court. That was the headline.

Meanwhile, back in D.C., Judge Bazelon did not announce the decision of his court until 8:00 p.m. The *Washington Post* won, the government lost. Judge Bazelon's court decided the government had not met the standard it was trying to prove, namely, "irreparable harm to national security," and so the *Post* was free to publish, while the *Times* was not.[12]

This standard was, of course, too low. It was another reason why both cases needed to go to the Supreme Court. It was important for the sake of the First Amendment to get a standard better than "irreparable harm," just as it was to get a standard better than "grave and immediate danger." The government, however, was not ready to give up that fast. It immediately got a stay to stop the *Post* from publishing while it considered whether to ask for a re-hearing of the Court of Appeals decision.

As Wednesday night ended, we didn't know then what would happen to our case or to the *Washington Post*'s. Would the Supreme Court hear our case? Would the *Washington Post* case go to the Supreme Court along with ours? If we made it to the Supreme Court, what would our argument be? And finally, would Bickel be with us or not?

CHAPTER XXV

A RUSH TO THE SUPREME COURT

On Thursday morning June 24, we woke up to find out that the Knight chain of newspapers in Miami, Akron, Tallahassee, Boca Raton, Macon (Georgia), Charlotte (North Carolina), and two in Philadelphia, had published new articles from the Pentagon Papers given to them by Ellsberg. We realized we had to move quickly to free ourselves from the Second Circuit's injunction or we would lose the story entirely. (The *Times* had not published for nine days.)

With that in mind, we had worked furiously through Wednesday night to prepare our appeal papers (a petition for *certiorari*) to the Supreme Court to avoid going back to the trial court. By dawn's light, they were driven by a Cahill associate to Washington D.C. to be filed with the Court. At 9:00 a.m. Thursday, we sent a letter to the Court telling it the petition was on its way.

Usually it takes years before a case gets to the Supreme Court, but here we were on our way only nine days after the case began. And it was only three months before that I had started thinking about the issues in the case. In the space of sixteen months, two major First Amendment cases that had begun with me—this and the *Caldwell* case—were on their way to the Supreme Court. Both were cases of first impression: there were no precedents to assist the Court in deciding these issues. We had to propose rules to the Supreme Court to aid it in its decision.

The Nixon administration had its hands full on Thursday morning. It had to decide whether to pursue the Knight newspapers. It had to be prepared for the arrival of the *Times* appeal papers to the Supreme Court, and it had to deal with the loss it suffered in the *Washington Post* case the day before. In short, it had to preserve its victory in the *New York Times* case and to reverse its loss in the *Post* case.

Its first move was to reverse its *Post* loss. At 10:30 a.m., the Justice Department notified Bill Glendon that it would ask the Court of Appeals to re-hear the *Post* case in the early afternoon.

But at noon, before the government had a chance to file re-hearing papers, it received the *Times'* petition to the Supreme Court. Now it not only had to chase the Knight newspapers but also respond to the *Washington Post* and the *New York*

Times almost simultaneously. For the Justice Department it was a combination of "The Perils of Pauline" and the Keystone Cops.

For whatever reason, the Justice Department decided not to pursue the Knight newspapers. Mitchell said those papers had not published classified information. This, of course, was totally untrue. The Justice Department had gotten itself into a knot which it could not untie.

The *Times* asked the Supreme Court to take its case because of the errors in the Second Circuit Court of Appeals decision. It focused on the illegality of the acceptance of the Special Appendix. It maintained that the standard used of "grave and immediate harm" to national security was too vague to be constitutional. And, among other things, it said that there was no power of the Executive to enjoin the *New York Times* without a statute.[1]

Griswold whipped off a quick response to the *Times*' argument in which he said that in national security cases, "legal nicet[ies]" need not be followed with respect to a Special Appendix.[2] This was infuriating. The solicitor general of the United States, the former dean of Harvard Law School, was saying that "legal nicet[ies]" did not apply in a major constitutional case. He had spent nearly all his professional life telling his students the exact opposite.

He also said the decision in New York allowing the use of the Special Appendix as supplemented by new items for a retrial was perfectly reasonable. All the decision directed was that Judge Gurfein be given another week, until July 3, to decide whether there was anything in the Special Appendix that damaged national security. What he did not say was that when sent back to Gurfein, the case would go on forever because the government would always be able to find a new threat to national security in the 7,000 pages.

Meanwhile in D.C., the Court of Appeals agreed with the *Post* and rejected Griswold's request for a re-hearing, which would essentially allow the *Post* to start publishing again.[3] But Griswold anticipated this response, and immediately appealed to the Supreme Court for a stay of that ruling until both cases were resolved.[4]

Griswold added to his request for a stay that he also wished to appeal the whole *Washington Post* case to the Supreme Court.[5] He allowed that he didn't have time to prepare a formal petition for *certiorari*. Effectively, he was saying, "This is a screwball case, I don't have time to prepare the correct papers, just consider this paper as the correct one (i.e., a petition for cert)." If the Supreme Court agreed with Griswold to accept the *Post* case and granted the *Times* request for *certiorari*, it could combine the two cases and deal with them as one.

The *Washington Post* was not pleased with Griswold's approach. It had won its case. It didn't want to go to the Supreme Court, where it might lose. It said all that Griswold wanted to do was make the Special Appendix apply to the *Washington Post*. It pointed out that much of the material from the Appendix had been taken from its case before Gesell.[6]

It said the very claims now made in the secret *New York Times'* Special Appendix had already been found in the *Washington Post* case not to damage national security. And so the *Post* asked, why would we have any interest in permitting a court to review this material again?

And so by the end of Thursday both the *Post* and the *Times* cases had been appealed to the Supreme Court. No one knew whether the Court would take them. If four members of the Court vote to take a case, then the full Court hears it. These votes take place at a conference called by the Chief Justice, who was then Warren Burger.

The whole country was now following every detail of these cases. The national press reported that the Court had met for three hours on Thursday afternoon in conference to decide whether to take the cases. Justice Douglas, who was in his home state of Washington, participated by telephone.[7]

The Court was nearing the end of its term. The following Monday was its last regular day. After that, the Court would be in recess for the summer. In order to meet that deadline, the Court would have to have to hear arguments, if at all, on Saturday or perhaps Monday.

The expectation of the national media was that on Friday the Court would decide to take the case and the argument would probably be the next day, on Saturday. This was our expectation, too. On late Thursday afternoon, Bickel decided he was coming back. He would take the red-eye from San Francisco and arrive in Washington, D.C. the next morning. The rest of the team, Bill Hegarty, Larry McKay, Floyd, and I, headed for Washington on Friday morning too.

At 1:15 p.m. on Friday, the Supreme Court announced that it would take both cases. It was a 5–4 decision.[8] It was a very unusual 5–4 decision, however. Four of the Justices—Douglas, Black, Marshall, and Brennan—did not want to take the case at all. Instead they wanted to free the *Times* and the *Post* to publish immediately.

The other five, Justices Burger, Blackmun, White, Stewart, and Harlan, wanted to keep the injunction in place until the case could be heard. That was an excellent result for us. Four of the Justices thought we should not have been enjoined at all. All we needed was one more vote and we would win the case.

That was the good news. The bad news was that the Supreme Court required the *Times* to respond to the Special Appendix. This response was to be in the form of a secret brief delivered to the Court at 10:30 the next morning, before the case was argued. It also permitted the government to designate other items it could put together that alleged damage to national security before 5:00 on Friday to supplement the Appendix, which the Court called a "Supplemental List." We would have to respond to that too.

This was a huge blow for us. How in the world were we going to respond to the items in the Special Appendix in that period of time? Where were we going to get the information to do that? How could we determine whether the assertions made by the government in the Special Appendix were true?

We had no right to a cross-examination. The Supreme Court, like every other appellate court, does not permit cross-examination. Worse still, how many items would the government designate before 5:00 p.m.? The government would now throw new unsubstantiated allegations at us in the Supplemental List, as well as force us to answer similar allegations in the Special Appendix. There was no due process in a national security case.

Again we broke our team into two—Max Frankel and Bill Hegarty were to write a secret brief responding to the secret Special Appendix and the Supplemental List, Alex would write the legal brief, Floyd would assist, and I would review and approve for filing.

At 5:00, Bill and Max received the government's new claims set out in the Supplemental List. There were forty-four of them, which, when added to the seventeen claims in the Special Appendix, made a total of sixty-one claims of damage to national security to be answered before 10:30 a.m. the next day. The government attempted to add three more claims after 5:00, but the Court refused to let the them do that (a very small victory for us).

The outrageous behavior of Nixon's lawyers radicalized us. We lost all faith in the government to act fairly. We had to respond satisfactorily to a secret list of new allegations by 10:30 the next morning, or lose the case.

The supplemental list was broken into thirteen categories and contained items that included: "Official communications which criticize present Vietnam officials or efforts by Vietnam government Agencies or officials affecting vietnamization programs…Documents relating to the military involvement of any foreign government in Vietnam (sic) other than U.S. and Vietnamese troops… Confidential information relating to peace negotiations assets or tactics."[9] The list also included the Llewelyn Thompson telegram, which had been part of the case before Gurfein.

These claims had a familiar ring. Many of them had been rejected by Gurfein and Gesell. The government, for example, continued to claim we had the four volumes relating to "peace negotiations" although we had told them repeatedly that we did not. Ellsberg had apparently taken them out of the copies given us.

Our denial fell on deaf ears, however. Griswold went ahead and repeated this claim in his own secret brief to the Court. As will be explained later, while Frankel and Hegarty worked feverishly to answer the forty-four claims, Griswold cut them down to eleven in his secret brief without telling them, of which one related to "peace negotiations."

The *Post* decided not to answer any of the allegations. It said in its secret brief: "[It] is clear from its Supplemental List of Special Items that the government continues to tilt at windmills."[10] For reasons of its own, the *Post* apparently had decided to broadbrush its response to the entire supplemental list as "tilt[ing] at windmills" and leave it at that.

Frankel and Hegarty, however, worked until the wee hours to rebut the government's allegations point-by-point. Frankel describes the frantic night in his book *The Times of My Life and My Life with The Times* as follows:

> Thus it happened that the most feverish piece of writing of my entire career…became the body of a top secret brief to the Supreme Court…. The government's annex began with a catchall list of what it claimed were taboo subjects, ranging from "details of bombing in Indochina" to "confidential information relating to peace negotiations, assets or tactics."
>
> We replied that if those broad subjects were declared off-limits to the press, the government would have succeeded in promulgating a dangerous code of censorship. Besides, we showed that those very subjects had been routinely addressed in the writings of present and former government officials, in open testimony to Congress, and in daily press coverage of the war.
>
> We also argued that the government had no standing to fret about the publication of "national intelligence estimates" and the "deployment times" of troops to Vietnam. Intelligence estimates were openly debated in the capital, and Nixon himself regularly boasted about the pace, size and timing of troop movements out of Indochina.[11]

Max showed particular relish in later e-mails to me that showed that the Thompson telegram did not damage national security:

> The Griswold complaint said the [Pentagon Papers] would reveal Thompson's still operative advice and analysis about the attitudes and policies of Soviet leaders during the Vietnam War. Our joker was to cite Nixon's own memoir, published in 1961, that revealed a great deal more of Thompson's secret advice to Nixon during Nixon's visit to the Soviet Union just two years earlier. We quoted Nixon's book, *Six Crises*, about what Thompson had told him, not Thompson's direct memos.
>
> All the other rebuttals similarly cited news stories or books about current CIA agents, or estimates of Soviet military installations and deployments, troop movements or "battle plans" or secret diplomatic letters and analyses (there were not forty-four because a couple of the alleged "secrets" were so vaguely cited by page number only that we didn't know what the references were).[12]

The exchange of the secret briefs on Friday-Saturday was a truly radicalizing event for all the lawyers on our side. However flimsy they deemed the government's case, they had never encountered such outrageous behavior as the introduction of new facts at every appeal stage, with barely a moment to seek clarification and time for rebuttal.[13]

Clearly, the government was playing by a very different set of rules than we were. If the *Times* could not satisfactorily answer even a single one of the allegations, the Supreme Court could send the case back to a trial court for special consideration of these allegations, which by one count would cover more than 2,000 pages of the Pentagon Papers.[14] In the real world, this would mean we had lost the case. It was an absolutely outrageous performance by the government. We blamed not only Seymour and the Second Circuit, but also Griswold for permitting this to take place on his watch.

CHAPTER XXVI
ALEX TO THE RESCUE

Alex had taken the red-eye back from California and arrived in the early morning. I met him in our hotel suite before noon. In order to win, we had to come up with a strategy to defeat the Seymour-Griswold tactic that permitted the introduction of new evidence. The only way to do that was to articulate a new test under the First Amendment akin to "clear and immediate danger." If none of the items in the Appendix or on the Supplemental List could meet such a test at first blush, then we would win.

I had decided to appeal the *Times* case because the standard used by the Second Circuit of "grave and immediate damage" was not adequate. I did not think that test was worthy of the First Amendment. It gave too much leeway for judges to stop publication.[1]

We needed a test that would permit the Court to look at the allegations made in the Special Appendix and the Supplemental List and be able to immediately decide that those allegations failed the test. This would prevent the government from making last minute allegations unless they implied a truly disastrous event for the country. Such a test could also meet my ambition that the only injunction permitted by the Court would be against a disastrous event such as the publication of the instructions for the development of a hydrogen bomb.

Alex knew all of this when he started writing his brief. The test he proposed to the Court was as follows: a prior restraint would be permitted "only when publication could be held to lead directly and almost unavoidably to a disastrous event" for the country.[2] The test of "grave and immediate danger" was not enough. It had to be "a grave and disastrous breach in the security of the country."[3] Further, the publication of an alleged violation of national security should "leap to the eye."[4] This meant that the item in question should be so obvious that the government should not have to ask the Court for time to point out the items it thought damaged national security, as it had in this case.

I was very happy with this articulation and with Alex's brief. He had finally written a great First Amendment brief in the bedroom of our hotel suite while I sat in the living room. When Alex worked, I imagined a sign outside his door: "Genius at Work—Do Not Disturb."

When he finished sections, he would send them out for my approval. I would interrupt him from time to time. On one occasion we agreed that our proposed test should "leap to the eye." We also discussed the test itself and concluded that we had a chance the Court would adopt it.

We knew, of course, we had to have five votes to win. We already had four, Black, Douglas, Marshall, and Brennan. We had them since they had indicated earlier in the afternoon that no injunction against the *Times* should be entered at all. In theory, they should vote for any test we proposed.

Black and Douglas were considered to be absolutists on the First Amendment. They believed that no restrictions on freedom of speech should be permitted. This was even more "radical" and "liberal" than the *Times'* position. From the beginning of the *Caldwell* case, Abe Rosenthal and I believed the *Times* should not take an absolutist position on the First Amendment.

The position we presented to the Court was not an absolute one. It would allow the government to permit an injunction under extraordinary circumstances. Nonetheless, Black and Douglas would vote for it. It would not meet their view of the First Amendment, and they would criticize the test, but they would not vote against it. While Marshall and Brennan were not absolutists, we thought they would come out roughly the same way.

But where was the fifth vote? We thought Chief Justice Burger, a Nixon supporter, was a lost cause. He was a very conservative judge. At that time, Justice Blackmun voted in tandem with Burger. The two were known as the "Minnesota Twins," since Minnesota was their home state. Alex thought a fifth vote might be Justice Harlan, whom he admired as much as any other Justice on the Court. I did not share Alex's enthusiasm for Justice Harlan.

That left two other Justices as a possibility for the fifth vote: Justices Stewart and White. White was a Kennedy appointee, although not as liberal as Kennedy. As a former prosecutor, he was tough on crime. He was also tough, personally. While attending Yale Law School, on the weekends he had played pro football for the Detroit Lions, then one of only ten teams in the National Football League. He was a former All American football player at Colorado and a Rhodes Scholar.

That left "my new best friend," Potter Stewart, who had much to my surprise told me at the Gridiron Club, "we won the Sullivan libel case for you," meaning the press. I had high hopes for Stewart as our fifth vote because he had been a newspaper man. He had been editor of the *Yale Daily News* and a summer reporter for the *Cincinnati Inquirer*. He seemed to understand the press and, of course, had voted for "us" in the Sullivan case.

Alex's brief followed the briefs he had written for Judge Gurfein and the Court of Appeals in New York City. He said that the Espionage Act did not apply, because, among other reasons, of its legislative history. The government had no power to enjoin the *Times* because there was no law supporting such injunction.

The Executive Order 10501 and the Freedom of Information Act were irrelevant. The brief ran sixty-two pages.

We did not receive the government's brief until shortly before the argument the next day. It was a surprise. They had completely dropped the Espionage Act argument. This, of course, was the act upon which the *New York Times* had been sued. It also had dropped its argument under the Executive Order 10501, the section over which Lord, Day & Lord had resigned.

Effectively, it relied on a version of a weak First Amendment, which justified the injunction. It said the First Amendment permitted the use of the test "grave and immediate harm" or with respect to matters covering foreign relations, a test of "irreparable harm." It also repeated the argument that the law of intellectual property and copyright, as strange as it seemed, was relevant. The brief was twenty-two pages.[5]

The *Washington Post* brief proposed a test that the government should show "serious, immediate and substantial harm" before enjoining the press.[6] And so the government would be required to show the prospective publication would "vitally effect" national security.[7] These tests were perfectly reasonable suggestions for the Supreme Court to consider. But they were inadequate to meet the *New York Times'* needs, or the needs of the First Amendment. The *Post*'s brief was twenty-six pages.

Glendon and Griswold worked under difficult conditions. Security guards watched their every move. When Griswold began to write his brief in the Solicitor General's office, he asked for a set of the Pentagon Papers. An army sergeant brought them in and sat next to them. Shortly thereafter, Griswold's secretary entered the room. The sergeant said, "Who is she?" Griswold replied, "She is my secretary." "Is she cleared?" asked the guard. "If she is not cleared, she cannot come in here."

Griswold, who was then faced with writing a major constitutional brief by hand, got upset and said, "In this office I'm in charge.... I cannot do my work without the aid of my secretary." He then ordered the staff sergeant to leave and asked him to report whatever he had to report to his superior. Much to Griswold's surprise, the staff sergeant didn't argue and left.[8]

Glendon had security guards watching his every move as he wrote his brief in his law office. He had also had a battle with one of the guards earlier in the week. He wanted to look at the secret affidavits the government had introduced in the *Post*'s trial before Judge Gesell. At first, the FBI would not let him. He was then allowed to look at them only at the Justice Department and as long as the FBI agent looked at them at the same time. As he started to take notes, Mardian burst in the room and said he couldn't take notes.

A shouting match ensued. Glendon told Mardian, "I'm under a lot of pressure; I'm going to take these notes and I'm going to walk out of the room with them. Now this fellow [the F.B.I. agent] here is a lot younger and bigger than I am, and I'm sure that you are going to try and stop me—if you do, there's going to be a helluva fight and I know I'm going to lose; but when I stand up in Court tomorrow and I've got a few bandages on me, I'm going to tell people exactly what happened: that I was beaten up by the Department of Justice."[9]

Our conditions were normal—if writing a major Supreme Court brief in a hotel bedroom is thought to be normal. As I was sitting in the hotel's living room waiting for pages of Alex's brief to appear, Larry McKay, who was sitting there with me, picked up the phone and said that Fritz Beebe, chairman of The Washington Post Company, wanted to talk with me. Fritz, a generation senior than I, gave me a cordial hello.

He then asked, "Jim, is it okay with you that we (the *Washington Post*) go first in the argument tomorrow?" I wondered if he was serious. It was, after all, my case. His case was important and useful to us, but basically, the *Post* was riding on my coattails. If it went first, it would appear to the nation to be the leader in opposition to this calumny committed by Nixon, rather than the *Times*. Equally cordially, I told Fritz we were going to go first.

In fact, Erwin Griswold went first for the government, Bickel followed, and the *Post* went last. We thought we were out of surprises in this case. But Griswold had another one for us, which he sprang at the very last minute before the argument began at 11:00 in the morning.

CHAPTER XXVII

THE DAY THE PIN DROPPED

We assembled the next morning in our hotel room before going to the Court. I found myself saying such sports banalities as "let's go get 'em!"—as though we were about to enter a football stadium for the big game. As we walked up the street to the Supreme Court, reporters and TV cameras followed, shouting questions. We did not pause. The argument at the Supreme Court was the major news event of the day and we could not escape press attention.

I felt as self-confident as I ever had been, or have been since. I thought we were going to win. I also thought, with a sense of egomania and no little conceit, that I had the country in my palm—no matter what direction I took, the team, the press, and the country would follow.

When we arrived at the Court, the atmosphere changed. It was like going from Yankee Stadium into a mausoleum. The animated crowds that followed us right into our courtrooms in New York City were gone. The Supreme Court was very quiet and dignified. No sooner had I sat down at the counsel's table with Alex than a clerk told me that a uniformed security guard had something for me. Griswold had another surprise for us: two new secret briefs in addition to his own. They were from the Departments of State and Defense.

I looked at them immediately. They designated eleven items, which appeared to be new allegations of breaches of national security. I did not have time to look at them carefully before the uniformed guard snatched them back. Alex didn't have a chance to look at them at all. Bill Hegarty told him that the eleven items appeared to expand on eleven of the forty-two items he and Max had spent all night analyzing. Alex was barely, if at all, familiar with Hegarty's secret brief. Now the government had expanded its claims minutes before the argument, and he had no idea what the nature of those claims was.

Griswold had broken the rules again. He was not allowed to deliver any new items after 5:00 in the evening the day before. Here he was introducing new unsupported allegations or expanded allegations in two "briefs" from the State and Defense Departments minutes before the Supreme Court was to hear his argument.

We had no chance to respond to this new information.[1] The former dean of Harvard Law School, now the solicitor general of the United States, had fallen into

Nixon's smear trap along with Whitney North Seymour, the U.S. Attorney for the Southern District—right in the middle of the Supreme Court of the United States.

As soon as Griswold stood up to argue, he explained why he had delivered the secret briefs at the last moment. The afternoon before, he had met with representatives from the NSA, and State and Defense Departments. (It turned out they were Gayler, Zais and Macomber.[2]) He asked them what the really important claims of damage to national security in the case were.

Griswold said he had looked at the Supplemental List for the first time at 8:00 in the evening. He thought there were too many items. He cut them down to "ten" (he meant "eleven") based on his conversation with Gayler and the rest.[3] He then had three new secret "briefs" to be prepared (while Max and Bill were frantically trying to respond to all forty-two items), including his own, elaborating on the reasons the eleven items violated national security. The two new briefs he submitted from the State and Defense Departments were in fact not briefs at all but new factual assertions, comparable to affidavits.

When Griswold got up in front of the justices for questioning, he was unclear whether he meant to rest his case on these eleven items. He said he did, and then he said he did not. This was unsurprising, since Griswold changed his position frequently in the case. He seemed to be reserving his ability to change his position once again.

Justice White tried to pin him down and asked, "If we disagreed with you on those which you have covered, the remainder of the items need not be looked at?" Griswold responded, "Mr. Justice, I think that the odds are strong that that is an accurate statement."[4] Either his statement was accurate or it was not. It was not a question of what the odds were that it was accurate.

White also wanted to know whether he was also relying on the Special Appendix and the seventeen items in it. This was the Appendix that had so bedeviled the *Times* in New York. Griswold said he was relying "on the items specified in the Supplemental Appendix [he meant "Special Appendix"] filed in the Second Circuit and on such additional items as are covered in my closed brief in this case."[5] And so he was relying on both, apparently.

This was a very confusing answer. What was he trying to enjoin? The eleven items of the forty-two in the Supplemental Appendix, or the seventeen in the Special Appendix? Or both? At first he had said he was indeed relying just on ten items (i.e., eleven). Then he said there was a "good chance" that he was just relying on the ten items (i.e., eleven). But in response to White's question, he said he was also relying on the Special Appendix that had caused us so much trouble in the Second Circuit.

In a sense, it made no difference to us how many items he was using. We had not been allowed to cross examine his assertions, or indeed, fully see his new ones before we argued. In a major First Amendment case in the Supreme Court, it would have been nice to know what the government was trying to stop us from doing.

Unbelievably, Griswold began the formal part of the argument by talking about intellectual property. Once again, out came references to Ernest Hemingway and other irrelevant items. At least he did not refer to Queen Victoria and Prince Albert, as he had in the Court of Appeals. Justice White asked him if his case depended on intellectual property, and he said "no." He also asked him whether his case depended on classification. He said "no" again.

Then Justices White and Stewart began to pummel him with questions as to what standard he thought applied to this case. Stewart asked him whether "grave and immediate danger"[6] was the proper standard. Griswold said, "I'm glad to proceed on that basis."

Stewart asked him a second time, "Your case depends on the claim, as I understand it, that the disclosure of information will result in an immediate grave threat to the security of the United States of America." Answer: "Yes, Mr. Justice."

But the third time Stewart asked him, Griswold suddenly changed his tune, "All right, Mr. Justice, I repeat, unless we can show that this will have 'grave,' and I think I would like to amend it, I know the Court's order has said 'immediate' but I think it really ought to be 'irreparable harm to the security of the United States.'"[7]

Griswold, in the space of a few minutes, had changed his theory of the whole case. He had switched from "immediate" to "irreparable harm." There is all the difference in the world between "immediate harm," which would be felt almost instantly upon publication, and "irreparable harm" that would happen months or years later. Griswold had suddenly given up on the first and grasped the second. Later in the argument, he said that Gesell had applied the wrong standard in the *Post* case. Gesell's standard, in addition to "direct and immediate harm," was that the government had to meet the conditions of "top secret."[8]

In his memoirs, Griswold said he was so pleased with his argument that every four or five years he would pull out a recording and play it.[9] I find it hard to believe that an argument in which he gave the Court two or three versions of facts he was relying on and the choice of two tests, or maybe even three, to apply to those facts, was something anybody would want to listen to at all, much less every few years.

There was extraordinary anticipation when Alex stood up. The audience thought that this was the moment they were waiting for, and they were right. Alex was very confident. He appeared more energetic than Griswold, who looked crumpled and fatigued.

Almost immediately, Justices White and Stewart pounced on him. They asked him twenty questions about his standard. Was "grave and immediate" the standard he was arguing for? White wanted to know.[10] Bickel said the government had to pinpoint a particularly grave danger to "the nation." He had argued in his brief that the standard should "lead directly and almost unavoidably to a disastrous event for the country." He was defending that standard.

Would the definition of "top secret" meet his test? White wondered. That definition penalized "unauthorized disclosure of which could result in exceptionally grave damage to the nation such as leading to a definitive break in diplomatic relations affecting the defense of the United States, an armed attack against the United States and its allies, a war, or the compromise of military or defense plans, or intelligence operations...."[11] Bickel would not agree.[12]

Then Stewart jumped in. Our ears pricked up. We had to get his vote to win. Would he be friendly or antagonistic? I had hopes for the former, because of our conversation at the Gridiron Club. In that conversation I formed a highly favorable impression of Stewart, not only because he said he won the Sullivan case for "us," but because he could be outgoing, serious, yet at the same time not take himself overly seriously. My impression of Bickel was the same.

Stewart's tone, however, was very stern. His voice was commanding—quite unlike when I met him earlier in the year at the post-Gridiron cocktail party:

> Stewart: Let me give you a hypothetical case. Let us assume that when the members of the Court go back and open up this sealed record we find something there that absolutely convinces us that its disclosure would result in the sentencing to death of 100 young men whose only offense had been that they were nineteen years old and had low draft numbers. What should we do?
>
> Bickel: Mr. Justice, I wish there were a statute that covered it.
>
> Stewart: Well there is not. We agree, or you submit, so I am asking in this case what should we do.[13]

You could hear a pin drop. For the First Amendment, the correct answer to this question was it made no difference whether a publication caused the death of soldiers or anyone else. The death of a soldier or the sinking of a troop ship did not "lead directly and almost unavoidably to a disastrous event for the country." On the other hand, if the answer was it made a difference whether soldiers died or not, it was a concession that our test was weaker than advertised. We would win or lose on his answer.

Stewart followed up his question by saying, "You would say the Constitution requires that it be published and these men die. Is that it?"

> Bickel: No, I'm afraid that my inclination to humanity overcomes the somewhat more abstract devotion to the First Amendment in a case of that sort...a troop ship is in a sense that 100 men for the location of a platoon is in a sense that 100 men...I do honestly think, that that hard case would make very bad separation of powers law.[14]

What a great answer. If he had said "yes," that the First Amendment protects the killing of soldiers, the headline the next day would be "*New York Times* Says It's OK To Kill People." If he had said "no," unconditionally it would have jeopardized our case. We needed a strong test to avoid being sent back to Gurfein. Bickel had answered the question both ways and satisfied the First Amendment and satisfied the public standing of the *New York Times*. More importantly, the answer seemed to satisfy Stewart.

There are those today who still criticize Alex's answer. First, he said it would make a "bad separation of powers law." He should have said it would make bad First Amendment law, too. He had argued in his brief that the interest of the First Amendment and separation of powers were intertwined. But it made no difference to me whether he used separation of powers or the First Amendment to justify his answer. His answer was correct. I thought his answer had won the case.

The following Monday, the American Civil Liberties Union (ACLU) filed a brief to the Supreme Court objecting to Bickel's answer. The ACLU effectively said that in a prior restraint case the Court should not take into consideration the possibility of death to soldiers.[15] Its test was simply that "publication of the remaining documents would jeopardize the ability of the United States to defend against hostile acts."[16] It did not suggest there should be an immediate nexus to a feared event, as the *Times* had. It was therefore inadequate.

Bill Glendon's argument was an excellent antidote to Erwin Griswold's and Alex Bickel's, who were essentially academics. Glendon was a tough and able trial lawyer. He reminded the justices of a simple maximum: to win a case, you have to prove it. The government had not proved its case.

Glendon, however, had the impossible job of telling the justices what First Amendment standard applied. Almost everyone forgave him his answers, since he was not a First Amendment lawyer. Nonetheless, the answers were somewhat embarrassing. He first stated that "irreparable injury to the United States" was the correct test.[17] He then agreed with Stewart that the test should be "grave, irreparable and immediate danger."[18] Then he said it didn't make any difference whether the standard was "gravely prejudicial to the United States" or whether a security breach "irreparably injured the defense." He also said the "top secret" standard was not met.[19] He then said he would accept that standard, although Bickel would not.[20] He also said Gurfein and Gesell used the same standard, which they did not.[21]

Glendon said that the government had changed its position so many times, he couldn't keep up with it. He asserted the government had argued in the Court of Appeals that once an item was classified, that was the end of it. Stewart told him that's not what the government had argued. Glendon seemed unfazed.

The *Post*'s brief had suggested reasonably acceptable tests for the First Amendment throughout the litigation. Every time Glendon got up to speak, there was a disconnect between what he said and what his briefs said. When he sat down, nonetheless, the sense was the *Post* and the *Times* had made a good defense.

We left the argument thinking we were in pretty good shape. Most of us thought we would get Stewart's vote and perhaps White's. I asked the *Times'* representatives their views as we left. Bickel thought we had won 5–4, Fred Graham 6–3, Bancroft 5–4, McKay 5–4, Frankel 9–0, Phelps 5–4, Wicker 6–3. Abrams and Hegarty, who didn't want to appeal anyway, thought we had lost 5–4.[22]

As soon as we had a chance, we looked at Griswold's eleven items to see if they presented a risk to our views on the outcome of the case. As far as we were concerned they were a big bust. They were: 1) the negotiating volumes, 2) the Thompson telegram, 3) the Gayler affidavit, 4) embarrassing statements about Australia et al., 5) statements about third-party POW negotiating efforts, 6) SEATO contingency plans, 7) confidential discussions between South Vietnam and Laos, 8) the names of C.I.A. agents, and 9), 10), 11) estimates of Russian and Chinese military capacity.

The first six items had come up in the case before and had impressed no one. Neither the *Times* nor the *Post* had the negotiating volumes. The government had been told this repeatedly. Nonetheless, the government requested the Court to enjoin the *Times* for something it did not have. Fortunately, the Court did not follow the government's suggestion.

It would have been a catastrophe had the Court done otherwise. It would have issued a decision enjoining material not in the *Times'* possession. It would then have had to issue another decision saying it was wrong. The process would have severely damaged the reputation of the Supreme Court.

Frankel had discovered the Thompson telegram had been previously published. Wilson had demonstrated the heart of the Gayler affidavit had also been previously published.[23] Gurfein and Gesell had been unimpressed by claims concerning the SEATO treaty, embarrassment for Australia et al., and the use of third-party countries in POW negotiations. The references to talks between South Vietnam and Laos were general and revealed no details. The *Times* had no intention, nor did the *Post*, of publishing the names of CIA agents. According to those who have searched all of the Papers, the only CIA name published was a Colonel Conein, who had already left the CIA.[24]

Of three intelligence estimates, the one of Soviet strength would be published by the government a few months after the *Times* series on the Papers. Of the other two, one only spoke in generalities and the other was highly hypothetical.[25]

For us the eleven items were just more unsupported allegations which, when examined, did not amount to much. They certainly did not meet Griswold's initial test of "immediate danger" and did not even meet his test of "irreparable harm" which he adopted at the last moment, halfway through his argument.

The most unsupported allegation of the eleven, was, however, the claim that we had broken Vietnamese codes. The government had repeated the substance of the Gayler affidavit in item number 10 of Griswold's secret brief. It did not tell the Court that the interception to which that item referred had already been published in the Congressional Record or that Judges Gesell and Bazelon ignored the allegation. Griswold did not tell the Court any of this and let it think the *Times* had broken codes. Again, he fell into the smear trap.

As noted earlier, in his memoir Nixon said a principal reason he brought the Pentagon Papers case was to protect against the disclosure of codes. He said that codes were a central part of the Pentagon Papers case right up to the last minute in the Supreme Court.

Whether the Supreme Court would be impressed by these unsupported allegations, however, was not clear. They were not, of course, subject to our right of cross-examination. Frankel and Hegarty had attempted to answer them, but under impossibly trying circumstances. It is fair to say, therefore, we all felt some tension as to what the Supreme Court would do with them, as well as with the Special Appendix. Would it follow the Second Circuit and send the case back for further findings, or would we win straight away?

CHAPTER XXVIII
THE HISTORIC VICTORY

We won 6–3. We got the news about 2:30 Wednesday afternoon, four days after the argument in the Supreme Court. Sydney Gruson, Harding Bancroft, Abe Rosenthal, Punch, and I had an impromptu celebration on the fourteenth floor of the *Times*.

We were slapping backs, high-fiving and generally acting like adolescents. We posed for a picture, arms extended with our palms on top of each other as though we had won the Super Bowl. Abe and I led the celebration since we thought the future of the *Times* and the newspaper business depended on the outcome. Gruson and Bancroft, having been against publication, were more composed. Punch Sulzberger looked relieved.

We got Stewart's vote, the one we really wanted, and White went along with him. Their votes plus Black, Douglas, Brennan, and Marshall made up the six. The latter four thought we should have never been enjoined anyway. Burger, Blackmun, and Harlan dissented. Our strategy had worked.

Even more exciting from our point of view was that Stewart had substantially adopted the test we proposed to the Court. All in all, six votes could be counted on to support this test. Not only did we win the case, but we had won a great First Amendment victory. It was a historic win.

There was some bad news, too. Mr. Justice White said a criminal action was possible against us and the *Post*. But that did not spoil our celebration. Exhilarated, Punch, Abe, and I went downstairs to the newsroom floor to face the cameras and the press who were clamoring for our comments as they pushed their way into the building.

In the best of all worlds, a Chief Justice of the Supreme Court tries to have all Justices sign on to one majority opinion, and the dissenting Justices sign on to another. Here there should have been one opinion signed by the six who voted for us and one signed by the three who voted against us.

Burger said that because of the pressure to issue an opinion speedily, he could not do that.[1] Instead, he asked each Justice to write his own opinion. He then issued all nine opinions as the opinion of the Court. He prefaced that opinion with a statement by the Court, technically known as a *per curiam* opinion.

This opinion said that prior restraint cases require a "heavy burden" of proof for the government. Six justices agreed that the burden had not been met. The other three dissented and sought further proceedings in the lower courts. The *per curiam* opinion by itself was meaningless. It did not tell us what test or standard "our" six justices would agree to.

Many in the press reading the *per curiam* opinion felt let down. In his excellent book *The Papers & The Papers*, written the year after the case, Sanford J. Ungar wrote:

> As months went by, legal scholars and journalists alike began to realize that the 6–3 Supreme Court decision in the cases of *New York Times v. United States* and *United States v. Washington Post* had been a rather hollow victory for the press.
>
> The unsigned opinion of the Court said only that the government had failed to carry its heavy burden of proof to obtain a prior restraint, and the individual justices' opinions had as many nasty words for the press as for the government. Many editors felt strongly that the newspapers were worse off after the Pentagon Papers case than they had been before.[2]

But this view was clearly wrong, and ignored a close reading of the six opinions supporting publication. It was clear they would all support Stewart's standard which was "direct, immediate, and irreparable damage to our nation or its people."[3] Bickel, by comparison, had proposed a test that would permit an injunction only "when publication could be held to lead directly and almost unavoidably to a disastrous event for the country." The tests were not dissimilar.

Stewart did not talk about a "disastrous event for the country." He did, however, talk about damage to "our nation or its people." Whether the death of a hundred soldiers in Stewart's hypothetical would amount to "damage to our nation or its people," remained an open question. The death of a hundred soldiers, or the sinking of a troop ship, is a terrible event, of course, but whether it constitutes damage to the nation or just personal tragedy for those who perish is another question. Arguably, this tragedy does not rise to the level set out in Stewart's test.

In terms of the rule of the case or the "law" of the case, it is what Stewart says in his opinion that counts, not what he said to Bickel in argument or what Bickel said to him. What he said to Bickel and vice versa aids us in understanding the *Times'* position in the case. It's interesting but it is not part of the law of the case.

"Immediacy" is the essence of the Stewart test, and Bickel's as well. Publications must cause "immediate" damage to national security to merit a prior restraint. A history, such as the Pentagon Papers, is incapable of causing such immediate damage. There is nothing current or immediate about history.

Bickel proposed that "publication" should "lead directly and almost unavoidably to a disastrous event." Stewart said that it will "surely" result in such event. "Surely" and "directly and unavoidably" are indistinguishable. They are, however, distinguishable from a publication that "could" result in, or could "pose" a danger, to national security—to use the language of the definition for "top secret" and that of the Second Circuit, respectively.

White joined in Stewart's opinion, providing a second vote for Stewart's standard. The other four Justices who voted for the *Times* all seemingly wanted a higher standard. The Stewart standard was the minimum. At the very least, they would support such a standard, and so the Stewart standard became the rule of the case.

My ambition from the beginning was to have the Court adopt a test that would only prevent publication of a story comparable to instructions on how to make a hydrogen bomb. Did Stewart's test reach that magnitude? It would have been better if he had used Bickel's phrase: "a disastrous event." But he didn't. That fact is not dispositive. No court properly applying the Bickel-Stewart test will ever grant an injunction—unless the case concerns something like a hydrogen bomb.

Justices Black and Douglas wanted no standard to be applied at all, and joined each other's opinions. They thought the First Amendment was absolute. Black said that "in revealing the workings of government that led to the Vietnam War, the newspapers did precisely that which the Founders hoped and trusted they would do."[4] The press had a duty, he said, "to prevent any part of the government from deceiving the people and sending them off to distant lands to die of foreign fever and foreign shot and shell. I believe that every moment's continuance of the injunctions against these newspapers amounts to a flagrant, indefensible, and continuing violation of the First Amendment."[5]

Douglas said Judge Gurfein's decision that the Espionage Act did not apply was "preeminently sound."[6] He added, "the dominant purpose of the First Amendment was to prohibit the widespread practice of governmental suppression of embarrassing information.... The stays in these cases that have been in effect for more than a week constitute a flouting of the principles of the First Amendment..."[7]

Marshall was persuaded by Bickel's separation of powers argument; he was the only one of the twenty-six judges who heard the case in New York and Washington who bought Bickel's argument. He said that since there was no legislative basis for bringing the case, there was virtually, if not absolutely, no way for the government to succeed. Presumably, if the government could have shown a national emergency as Bickel had suggested, Marshall would have qualified his separation of powers argument. He did not suggest that exception in his opinion, however. He was as absolutely against an injunction, as were Black and Douglas.[8]

Brennan said, "[T]he First Amendment stands as an absolute bar to the imposition of judicial restraints in circumstances of the kind presented in these cases.... [T]he error that has pervaded in these cases from the outset was the granting of any injunctive relief."[9]

Brennan's view of the First Amendment, however, was not absolutist. He would permit an injunction, but only when "governmental allegation and proof that publication must inevitably, directly, and immediately cause the occurrence of an event kindred to imperiling the safety of a transport at sea."[10]

His test was similar to Stewart's. In a later case (*Nebraska Press Association v. Stuart*), Brennan changed his view to eliminate troop ships. He said in *Nebraska* that Stewart's opinion in the Pentagon Papers case stood for the "rule."[11]

Since all these Justices supported, or would support, the Bickel-Stewart-White test, all of them can be counted in favor of it. The Pentagon Papers thus has become known as the case which stands for the rule that no prior restraints can be granted unless as Stewart said, publication "will surely result in direct, immediate, irreparable damage to our nation or its people."[12]

In their dissents, Burger, Blackmun, and Harlan complained about the unseemly haste in the case. They voted to send it back for further hearing on the Special Appendix and the Supplementary List. Burger said that because of the rush, some of the lawyers did not have a full grasp of the case. He was particularly shocked at the behavior of the *New York Times*. The *Times*, for example, was claiming the public's "right to know" was absolute. The *Times* didn't make that claim.

Burger's dislike of the press was well known. He was involved in a notorious incident during the Pentagon Papers case in which he greeted *Washington Post* reporters at his door with a shotgun. After the D.C. Court of Appeals had ruled in the *Post*'s favor on Wednesday evening, the *Post* had sent two reporters to his house. They had thought the Justice Department would apply for an order to stop publishing to the chief justice himself. When they knocked on his door, Burger apparently thought they might be intruders. When he discovered they were reporters, he held the shotgun by his side and told them they should not have come. They could wait outside his gate if they wanted to stay around.[13]

A month before the Pentagon Papers case, Burger had given an extraordinary anti-press speech in Washington D.C. at the American Law Institute. He said that in 19th century Britain, "it was not uncommon for political leaders to horsewhip newspaper reporters." He aimed this remark at "newspapers not too distant from this building where I speak" (i.e., the *Washington Post*).[14] He was thought to be Nixon's voice on the Court, and he certainly sounded like it in that speech and in his opinion.

He berated the *Times* for not returning the Pentagon Papers to the government. He said he thought any "taxi driver" would do that: "To me it is hardly believable that a newspaper long regarded as a great institution in American life would fail to perform one of the basic and simple duties of every citizen with respect to the discovery or possession of stolen property or secret government documents. That duty I had thought—perhaps naively—was to report forthwith, to responsible public officers. This duty rests on taxi drivers, justices, and the *New York Times*."[15]

Blackmun, who then was known for consistently following in Burger's footsteps (as a "Minnesota Twin"), echoed Burger's comments. He blamed the *Times* for the haste of the case. The *Times* had had the documents for three months, but wanted the courts to render instant opinions. His cursory review of the Pentagon Papers led him to believe there might be material there which would cause "the death of soldiers, the destruction of alliances, the greatly increased difficulty of negotiation with our enemies, the inability of our diplomats to negotiate."[16] For these reasons, he wanted further hearings.

Justice Harlan had worked with Herbert Brownell at the New York firm then known as Root Ballantine. They were friends. Brownell had supported Harlan for the Supreme Court when Brownell was attorney general. It is possible Harlan knew that Brownell had resigned from the case, since that knowledge was notorious at the time. It is doubtful, however, that Harlan was influenced by it.

Bickel had hoped to get Harlan's vote, and was very disappointed he did not. Harlan was offended by the speed of the case, which he thought was driven by a "torrent of publicity." Courts should defer to the Executive in a case such as this, which involved foreign policy. Harlan wanted the case retried on this basis. Under this view, however, it is doubtful the press would ever win.

The greatest concern for the *Times* was the threat of criminal prosecution set out in Justice White's opinion. This opinion was joined by Stewart. Burger and Blackmun also thought there could be a criminal prosecution. Even Douglas agreed there might be one part of the Espionage Act—codes—applicable to criminal prosecution of the newspapers.

This meant there were four votes and possibly a fifth, Douglas, who *thought* there *might* be a criminal prosecution under the Espionage Act. However, what Justices think and what they decide are two different things. Since the application of a criminal statute had not been argued before them, they could not decide whether it applied.

All they could do was say what they thought, "dicta," as lawyers call it, which does not have the force of law. White, a former prosecutor, seemed most taken with the idea of criminal prosecution. He devoted four of his seven pages laying out the criminal statutes that might be applicable to the publication by the *Times* and the *Post*.

Judge Gurfein had decided that 793(e) of the Espionage Act did not cover publication. White thought it could, nonetheless, cover the mere possession of classified information. Bickel had dealt with the issue of possession in his argument before the Second Circuit saying that 793(e) was too vague to apply to mere possession. When I advised the *Times* with respect to the scope of this statute, I too thought it might be too vague to be constitutional.

White also indicated that Section 798, which covered publication of information relating to codes, could be applicable in this case, as Douglas also noted. The government had asserted throughout the case that there were issues concerning codes. It had no proof at any time to support these assertions.

The government had used its best efforts to prove there were intercepts in the Pentagon Papers, as set out in Admiral Gayler's affidavit. But it ended up with egg on its face before Judge Bazelon when it tried to prove the intercepts were secret. In the years following publication of the Pentagon Papers, no one has been able to show there was any basis for the claim that codes were involved in the Pentagon Papers case.

We were concerned, nonetheless, that Mitchell, on the basis of White's opinion, would take criminal action against us or even our reporters. He did not disappoint.

According to legal circles around the Justice Department, Attorney General John Mitchell was elated when he read Justice White's opinion.[1] The Nixon administration had been bruised by the Pentagon Papers case. White's opinion provided a roadmap for a criminal action against the *New York Times* and *Washington Post*. Nixon could recoup his loss. Mitchell made ready.

Within twenty-four hours of the issuance of the Supreme Court opinion, Mitchell issued his own statement, which the *Times* headlined on page one, "Mitchell Will Prosecute Law Violations in Leaks." The statement said, "Since the beginning... of the unauthorized disclosure of the Pentagon's classified documents, all avenues of criminal prosecution have remained opened.... The Department of Justice...will prosecute all those who have violated Federal criminal laws in connection with this matter."[2]

We battened down the hatches. There was no doubt Mitchell and Nixon meant to prosecute the *Times* and the *Post*. Ellsberg had already been indicted before the Supreme Court heard our case. I advised that no one should make comments on the case. They could be used against us.

Nixon had always wanted to indict the *Times*.[3] Now he had his chance to go full steam ahead. His administration was angry. The same day Mitchell announced he would "prosecute...leaks," *Washington Post* reporter Ken Clawson joined Assistant Attorney General Richard Kleindienst at a concert for the Wolf Trap Grand Opening in Virginia. He told Clawson "[I]t was only a matter of time before government obtain[ed] evidence of a type in which it could not avoid proceeding with a criminal prosecution against the newspapers.... The President is going to pick up a stick and start fighting back."[4]

These remarks were reported to Katherine Graham. She told us several weeks later at lunch at the *Times* that Nixon was not only going to prosecute the *Times* and the *Post*, he also wanted the Pentagon Papers back, and he wanted the *Post* not to publish certain offensive material.

I reported Graham's conversation to Punch as she told it to us:

Mitchell and Nixon were also contemplating criminal action to get the Papers back and accordingly wanted them delivered to the appropriate officer of the *Washington Post*'s choice. Mrs. Graham said the offensive material concerned two diplomatic cables.

The *Post* decided to call Bill Rogers (former *Post* attorney). He was told the *Post* had no intention of using the two objectionable matters and Rogers replied, "Well that ought to take care of this matter." The *Post* decided deliberately to ignore the request for the documents.

Kleindienst called Graham and said he still wanted the documents back. Graham told us the *Post* "discussed the matter at length internally but finally concluded not to comply with the government's request."[5]

The *Times* also concluded not to return the Papers, but received no threats. Mardian, however, demanded that the *Times* return its copies of the government's secret briefs, the Special Appendix and the Supplementary List. I refused at first, but then after some thought consented to return the documents, subject to my right to get them back for purposes of defending the *Times* in any criminal action.[6]

Mitchell directed Richard Kleindeinst to ask Whitney North Seymour, Jr. to impanel a grand jury in New York. The jury would indict those at the *New York Times* who received the Papers. Seymour refused, saying, "not in this district."[7] Seymour was admirably asserting the traditional independence of Southern District U.S. Attorneys. We frequently commented on Seymour's lack of independence. We unrealistically thought that Seymour should have resisted trying to restrain the *New York Times* from publication.

After failing to get Seymour to prosecute the *Times*, a few days later, on July 7, Mitchell took his case to Boston. The *New York Post* headlined, "Jury Weighs Indictment of the *New York Times*."[8] The story was based on a leak, ironically, from the grand jury to the ubiquitous Ken Clawson. He said it was investigating possible criminal charges against "the *New York Times*, the *Washington Post* and the *Boston Globe*." He also reported that Neil Sheehan and his wife Susan "were also named in the government's case before the grand jury last week."[9]

The next day there was another story, this time in the *Times*, headlined: "U.S. Said to Be Planning to Seek Indictment of a Times Reporter." It read: "Mr. Sheehan… was the main subject of information presented to the jury…the presentation…was aimed at an indictment charging that Mr. Sheehan had violated statutes against moving stolen property in interstate commerce by receiving secret documents taken from the government without authorization."[10]

I moved quickly to prepare the *New York Times* and Neil Sheehan against possible prosecution. I engaged Mitch Rogovin of the D.C. firm of Arnold & Porter to represent Sheehan and Mike Harrington of Ropes & Gray of Boston as the *Times'* local counsel.

The first step in preparing our defense was to review the advice that I had given the *Times* in light of the Supreme Court decision. I had initially advised the *Times* no jury would vote to convict it. This was based on my judgment that jurors would not convict the publisher of a truthful history of the Vietnam War, and that the ambiguity of the law that applied to such publication. While the papers reported that Sheehan was sought for "moving stolen property in interstate commerce," it turned out the government was really just using the two statutes I had originally found: § 641 relating to the theft of government property, the Espionage Act § 793(e), and a conspiracy to breach those statutes.

The government's theory was set out in a preliminary opinion by the supervising judge, W. Arthur Garrity.[11] I did not focus at that time on the fact that the government was trying to prove a conspiracy to violate the Espionage Act. As we shall see later, this theory has become extremely important in the government's threatened prosecution of Julian Assange and WikiLeaks.

When I reviewed my thinking on § 641 and § 793(e), I didn't see any reason to change my mind that they did not apply to Sheehan or the *Times*. I did not believe that the *Times* or Sheehan ran a real risk under them. The real risk was whether the *Times* and Sheehan could withstand the pressure from a harassing grand jury.

When I first looked at § 641, I concluded that it criminalized people who stole jeeps and other tangible government property. It did not apply to Xeroxing of the Pentagon Papers. If the government was really serious about getting Sheehan for trading in stolen property, it would have to find language in § 641 that was not there.

In a nutshell, there were no laws that directly covered leaks. When Daniel Ellsberg sat down with his attorney, Leonard Boudin, to discuss his liability, Boudin had told him, much to his surprise, there were no laws that covered his actions. He had not broken the law. This surprised Ellsberg, because he thought he was acting illegally.[12]

However, just because there were no laws that were directly applicable did not mean that in its war against the press, the Nixon administration couldn't stretch existing laws to fill the void. This is what they attempted to do. It gave us many anxious moments concerning Neil Sheehan's well-being.

Rogovin interviewed Neil to see how he had actually obtained the Pentagon Papers. That interview highlighted the then-unknown role of the Institute for Policy Studies (IPS) in Washington, D.C. The IPS was a leftist antiwar organization. It was founded by Richard J. Barnet and Marcus G. Raskin. I knew Raskin from law school. He seemed then a liberal duck out of water in an extremely conservative law school. Raskin and Barnet ended up on Nixon's list of enemies.

Ellsberg had given Raskin a small part of the Pentagon Papers covering years 1961–65, including the Tonkin Gulf Study. The IPS was working on a book titled *Washington Plans an Aggressive War* that was published in September 1971, after the Pentagon Papers. Raskin, who had been impressed by an antiwar piece written by Sheehan for the *New York Times Book Review*, told Ellsberg he should consider sharing the Pentagon Papers with Sheehan. Sheehan and the *Times* then could "publish" the Pentagon Papers.[13]

In February of 1971, Ellsberg offered to make the Papers available to the *Times* if, according to Rogovin's memo, the *Times* would "handle it properly."[14] On March 3, 1971, Neil "first broached the subject of publishing"[15] to Bob Phelps of the Washington Bureau. Phelps referred him to Tom Wicker and then to Scotty Reston. Sheehan gave Frankel materials given to him by IPS concerning the Tonkin Gulf incident. Frankel "told Neil later that on March 13, the night of the Gridiron Dinner, he called Jim Goodale aside and told him to read the law on classified documents because they might have a story involving a lot of classified documents."[16]

I did not realize until I read this memo that when Frankel had told me to check the law on classification, the *Times* itself did not have any copies of the Pentagon Papers given to it by Ellsberg. All it had were chapters given to IPS by Ellsberg. Sheehan then did not have the Papers—more importantly, he did not have Ellsberg's consent to use them.

Sheehan took some part of the month of March to get copies of the Papers. He got a key to an apartment from Ellsberg where Ellsberg kept the Papers. Ellsberg did not give him permission to copy them, but Neil did anyway.

He was able to copy them since, according to Rogovin's memo, he "called Bill Kovach [the *Times'* Boston reporter] and asked him to obtain a xeroxer for him (on an assumed name) and get money from New York to pay for reproduction [on March 23]."[17] It has been rumored for years that this "xeroxer" was Dun Gifford, who, as we will learn later, was subpoenaed by the Boston grand jury. "Early on the morning of March 23, Neil called Phelps and told him he was almost finished and would be returning home soon. That night he called Frankel to say, 'I got it all.'"[18]

At first the materials were kept at the Hotel Jefferson and in Neil's home. Eventually Gerald Gold, of the *Times* office, took the originals to New York in his car to make a copy. The "originals"[19] were returned to Neil. Gold made "another copy for safe keeping at 229 West 43rd Street [the *New York Times'* office]. All the xeroxing was done on Arthur Och's Sulzberger's machine on the fourteenth floor of the *Times* by the two secretaries and the news clerk from the Foreign News desk."[20]

If Punch Sulzberger knew that reporters from the newsroom had used his personal xerox machine, his anger might have overridden the subsequent request for publication. He could have very well thought that the use of his personal Xerox machine would somehow create criminal liability for him. He would have been furious.

During this period Ellsberg did not know that Sheehan had photocopied his documents. "He [Sheehan] was worried about the position he would be in, if after extensive work by Gold himself, the source [Ellsberg] still refused permission to print."[21]

During the month of May "the pressure to meet deadlines started to build. In the meantime Neil was still unable to get permission from the source...."[22] Neil finished his first piece May 26 and "on May 27 Neil's source gave him 'official permission' to possess the papers.... On June 6, Neil finished his second piece."[23]

I had wondered after the brouhaha with Lord, Day & Lord on April 29 why I had not heard much on the project during the month of May. The answer was, in some part, because Neil could not get permission from Ellsberg to publish the Papers.[24] Also, for whatever reasons, including the pressures asserted on him by Ellsberg, he was unable to get his writing done until June 6—a scant week before the publication date.

Because of all the leaks from the Boston grand jury, it was disbanded a few weeks after it started up. A new one was impanelled to take its place. Three new U.S. attorneys, David R. Nissen, Warren P. Reese, and Richard J. Barry, took over the jury. They immediately subpoenaed a variety of people they thought knew that Ellsberg had been in possession of the Pentagon Papers.

Four of those subpoenas were for those who worked or were connected with IPS: Ralph Stavins, Richard Falk, Leonard Rodberg, and Harvard Professor Samuel Popkin. Other subpoenas were issued to MIT professor Noam Chomsky, an antiwar activist, David Halberstam, a former *Times* reporter, and L. Dun Gifford, a Boston lawyer who had worked with and was reputedly close to Ted Kennedy.

The government wanted to find out how Sheehan got the Pentagon Papers from Ellsberg. They couldn't call Ellsberg and Sheehan to the grand jury because both would take the Fifth Amendment. Furthermore, Ellsberg had already been indicted in Los Angeles.

The government sought to learn by asking those named above what they knew about the Papers in advance of their publication by the *Times*. Among the antiwar community, there was knowledge that the IPS had material from the Pentagon Papers. The government also wanted to know if those antiwar activists named above and others conspired to violate the Espionage Act.

The U.S. attorneys met furious opposition from the people they had subpoenaed. The greatest resistance came from Rodberg, who had previously worked at IPS, but at the time was on the staff of Alaskan Senator Mike Gravel. Gravel had read the Pentagon Papers into the legislative record a few days after our Supreme Court argument. Gravel then intervened on behalf of Rodberg in the case before the grand jury. His claim was that legislative privilege protected both himself and Rodberg from testifying.

Judge W. Arthur Garrity, overseeing the Boston grand jury, denied Gravel's claim. The case was appealed to the Court of Appeals in Boston. That court stopped the grand jury from moving forward for thirty days, and then permitted it to go forward without Gravel or Rodberg's testimony. It then ruled that Gravel and Rodberg did not have to testify before the grand jury, but that decision was reversed by the Supreme Court the following June.[25]

Stavins, Chomsky, and Falk all claimed a First Amendment privilege not to testify. They said they would be unable to conduct their scholarly research if they testified, since their sources of their research would be disclosed. They lost, and were ordered to testify. Each of the three then alleged they had been illegally wiretapped, and Garrity did not pursue their testimony any further. Gifford claimed a First Amendment privilege not to testify because he was working for an experimental newspaper, *Morning News*. David Halberstam also claimed a First Amendment privilege as a journalist and was given a three month continuance to prepare his case.

While all this was going on, Rogovin was preparing Sheehan's defense, with my input. He was increasingly pessimistic about keeping Sheehan from being indicted. We all shared his view.

One of Rogovin's problems was that I could not tell him about what really went on in the Pentagon Papers case, because much of it was classified. This made it very difficult for him to prepare his defense. He was particularly angry that I had agreed with Mardian to return the government's secret briefs, and only Floyd Abrams and myself had access to them. He thought he should have access to the documents too. He threatened to, but ultimately did not, sue the *Times* and me for such access. By the time we reached February, 1972, we had all concluded that Sheehan would be indicted. Accordingly, we prepared the following statement to be issued by Punch:

> The indictment of Neil Sheehan for doing his job as a reporter strikes not just at one man and one newspaper but at the whole institution of the press of the United States. In deciding to seek Mr. Sheehan's indictment, the administration in effect has challenged the right of free newspapers to search out and publish essential information without harassment and intimidation.
>
> Neil Sheehan is not a criminal. He is a newspaper reporter for the *New York Times* who acted in the finest tradition of American journalism. The *Times* published the Pentagon Papers after a thorough review by the paper's responsible executives…because we felt it was our duty in the public interest to do so.
>
> During its effort in court to prevent publication of the Pentagon Papers, the Government asserted that dire consequences might result from disclosure of this material. The *Times* had carefully considered this possibility and had concluded there was no such likelihood…. What did happen was that this large and significant body of information bearing on a vital national question was made available for the first time to the American people and to historians and analysts now and in the future.

The administration's ultimately unsuccessful effort to prevent publication of the Pentagon Papers was without precedent in this country. Now the administration has gone a big step further by seeking to punish a reporter personally for his part in a major story.... The course that the administration has set for itself is dangerous. A free press is at the very heart of a free society.[26]

We waited for the other shoe to drop, but it did not. In March, Samual Popkin finally testified. He sent us a transcript of his testimony.[27] The government had asked him multiple questions about Sheehan, but Popkin provided no help. When asked about a source, he refused to answer and so he was held in contempt.

His contempt conviction was upheld by the Federal Court of Appeals in Boston. It was then appealed to the United States Supreme Court. On November 21, 1972, the Supreme Court declined to hear his case and Popkin was ordered to jail.[28] He served for seven days until November 28, 1972, when, much to the great surprise of everyone, the government announced that it was permanently disbanding the Boston grand jury.[29]

It said that the reason for this action was that the grand jury interfered with Ellsberg's trial in Los Angeles, which was about to begin. No one knows whether this is the real reason. In April 2010 I asked one of the Boston prosecutors, David Nissen, what the real reason was and he slammed down the phone. Barry, one of the other prosecutors, could not remember what had happened. The third, Warren Reese, had died.

It is probable that the reasons the Justice Department gave for disbanding the grand jury were in some part correct. Nissen and Reese were responsible for trying the Ellsberg case, too. They were getting nowhere with the Boston grand jury. It would have been very difficult for them to shuttle between Boston and San Francisco to keep the Boston grand jury alive and conduct Ellsberg's trial at the same time. Additionally, their legal theories supporting action against Sheehan were weak, and to the extent the case against the *New York Times* was still alive, that was weak, too.

On May 1, the *New York Times* was awarded the Pulitzer Prize for its publication of the Pentagon Papers.[30] Punch shared the prize with those who had worked on the publication: Sheehan, Rosenthal, Frankel, Greenfield, me, and others. While we do not know the reason the prosecutors dropped the case against Sheehan, we do know no prosecutor will walk away from an indictment he is sure he can get. It seems highly unlikely any grand jury would indict a reporter, or indeed a publisher, for publishing material that won a Pulitzer Prize. Nissen, Reese, Barry and, indeed, Mitchell and Nixon, must have known that.

*   *   *

It is well known that the trial to convict Ellsberg was a disaster. As a consequence of the Pentagon Papers, Nixon formed a group known as the "Plumbers" to plug leaks. Among a host of other illegal acts, this group broke into the offices of Ellsberg's psychiatrist.

When Judge Byrne, sitting on Ellsberg's case, learned of the break-in as well as the illegal wiretaps that went back years, he dismissed Ellsberg's case. The Plumbers subsequently broke into the Democratic National Committee headquarters at the Watergate Hotel in D.C. It was this break-in and subsequent coverup that led to the resignation of President Nixon. All these events began with the decision to print the Pentagon Papers, and to resist Nixon's efforts to stop that publication.

While the Pentagon Papers case was a terrible defeat for Nixon, his efforts to get reporters to reveal their sources turned out differently. It was a victory for him—at least, so it seemed at first. Would the press take this loss sitting down or would it fight? And after the Pentagon Papers case, would the Nixon administration take its loss sitting down or would it, and succeeding administrations, continue to fight to stop leaks?

Nixon got his revenge eight months after the Pentagon Papers case. His Justice Department won the Branzburg (Caldwell) case. The decision was close: five to four, with a concurrence from Justice Powell—a concurrence the press would later make much of in an effort to turn around its loss.

Over the preceding eight months, the Court had changed—for the worse, as far as we were concerned. Justices Black and Harlan had left. They were replaced by William H. Rehnquist and Lewis F. Powell, Jr. Rehnquist was highly conservative, and Powell was somewhat conservative.[1] Black's departure was a huge loss, since he was an absolutist on First Amendment questions. We needed him to be a fifth vote on our case.

White wrote the opinion in *Branzburg*. While he had reluctantly voted with us in the Pentagon Papers case, he did not vote for us this time. The conservatives—Blackmun, Burger, and Rehnquist—voted with him and Justice Powell wrote a concurrence to make up the fifth and deciding vote. Stewart wrote a dissent, which Marshall, Douglas, and Brennan joined. We were excited by Stewart's dissent. He adopted the three-part test that we proposed to the Court verbatim. This was very much like the Pentagon Papers case, when he had also substantially adopted the test we proposed.

Justice White, writing for the majority, said that in criminal cases reporters had to testify just like anybody else; he was not about to give them a special privilege to avoid testifying. Justice Powell's opinion was more enigmatic. He said the press had First Amendment rights to gather the news. He also said that the press could not be harassed to give up their information.

Before the argument in *Branzburg*, we had to round up other media companies to join us in the amicus brief written by Alex Bickel. Alex had come to my office on Monday, June 13 to discuss this case with the TV networks and me. He did not know that thirteen days later he would be in the Supreme Court, arguing a different case, one of the Court's greatest constitutional cases. After the Court's decision in the Pentagon Papers case, we had to return to the task of getting amici to sign on to our brief so that we would have an industrywide position.

Bickel by then had become a national figure. His brief for *Caldwell* was excellent, and it was then a much easier sell to get media companies to join on it. We ended up persuading ABC, NBC, CBS, the *Chicago Daily News*, the Associated Press, and the Associated Press Managing Editors Association to be a part of our group. *Newsweek* and the *Washington Post*, however, would not join, nor did we want them to.

We argued, as we had when Nixon sought our sources in the Pentagon Papers case, that reporters could testify if 1) there was a compelling state interest; 2) the information sought was highly material and relevant; and 3) such information could not be obtained from alternate sources. This was the three-part test Stewart later adopted for the minority four justices. The *Post* and *Newsweek* would not accept the qualified position we proposed.

The *Post* wanted an absolute First Amendment privilege. This was inconsistent with the position it took in the Pentagon Papers case. There, in its brief, the *Post* had argued for a qualified First Amendment position for prior restraints. That position, however, was muddled when it was presented in the argument to the Court, since the *Post* lawyer Bill Glendon took contradictory positions on what he thought the First Amendment required.

We had asked for oral argument for Alex Bickel in the Supreme Court in the *Caldwell* case. When he heard this request, Fritz Beebe of the *Washington Post* then asked for an oral argument for the *Washington Post*. This request did not make us happy. We wanted the press to take a common, unified position. In any event, our unhappiness with the *Washington Post* was short-lived. We were both denied the opportunity to appear before the Supreme Court. The Court would hear argument only from the lawyers representing the reporters directly involved—Caldwell, Branzburg, and Pappas—and so the *Times* was no longer directly involved in the case (fortunately, as it turned out, since Caldwell's destruction of his notes meant that we would have been unwittingly lying to the Supreme Court).[2]

When the Court announced its decision, there was deep gloom in the journalistic community. How was the press going to get out of the mess caused by this case? I was the one who had gotten the press to bring this case in the first place. It was now up to me to figure a way around it.

Regardless of the decision, the *Times* was not going to give up its sources and its notes without a fight. Our problem was in the federal courts. In the state courts, we could urge legislatures to pass shield laws. Earlier, we had persuaded New York State to adopt a law to shield our sources and our unpublished information. It was an absolute shield law which allowed for no exceptions under which we would be required to turn over information.

Lawyers try to limit decisions they don't like. The *Branzburg* case involved three reporters who were required to testify before a criminal grand jury. Earl Caldwell and Paul Pappas had been inside the Black Panthers' headquarters and were asked to testify about what they saw there. Paul Branzburg took a picture of someone making hashish. He was asked to tell a grand jury what he had seen.

Therefore, we had to concede that when reporters were called to testify about what they'd seen in a criminal case, they would have to testify. But that's all we would concede. The idea was to limit the *Branzburg* decision to those very circumstances and then figure out a way to fight like hell on all other cases.

Lawyers don't need reporters to testify in the vast majority of their cases. Reporters were easy targets. With the ubiquity of TV, radio, and newspapers, it was very easy for lawyers to find out what reporters knew about the cases they were involved in.

Rather than do the hard work of investigating the facts of their cases, they would let the press do it for them. Calling reporters to testify was a new phenomenon. Lawyers had tried cases for centuries without the help of reporters. I did not think they needed reporters now.

I had never thought that the testimony of Caldwell, Branzburg, and Pappas was that important. Indeed, after the Supreme Court handed down its decision, the United States Justice Department, the State of Kentucky, and the Commonwealth of Massachusetts completely forgot about Caldwell, Branzburg, and Pappas. The government made no effort to get them to testify. If the three reporters were so important to their respective cases, one would have thought they would have been pursued. A mountain had been made out of a molehill.

The key to the continued resistance by the press to subpoenas lay in Powell's opinion. He explicitly said that the First Amendment protected newsgathering. It followed that if reporters had a right to gather news, then they had a qualified privilege not to testify when that right was threatened.

And so, in situations other than the particular conditions of the Branzburg case, the Supreme Court had indeed decided that there was a qualified privilege for reporters not to testify. This was because if you added Powell's vote to the four dissenters, there was a majority of five for Powell's view.

What was not clear, however, was the precise nature of Powell's view. When we parsed his opinion carefully, we could see remnants of the three-part test in it.[3] Accordingly, the press could continue to argue a somewhat diluted view of that test.

In Powell's view, anyone who wanted to get reporters to testify would have to show a compelling need for such testimony, i.e., that it was 1) highly material, 2) highly relevant, and 3) not available from any other source. Accordingly, the press would fight all cases other than the ones similar to the Branzburg, Caldwell, and Pappas cases to see if a body of case law or common law could be developed to protect reporters.

I subsequently wrote a *Law Review* article that encompassed these ideas. It became a bible for fighting subpoena cases.[4] One way to quantify these fights is to look at the number of cases brought before *Branzburg*—just two or three. Since

Branzburg, there has been an astounding 1,000 cases brought and fought, based in some part on my article.[5] The press has won a majority of these cases.[6]

In legal circles, law review articles can carry great weight. The analysis in such articles can become authoritative if courts and lawyers use them as they would legal precedents. Lawyers know that for an article to be published in a law review, it has to be thoroughly vetted and effectively subjected to peer review. This article had the good fortune of becoming authoritative.

Believe it or not, the first big test case of my theory involved Vice President Spiro Agnew. It was, after all, Agnew who had started Nixon's war against the press in the 1968 campaign. The *Times* was not far off the mark. In early 1973, the Justice Department investigated allegations of corruption against Agnew. Leaks from the Justice Department accused him of "bribery, extortion, fraud and conspiracy in connection with construction industry kickbacks during his tenure as Governor of Maryland."[7] The *Washington Post* and the *New York Times* published these leaks. Agnew was furious.

He subpoenaed both the *Times* and the *Post* for the sources of these leaks. Agnew's request for information, while in the context of a criminal investigation against him, was a personal subpoena authorized by a federal court, from him to the newspapers. It was not a criminal subpoena from a grand jury.

This being so, it seemed to me that *Branzburg* did not apply. We had a new civil case in which we could argue a version of the three-part test which Stewart found so appealing. By this time, the *New York Times* had replaced Lord, Day & Lord with Floyd Abrams and Cahill Gordon, and the *Post* had replaced Royall, Koegel & Wells with Joe Califano and Williams Connolly & Califano. Joe was a former assistant for domestic affairs to President Lyndon Johnson (and later Secretary of Heath, Education, and Welfare under Jimmy Carter) and Williams was a noted criminal lawyer. Both Califano and Williams were friendly with *Washington Post* personnel, particularly with Ben Bradlee. When Califano took over, the legal rivalry between the *Post* and the *Times* ended.

I wanted to play hardball with Agnew, just as he had with the *Times*. He had threatened to sue us, he had called the press "nattering nabobs of negativism" and was a member of the Nixon administration that had brought the Pentagon Papers case. Agnew wanted our reporters' notes. The *Times* would claim, as we had in the *Caldwell* case, that we owned our reporters' notes. I suggested to the *Post* that it do the same. The *Post* and the *Times* would take possession of the notes containing the leaks and give them to Katherine Graham, publisher of the *Washington Post*, and Arthur Ochs Sulzberger, publisher of the *Times*.

Graham and Sulzberger would then put the notes in a safe and they would refuse to turn over the notes to Agnew. Agnew would succeed in having a court hold Graham and Sulzberger in contempt. Graham and Sulzberger would be threatened with jail sentences. This would be a delicious government press battle that we would win, and Agnew would back down.[8]

Joe, Floyd, and I went to Baltimore for the hearing on our motion to quash Agnew's subpoena. There were crowds of reporters and others outside the courtroom. They were there to see another stand-off between the Nixon administration and the press.

We fought our way to the courtroom ready to make our arguments. Suddenly Agnew's lawyer, Jay Topkis, addressed the court and said that Agnew had resigned as vice president and pled no contest to income tax invasion. The courtroom was in a hubbub. Reporters streamed for the phones. He was the first sitting vice president to be convicted of a crime. This was one of the biggest stories of the year.

We were as stunned as everyone else at the news Agnew had resigned. Our case was over. We would not have the opportunity to make it into a test case at the Supreme Court for the protection of reporters. Our combative strategy, however, was well reported. The *Times* said, "Mr. Sulzberger and Mrs. Graham were prepared to go to jail with the reporters involved rather than disclose the sources and give up the reporters' notes and records."[9]

It noted that *Branzburg* was a narrow decision—the classic question of whether a reporter should disclose his sources was not answered. It said further, "The Supreme Court ruled in 1972 on the narrower issue of whether Mr. Caldwell should appear before a grand jury for questioning, and whether, once he appeared, he should answer questions concerning the commission of a crime he might or might not have witnessed."[10]

Lastly, our desire to make the Agnew case one of high drama was also fully reported: "Among other things, it was hoped that the sheer drama of the publishers of two of the most influential newsgathering organizations possibly going to jail would have some subtle effect on the Supreme Court's deliberations, and at the same time perhaps force Congress and the public to consider more seriously any attacks on the First Amendment."[11]

While we had failed to bring this test case to fruition, the question remained as to how the press would fight future cases. Could the press go into contempt and not obey unconstitutional orders as a strategy to take on the government and others to win First Amendment cases? And more to the point, could I get representatives of the press on the same page to fight First Amendment cases, including by going into contempt?

If Kay Graham and Punch Sulzberger were willing to risk jail sentences to protect freedom of the press, would other publishers and editors do the same? I set out to organize the press as a group to fight for press freedom, including going to jail, if necessary.

A principal objective was to persuade lawyers for the press and their clients to use the power of contempt to stop the government from enjoining the press and forcing disclosure of its sources. If the government issued illegal orders not to print or to disclose sources, we would disobey.

In the Pentagon Papers case, courts issued prior restraints against a newspaper for the first time in the history of the nation. I did not want other courts to follow that example, even if those restraints were overturned on appeal (as in the Pentagon Papers case). Otherwise the legacy of the Pentagon Papers case would be that the nation would have ended up with a system of censorship, albeit temporary. Courts could grant a temporary restraining order, then after a few days of thinking it over, or after an appeal, the temporary restraint would be lifted. In the meantime, a publisher or a broadcaster had been censored. As Justice Black said in the Pentagon Papers case, "[E]very moment's continuance of the injunctions against these newspapers amounts to a flagrant, indefensible, and continuing violation of the First Amendment."[1]

My other concern was that after the *Caldwell* case, the press would give up fighting subpoenas. I had to communicate to press lawyers in person how they could avoid the ruling in the *Caldwell* case and advise their clients to go into contempt if necessary.

I wanted press lawyers throughout the country to take the principles set forth in my *Law Review* article on reporter's privilege and persuade every state court and every federal court (and every state legislature) in the country that I was right. This way, the press would end up with a "reporter's privilege" in every court in the country, despite the Supreme Court ruling. And perhaps someday we could persuade Congress to adopt a federal shield law.

To achieve this end, I would have to convert press lawyers, who typically represented business interests of their clients, to become First Amendment lawyers. The press could not afford to have high-priced law firms that traditionally represented media clients without First Amendment expertise. Nor could the press rely on the ACLU, whose interests, as pointed out earlier, were not the same as the interests of the press.[2] In short, I would have to create a First Amendment Bar; that is, a group of lawyers devoted to the same area of the law.

In November 1973, a few months after the Agnew case, I gathered a group of lawyers for the press, editors, and others, for this purpose. Alex Bickel, Floyd Abrams, Tony Amsterdam spoke, as did Norman Dorsen of New York University Law School, Fred Friendly of the Ford Foundation, and others. I convened this group regularly for forty years under the umbrella of the Practising Law Institute. It succeeded beyond my wildest expectations. It turned out that because of the notoriety of the Pentagon Papers case, lawyers for large media corporations liked being called "First Amendment lawyers," the phrase now regularly used to describe them in the press.

As noted, I believed prior restraints should be disobeyed except in an extraordinary national security case. I told the assembled lawyers that we should disobey these orders until we got a ruling out of the Supreme Court that approved such disobedience.

I explained the risks inherent in the Pentagon Papers case to the lawyers and others at our first gathering. The choice we had faced was to appeal temporary injunctions, or disobey them. I urged lawyers to advise their clients to disobey them, risk a fine, and make it clear that under the First Amendment the imposition of such a fine was unconstitutional. In a sense, this was easier said than done. Whether, in fact, such a fine was unconstitutional was a matter of "first impression." That is to say, it was very much like the Pentagon Papers and *Caldwell* cases. The Supreme Court had never decided such a case involving the press.

I told the lawyers at the seminar what I had done a few months after the Pentagon Papers case, when I had received a frantic call from the city desk saying that a State Court Judge, George Postel, was attempting to enjoin the *Times*. Since the Pentagon Papers case was fresh in our minds, we were not inclined to be enjoined again.

Postel had ordered Lacey Fosburgh, a *New York Times* reporter, not to refer to Carmine Persico, the purported Mafia leader, as "The Snake." He also ordered her not to publish his past criminal record. Persico was on trial for thirty-seven counts of extortion, coercion, criminal usury, and conspiracy, and Fosburgh was covering the trial.

Persico was a notorious figure in the '60s and '70s. He survived an attempt to blow up his car and was shot at various times in the face, hand and shoulder. Fosburgh had published a story reporting many of these details.

Persico's lawyer, Maurice Edelbaum, asked for a mistrial because of the story. He said that the jury would not give Persico a fair trial. Postel said he hadn't read the *Times'* story, "but it's up in my chambers. It was too long to read." Edelbaum saved the judge a trip to his chambers. He read the *New York Times* article aloud to him.

After hearing it, Postel said, "[If] they report anything other than what transpires in the courtroom I shall hold the individual reporter in contempt." The reporters sought clarification in his chambers during recess. "Don't I speak English?" he said. Asked what legal authority he had for his order, he snapped, "Postel's Law." He then said the reporters would be thrown "in the can" if they violated his order.[3]

I told the City Desk to disobey the order. It was unlike the order in the Pentagon Papers case. There, the secret for making the hydrogen bomb could have been concealed in its 7,000 pages, a threat absent in this case. The *Times* went ahead and published, reporting that Persico was known as "The Snake." The next day, Postel was furious, but he did not throw Lacey Fosburgh "in the can" as he said he would. Instead, he barred the press (and the public) from his courtroom.[4]

The *Times* appealed his action to New York's highest court, the Court of Appeals.[5] That court decided Postel could not, under the First Amendment, threaten reporters with contempt as he had, nor could he close down the courtroom to the press and the public.[6] My strategy had worked. The judge backed down.

Persico had a storied career following this case, in which he was acquitted. The next time around, he presented his own defense for murder, was found guilty, and sentenced to one hundred years in prison. He is presently in federal prison in Butner, North Carolina, where reportedly he has struck up a friendship with Bernie Madoff.[7]

I had hoped that Postel *would* hold the *New York Times* in contempt, but he did not. I wanted to establish that prior restraints in cases not of the magnitude of that of the Pentagon Papers could be disobeyed. As lawyers at my seminar began to cause media companies to disobey these orders, I had occasion to make my strategy more nuanced. The reason for this was the ubiquitous Justice Potter Stewart.

I had met Stewart again at a seminar I had instigated and was organized under the creative genius of former CBS News president, Fred Friendly.[8] We gathered at the Homestead resort in Hot Springs, Virginia, in 1975. That seminar was called "The Media and the Law." (Those seminars continue to air on PBS TV as the Fred Friendly Seminars.) It presented freedom of the press hypotheticals, written by me and by others, for discussion. Among the attendees were Kay Graham, Robert Bork (Solicitor General), William Colby (Director of the CIA), Jim Lehrer (Sr. Correspondent, PBS), and Justice Potter Stewart.

One of the hypotheticals raised the question of whether an order such as the one directed to Lacey Fosburgh should be entered at all. The participants generally thought that it should be. I however, objected. In the conversation I had with Potter Stewart on the issue, I said, "Not only was such an order unconstitutional, it should be disobeyed."

Stewart's view was that in the federal courts, one cannot disobey a temporary injunction restraining First Amendment rights without first trying to appeal that order. If the appeal efforts were unsuccessful before reaching a publishing deadline, it was okay to publish. The idea was for a newspaper to make its best efforts to conform with the rule of law by appealing but, failing that, disobedience was permitted under the First Amendment.[9]

As a consequence of my conversation, I decided that the next time the *Times* had a chance to disobey an order not to print, it would adopt Stewart's approach. This opportunity came the following year when a *New York Times* reporter, Dena Kleiman, was covering a murder trial in Queens.

The presiding judge, John H. Starkey, ordered her not to print a prior conviction of the defendant for kidnapping.[10] This time, before disobeying the order, I adopted Stewart's more sophisticated strategy of disobedience. Applying Stewart's view to Dena Kleiman's case meant the *Times* had to exhaust every avenue of appeal before it published. We had to act quickly. Judge Starkey's order to Kleiman was issued in the late morning. We had to exhaust our appeals before deadline later that evening.

At 2:00 p.m. we asked Judge Starkey to rescind his order. He said, "no." We immediately telephoned the next highest court, the Appellate Division, to reverse him. That court refused to hear our appeal. We then asked Jacob Fuchsberg, the Chief Judge of New York State's highest court, the Court of Appeals, to let the *Times* print.

We reached Fuchsberg at about 4:00 p.m. He had been at a Fred Friendly Seminar the year before when the same hypothetical had been discussed. Therefore, he knew we were trying to exhaust our appeals so that we could publish. He told us it was too late in the day to call each member of his court to hear our appeal. He said we'd done our best to appeal.

He did not criticize these unorthodox steps I had employed to bypass Starkey's order. I had made up a procedure (as suggested by Stewart) to reconcile the First Amendment with the rule of law. I had bypassed all the usual steps of appeals which take months to achieve—such as briefs, appellate arguments, etc.

After talking to Fuchsberg, we published in defiance of the court. Again, it was my hope that Starkey would hold us in contempt. We would then be able to take our case to the U.S. Supreme Court. My further hope was the Supreme Court would make it clear it was appropriate to disobey a court order under these circumstances. Judge Starkey ignored us. For the record, we made a formal appeal with briefs and all the paperwork to the next court, the Appellate Division. That court dismissed Starkey's order as inappropriate. It did not approve our contumacious behavior, as we hoped it would.

However, one of the judges, J. Irwin Shapiro, noted that our disobedience "[s]hould never be a matter for court decision...[the] narrowly defined exception to the ban to the First Amendment on any prior restraint order is not really an exception. For every government has the inherent right to take measures against its own self-destruction."[11] In other words, Starkey had no business enjoining us, even temporarily. We did not have to obey his order. It would have been better if the Supreme Court said that. But it didn't have the opportunity.

Following the Kleiman case, I wrote a law review article published by Stanford Law School setting out a protocol to disobey a prior restraint, as suggested by Stewart. I explained it to my annual gathering of press lawyers, urging them to follow it. Many did, including the *Providence Journal*. A decision by the First Circuit Court of Appeals based on my article said as I urged: orders not to print could be disobeyed in the federal courts of Massachusetts, New Hampshire, Maine, and Rhode Island—"the Federal First Circuit."[12]

In virtually every case in which lawyers advised their clients to disobey orders not to print, they won.[13] In other cases, lawyers chose to appeal rather than fight, and they won every case to have the orders overturned, except one where the appeal was incomplete.[14]

They even won on appeal for a case in which I conceded that the First Amendment did not apply. In 1979, the government tried to stop *The Progressive* magazine from publishing information about making a hydrogen bomb. *The Progressive* published extensive diagrams and other information as to how the bomb could be constructed. A federal court in Wisconsin enjoined publication.[15]

During the appeal, it became clear the information was culled entirely from public sources. Many of the diagrams in *The Progressive* article came from the widely available *Encyclopedia Americana* and a detailed report on making hydrogen bombs was found sitting on an open shelf at the Los Alamos public library. In addition, a nuclear "hobbyist" had published the same information in his own magazine. As a consequence of these disclosures, the government dropped the case.[16]

While I urged the group to continue the fight against prior restraints, my colleague Floyd Abrams told the group that disobeying court orders was very dangerous, and he urged them to appeal instead of going into contempt, which most of them did. He was right that it was dangerous. And from his point of view, representing many First Amendment defendants, he rightfully did not want to be seen as an unreasonable firebrand when he came into court to defend those companies.

This branch of the fight against censorship is not over. In the federal courts, prior restraints in the states within the First Circuit can be disobeyed and, in New York State, temporary prior restraints are generally disobeyed rather than appealed.[17] But this battle against censorship will not be won until the Supreme Court takes a case and vindicates this disobedience.

Apart from urging the disobedience of orders not to print, another purpose of my annual gathering of lawyers was to persuade press lawyers to accept my view of the reporter's privilege (namely, a three-part test of materiality, relevance, and availability from other sources). They could then use the test to fight subpoena cases state by state and federal district by federal district. The hidden power of contempt was to be used to persuade each state and each federal district to adopt a qualified reporter's privilege.

When I started this group, reporter's privilege cases involving a refusal to reveal sources and other unpublished information were being decided at the rate of about ten a year. This number doubled as time went on. By 1978, there had been sixty-two decided cases. The press won most of them. Many were based on the three-part test I suggested. During this period of time, reporters went into contempt forty times and to jail more than a dozen times.[18]

In 1978, I had a chance to put my money where my mouth was and demonstrate that disobedience in a reporter's privilege case was appropriate. In New Jersey, *Times* reporter Myron Farber defied a court order and went to jail. The *Times* also defied a court order and was fined hundreds of thousands of dollars. Farber had written a story about Dr. Mario Jascalevich, a doctor at a local New Jersey hospital. He said that Jascalevich had intentionally killed five patients with curare, a muscle relaxant. Farber based most of his story on a transcript of an interview with Jascalevich, which he had obtained from an undisclosed source.

The district attorney who had investigated the deaths and made this transcript had given it to his office, which then lost it. After Farber published his story, the State of New Jersey indicted Jascalevich. His lawyer, Raymond A. Brown, wanted to know from whom Farber got the transcript. Farber would not tell him.

By the time this case started, I had been promoted to executive vice president of the *Times* (then subsequently its vice chairman) and had the corner office on the executive floor; Punch Sulzberger had the other corner office. This case was Punch's finest hour. He read the New Jersey shield law word for word and said, quite properly, the law gave Farber total protection.

Punch became well-versed in what the New Jersey Courts were doing to his reporter. He followed every step. He went to the argument at New Jersey's highest court. Not many chief executives would have taken the time to do what Punch did. This compared favorably with his ambivalence in the Pentagon Papers case, when he did not go to any of the arguments.

The strange part about this case is that while the newly formed band of media lawyers was going from state to state to obtain a qualified reporter's privilege, New Jersey already had an absolute privilege passed by the New Jersey legislature. When we explained to Judge William J. Arnold of the New Jersey Superior Court that the shield law absolutely protected Farber, he said he wanted to see Farber's notes (and relevant material in *New York Times* files) before he decided whether the shield law protected them. This made no sense to us at all. The New Jersey shield law did not say that. Farber and the *Times* were protected under all circumstances.

We said we were at least entitled under the First Amendment to a hearing to decide whether Arnold was correct or not. At such a hearing, Jascalevich would have to show that my three-part test of materiality, relevance, and unavailability from other sources had been met. If so, the *Times* would then turn over its material and the notes, which included the name of his source, to Arnold. If Jascalevich really needed to know who Farber's source was, he had to jump these hurdles.

But the court didn't do any of that and instead held Farber and the *New York Times* in contempt. It started assessing a fine of $100,000 plus $5,000 a day against the *Times,* and it jailed Farber.[19] We asked different justices of the United States Supreme Court three times to stop Farber from going to jail, pending a full appeal to that court. We were turned down each time.

The last denial was issued by Potter Stewart, and received by Judge Arnold's clerk. This clerk whispered to Arnold that Stewart had refused to act on the *Times'* request. Arnold—who clearly was not familiar with the world beyond his courthouse—in a loud voice, audible to everyone in the court, said, "Who is this Stewart Potter, anyway?"[20]

Ultimately the case ended up in the New Jersey State Supreme Court. It decided that the three-part test applied. It said, however, it would apply the three-part test *the next* time around. That court, unbelievably, concluded that Judge Arnold already knew enough of the facts to decide the three-part test had been met. Farber had to spend more time in jail, forty days in all. Jascalevich was acquitted.

This case ended as do many reporter's privilege cases. The reporter ended up in jail but no one else did. Jascalevich did not need Farber's source to prove his innocence. He was found innocent without it. This was very much like the notorious Judy Miller case in 2005, in which she went to jail for refusing to disclose her sources in a case involving Valerie Plame, a CIA employee. She was the only one in the case to go to jail.

In the long run, the *Times* won the Farber case. The State of New Jersey returned the fines. The State Legislature amended the shield law. It retained absolute protection for reporters, with one exception: in criminal trials the defendant was given the right to obtain sources of a reporter, but only after a hearing that showed the three-part test had been met, which was exactly the position we took in the case. This case proved if you fought privilege cases to the end, paid fines and served jail time, in the long term you would win and clarify the law as to protections under the First Amendment.

For thirty years, until 2000, the press was on a winning streak. Through the efforts of the First Amendment Bar, which I created, the reporter's privilege was recognized in all but two states: Wyoming and Hawaii. Forty states have passed a shield law, up from six at the start of the *Caldwell* case.[21]

It was also recognized in some form in all eleven federal districts plus the District of Columbia.[22] In that period, there had been over 800 cases contesting the reporter's privilege. In order to defend their rights under the First Amendment, reporters had gone into contempt over sixty times.[23] Foreign countries had also begun to recognize the privilege.[24]

The Espionage Act appeared to be a dead letter. It had been used for the first time against Daniel Ellsberg, unsuccessfully, and then only once more in thirty years against other leakers. No one had thought at that time it could be used against the press as the recipient of leaks. Nixon's attempt to convene a grand jury to indict the *Times* and Neil Sheehan had failed. No one was about to attempt to do it again.

The organization of the First Amendment Bar had been a great success. The attendance of the seminar grew until it averaged over 300 participants every year. The lawyers and the press who attended the seminar, which I ran annually, exceeded 9,000 (without discounting the same lawyers who attend it annually) in that period of time. The short volume of essays we prepared for panelists the first year grew from 500 to more than 3,000 pages per year. Through 2000, we published more than 80,000 pages, or twenty-four million words, on how to fight for press freedom.

When George W. Bush came into office in 2000, there was a noticeable chill. The press had to fight all over again for rights it thought it had won.

CHAPTER XXXII

BUSH'S WAR AGAINST THE PRESS

Following 9/11, the press had come full circle. After that event, President George W. Bush began his war against the press. It was very much like Nixon's, but there were some differences.

Bush was a conservative Republican, as was Nixon, but he was not out to destroy the Eastern establishment and the liberal press, as Nixon had been. He wanted to intimidate it in order to permit him to be free to carry out any actions as he saw fit in this war against terrorism.

From the point of view of the press, it made no difference what the motivation of Nixon or Bush was. It was under attack, in each instance. It did not follow that because the country was involved in war that its leadership could trample on the First Amendment rights of the press. When the press reported leaks on his illegal actions in setting up secret prison camps to torture detainees, and on his establishment of a secret wiretapping system, Bush was furious. His attorney general Alberto Gonzales went on national TV to threaten to prosecute the press.

During wars such as the war against terrorism and in Afghanistan and Iraq, First Amendment standards such as clear and present danger do not change. In such times, it is as important to fight for the First Amendment as it is in peacetime. Under Bush, the First Amendment suffered a significant setback in a case about AIPAC (American Israeli Public Affairs Committee). That case permits criminal actions against those who receive national security leaks such as the *New York Times* did in the Pentagon Papers case for the first time. The AIPAC case is a Bush legacy, and a bad one.

While Bush was not out to destroy the liberal press the way Nixon was, he clearly did not like it. He made it clear that he disdained the press by saying he didn't watch TV, listen to the radio, or read newspapers.

At a White House barbecue for the press in April 2004 he was asked how he could know "what the public is thinking" if he did not read newspapers, listen to the radio or watch TV. Bush replied, "You're making a powerful assumption, young man. You're assuming you represent the public. I don't accept that."[1]

While Bush did not have an Agnew to insult the press, it was no secret that the liberal press, including the *New York Times*, was as much the Bush administration's enemy as it had been Nixon's. The "Bushies" took delight in telling the world that the televisions in the White House had been switched to the conservative Fox News.[2] The Republican Party's associates on the far right, William Bennett and Bill Kristol, kept up a drumbeat of attacks on the *New York Times*.[3] Bush's attacks were aided by a conservative judiciary appointed by Reagan and the two Bushes.

One of these judges, Richard Posner of the Seventh Circuit, concluded in 2003 that *Branzburg* had not adopted a qualified privilege for the federal courts. He said flatly that there was no privilege at all, despite the fact there had been over 800 cases in the thirty years before that held the contrary.[4]

Posner was a polymath, a highly conservative part-time member of the faculty of the University of Chicago Law School and well respected in conservative legal circles. But his analysis of *Branzburg* was shallow. He said the Supreme Court in that case had decided that sources were not protected.

This was wrong because neither Branzburg, Pappas, or Caldwell had asked the Supreme Court to protect their sources. All they requested was not to appear before a grand jury. Posner also gave short shrift to Powell's concurring opinion. Counting Powell's opinion as a vote for the press, it won (in part) 5–4. Counting it Posner's way, it lost everything, 5–4.

A Hofstra law professor and expert in the reporter's privilege, Eric M. Freedman, had discovered extraordinary new evidence regarding Powell's opinion. Scouring through Powell's papers he found a note saying that his concurring opinion in *Branzburg* was meant to create "a privilege analogous to an evidentiary one" for sources.[5]

Powell further said that such protection should be decided on a case-by-case basis, which was precisely how I had interpreted it. While this note is not conclusive, since it is not part of his opinion, it is persuasive.[6] It supports my view that Powell intended to effectively create a reporter's privilege with his concurring opinion.

Posner's opinion did not stunt the continued recognition of the reporter's privilege. It did, however, have an effect on conservative judges of the federal courts in Washington, D.C., particularly in two cases, one involving Wen Ho Lee, a former nuclear engineer, the other, Judy Miller.

On December 21, 1999, Lee sued the federal government for invasion of privacy after it indicted him on fifty-nine counts of illegally removing highly classified material from a Los Alamos weapons laboratory. Along with others, the *Times* had published a leak which described what the government alleged Lee had done before it had become public. He subpoenaed five journalists in 2003, including two from the *New York Times*, for the confidential source of the leak.

The court, perhaps influenced by Posner, questioned the validity of the reporter's privilege in the District of Columbia—a privilege recognized there for decades. Ultimately, the case was settled by the government for $1.7 million, of which five news organizations paid $750,000. This settlement protected reporters from disclosing their sources.

All of this set the background for the notorious Judy Miller case. Judith Miller was a national security reporter. Her beat depended on leaks, and particularly leaks of classified information. National security reporters are extremely important for the formation of public policy. As Max Frankel pointed out in his affidavit in the Pentagon Papers case, such reporters provide the public with information they would not otherwise have because it is classified.

Patrick Fitzgerald, a federal prosecutor in George W. Bush's Justice Department, brought two cases against Miller. The one involving "Scooter" Libby was well known, the other was not. He won both. In the first, as a member of Bush's Justice Department, he wanted Miller's sources of a raid he was going to make on an Islamic charity. In the second, acting as an independent prosecutor appointed by Bush's Justice Department, he sought the source in the Libby case.

Lewis "Scooter" Libby, chief of staff to Vice President Richard Cheney, had targeted Miller for such a leak. He wanted to show her parts of the 2002 National Intelligence Estimate (NIE) that were classified. This estimate was given to Congress and had been used to support the authorization of the war against Iraq. He wanted to show her parts of it to support the Bush administration's position on weapons of mass destruction, which was then heavily criticized. He asked President Bush to declassify the estimate so that he could show it to Miller. She, however, did not know it was declassified. She thought it was classified. In other words, she thought the main purpose of the meeting was to leak to her classified information—not any other purpose.

In passing, Libby also told Miller that Valerie Plame, the wife of former ambassador Joe Wilson, was a CIA agent. On July 6, 2003, Wilson had written an op-ed in the *New York Times* entitled "What I Didn't Find in Africa" in which he described his top secret mission to Niger at the behest of the government to find out whether Iraq had purchased uranium from the African nation. Wilson claimed Bush's statement in his 2002 State of the Union Address that "Saddam Hussein recently sought significant quantities of uranium from Africa" was a lie. Libby, who rejected this claim, was looking for payback.

Libby had directly sought out Matthew Cooper of *Time* and Tim Russert of NBC News for the sole purpose of leaking Plame's name to the press. It was illegal to disclose the name of a CIA agent, and Fitzgerald indicted Libby for lying about those to whom he had leaked Plame's name.

Although Miller never even wrote an article on what Libby told her, she declined to name Libby as her source when Fitzgerald indicted him. She went to jail for eighty-five days before Libby permitted her to disclose his name. All of us who knew Judy supported her decision to go to jail and be in contempt. As a matter of principle, I told her that reporters should go into contempt if the information was not needed, as in this case. Further, I told her the hubbub would result in an increase in shield laws, which it did, and hopefully a federal shield law would come out of it.

Clearly, her testimony was not necessary for the prosecution of Lewis Libby. When the indictment was issued her name had scarcely been mentioned. When the trial was conducted she was called for a small supporting role. She was asked to confirm testimony already given. Seven government witnesses and two journalists testified that Libby had lied.[7] If Fitzgerald had not called Judy Miller, it would have made no difference whatsoever to his case.[8] On principle, however, Miller refused to name her source.

Miller was treated like a common criminal when she was sent to jail. She had a small dark cell with a slit to see outside. There was an open toilet, which she shared with other cell mates, who were usually immigration suspects. She was allowed to watch television three hours a week in a communal room, and slept on two thin mats on a concrete slab. When visitors came to see her, they had to go into a room which separated Miller from the visitor by glass. By the end of her stay, she had lost so much weight her clothes no longer fit. Her treatment was far more harsh than that afforded Myron Farber when he went to jail for refusing to disclose his source in the 1978 Jascalevich case. Farber had been housed with a television in a comfortable conference room.

Miller's courageous behavior to stand in contempt and go to jail contrasted with Norman Pearlstine's behavior with respect to Matthew Cooper, one of the other journalists approached by Libby to leak Plame's name. Pearlstine, who was editor-in-chief at *Time* magazine, was Cooper's boss and controlled some of Cooper's emails. The emails recounted conversations he had with Libby. Time Warner therefore owned the emails, as indeed the *New York Times* had owned Earl Caldwell's notes or the reporter's notes given to Punch Sulzberger during the Agnew case.

Rather than cause Time Warner to go into contempt, however, as I had caused the *Times* to go into contempt in the Farber case and as Sulzberger threatened to do in the Agnew case, Pearlstine turned the emails over to Fitzgerald despite his reporters' objections. Pearlstine then justified his behavior by concluding that *Branzburg* did not adopt a qualified privilege, following the reasoning of Judge Posner. Pearlstine also slammed my decision not to turn over material to the court in the 1978 Farber case. Pearlstine told the *New York Times*, when trying to justify his own decision, "If I were the *New York Times* in 1978 I would have turned over the information."[9]

After twenty-seven years, this was quite a turnabout. It reflected the tenor of the times, when the press was not only under pressure from the Bush administration because of 9/11, but also under economic pressure. It was exacerbated by the climate of fear that ensued after 9/11, in which courts tended to view assertion of individual rights more harshly than before. Further, the Internet was making inroads on the printed press such as *Time* magazine, which employed Matt Cooper. Media companies seemingly had less money to support press freedom litigation.[10]

A few days after Miller went to jail, on August 4, 2005, Bush's Justice Department, under Attorney General Alberto Gonzales, indicted two members of a lobbying firm, AIPAC, for receiving leaks under the Espionage Act. A shudder went through the press. No one had ever been indicted before for *receiving* leaks.

The two AIPAC employees indicted, Keith Weissman and Steve Rosen, were paid lobbyists for Israel. A Defense Department employee, Lawrence A. Franklin, had leaked classified information to them about U.S. deliberations on its Iran policy.[11] Rosen and Weissman had passed this information on to Israel.

It didn't take much imagination to realize that if the courts would permit an indictment of a lobbyist receiving classified information, that they would permit an indictment of a newspaper to whom classified information had been leaked. This was an unprecedented interpretation of the Espionage Act.[12] Nixon was unable to persuade a Boston grand jury to indict the *Times* under the Espionage Act, but Bush was able to indict Weissman and Rosen.

When Nixon attempted to indict the *New York Times* in Boston following the Supreme Court's decision in the Pentagon Papers, it would have rounded out his ambition to destroy eastern liberal papers. Bush, on the other hand, was not necessarily trying to destroy the *Times* by threatening it with prosecution, but rather trying to enhance the national security of the United States. Regardless of the difference in motivation, however, a successful criminal prosecution under the Espionage Act would be highly offensive to the First Amendment and effectively create an Official Secrets Act.

In the UK, under its Official Secrets Act, a newspaper can be enjoined before publication and criminally prosecuted after publication. Nixon lost his bid to permit an injunction against the press and so that part of the Official Secrets Act cannot under the First Amendment be enacted in this country. In the UK, of course, there is no First Amendment.

Bush, on the other hand, convinced a lower federal court in Virginia that there could be a basis for criminal prosecution of an entity (such as a newspaper) which had received a leak. And so Bush succeeded in a way that Nixon was never able to in effecting an Official Secrets Act at least in so far as it applies to criminal action *after* publication.

It was clear to most press observers that if Bush could win the AIPAC case, the next such case would be against newspapers, particularly the *New York Times*. A few months thereafter, the Bush administration had its chance. The *Times* published a story saying the Bush administration was illegally intercepting phone and email messages.[13] After 9/11, the Bush administration had caused a facility to be built with telephone company systems that would intercept all emails and phone calls. This was against the law.[14] Congress had specifically provided that interception of communications could be achieved only with a warrant. It had set up a special court particularly for the interception of phone calls in Washington, D.C., where such warrants were rapidly processed.

With the onset of the digital age, the Bush administration thought the old system was unwieldy as applied to emails. They could be put into a database and then searched by a computer. This was a new technology to which the old phone-only setup was not fully applicable.

Accordingly, the Bush administration decided to entirely ignore the law that applied to the interception of emails. It did not seek approval from the special court before intercepting emails and phone calls. These interceptions became known as "warrantless wiretaps," since they were achieved without a search warrant authorized by the special court. This information was leaked to *New York Times* reporters James Risen and Eric Lichtblau.

In a departure from the practice used at the time of the Pentagon Papers, the *Times* discussed its leaked information with the government before publication. Because of the Pentagon Papers case, the *Times* and the government knew the government could not get a prior restraint order against the *Times*. This permitted the *Times* and the government to have conversations about whether the information damaged national security or not.

The story was ready to be published just before the 2004 elections. For a year, the Bush administration talked the *Times* out of publishing it. In December 2005, George Bush even had an Oval Office meeting with Arthur Ochs Sulzberger, Jr., the editors, and writers, to permanently scuttle the story.

He told them if the *Times* published and there was another terrorist attack the paper would "have blood on…[its] hands."[15] The *Times* finally published anyway, but only after one of its reporters, James Risen, was about to publish the same information in a book. With the new-found love felt by the Bush Administration for the Espionage Act, and particularly 793(e), the *Times* risked criminal action, just as it had in the Pentagon Papers case. Probably more to the point, there was a risk of prosecution under 798, the code section. This section, it may be recalled, was batted around during the Pentagon Papers case.

The government tried its best in the Pentagon Papers case to persuade the courts to enjoin the *Times,* asserting that there were codes in the Pentagon Papers. Section 798 is a very broad statute. It is hard for me to believe that this statute is constitutional. So much of what it covers is published daily in the *Times,* and certainly on the Internet.

The government told the *Times* it should not publish the fact that communications including emails were being intercepted. It would tip off the terrorists that we were intercepting their emails. I found this an unpersuasive argument. It would have to be a pretty dumb terrorist to think that the government could not access emails.

In fact, the terrorists were as sophisticated about technology as we were, if not more so. Khalid Sheikh Mohammed, a trained engineer and the leader of the 9/11 plot, used encoded emails as far back as 1995. We know this because the emails of his nephew Ramzi Yusef to K.S. Mohammad were discovered in Yusef's computer when he was tried for the first bombing of the World Trade Center in 1995. Evidence of encoded emails was introduced in Yusef's trial.

We also know that Khalid Mohammed told fellow 9/11 conspirators not to use encoded email with the plotters of 9/11, because they would be easily discovered. If such discovery were made, it would lead the United States to the destination of the emails, even though it couldn't read them. K. S. Mohammad obviously told other members of Al Qaeda all this because he thought there was a possibility his emails were being read. Accordingly, to argue that a *New York Times* story would tell the terrorists that their emails were being read does not seem believable.[16]

The government did not bring a criminal action under the Espionage Act against the *New York Times*. It was bluffing. There were similar threats against the *Washington Post* for publishing stories about where the CIA kept its secret prison camps abroad. That also was a bluff.

The Bush administration, however, was not bluffing when, near the end of Bush's term, it said it would hold *San Francisco Chronicle* reporters Mark Fainaru-Wada and Lance Williams in contempt. Neither had disclosed their source in leaked grand jury testimony by Barry Bonds of the Giants, Jason Giambi of the New York Yankees, and others during an investigation into the use of steroids by professional baseball players. Almost everyone agrees the *Chronicle* did a public service in publishing this information.

It led to congressional hearings and the adoption of drug testing standards by Major League Baseball. Despite the benefits of such publication, Attorney General Gonzales personally sought the imprisonment of the two *Chronicle* reporters. Almost literally as they were being taken off to jail, the source of the leak came forward and identified himself, and the court dismissed the case against the reporters.[17]

Bush's war, however, had exposed a chink in the armor of the press. It needed a federal shield law to protect reporters such as Judith Miller from jail sentences in leak cases. It also needed to codify and improve the three-part test to the extent it existed in other federal districts before conservative judges such as Judge Posner took it away from those districts.

The press breathed a collective sigh of relief with the end of the Bush presidency. It looked forward expectantly to the election of Barack Obama. But has Obama proven to be any better?

CHAPTER XXXIII

IS OBAMA ANY BETTER?

President Barack Obama has seamlessly carried forward the main ingredients of Bush's war against the press. As a candidate, he supported the federal reporter's shield law and criticized Bush's use of state secrecy to cover up administration failures. When he became president, he unexpectedly took a hard line on national security cases. He watered down a proposed federal shield law for national security reasons and began an unprecedented campaign against leaks of classified information to the press.

Obama was barely into his first thirty days of office when he tipped his hand on national security cases. His Justice Department lawyers stunned a Ninth Circuit hearing on a state secrets case.[1] They said the Obama administration would continue to follow the Bush policy of refusing to disclose the Bush "extraordinary rendition" program to the courts or anyone else. It was a state secret.

This rendition program, or as it's known to its critics, "torture by proxy," was set up by Bush's Central Intelligence Agency after September 11, 2001. CIA operatives abducted terrorist suspects from all over the world and flew them to prisons ("black sites") outside of U.S. jurisdiction. "The most common destinations for rendered suspects," Jane Mayer of *The New Yorker* reported, "are Egypt, Morocco, Syria and Jordan."[2] All of these countries have been cited for human rights violations by the State Department.

Five of the detainees, some of whom were later released without any charges, sued the airline companies who helped the CIA with their abductions.[3] They alleged that the airlines were complicit in helping the CIA wrongfully imprison and torture them, despite the lack of evidence against them. The Bush Justice Department intervened and asked the courts to dismiss the lawsuit entirely. This was because the subject of the case involved "state secrets." The actions of the government were classified and were not subject to lawsuits in federal courts.

Dana Priest of the *Washington Post*, Jane Mayer of *The New Yorker*, and many others have written in detail about these programs. They were not secret—everyone knew about them. Many foreign governments published official reports corroborating the plaintiffs' claims, and even Bush himself acknowledged the program's existence. It was therefore ridiculous in the eyes of many observers to claim they were secret. Bush did not want the programs exposed further. Such disclosure would be embarrassing to the United States.

During his first campaign for president, Obama criticized Bush's excessive use of the state secrets doctrine.[4] When, on February 10, 2009, Obama lawyers appeared in the Ninth Circuit Court of Appeals in California, the expectation was that Obama would follow his campaign rhetoric and reverse course on the case.

Not so. A Justice Department lawyer continued to take the same position Bush had. Judge Mary M. Schroder could not believe her ears. She asked if anything "material" had happened that might have caused the Justice Department to shift its views. "No, your honor," replied the Justice Department lawyer. She then asked, more pointedly: "The change in the administration has no bearing?" Again, the answer was no.[5]

Later, Obama was asked during the press conference on his hundredth day in office why he had not kept his campaign pledge on state secrets. He said that the case in California had come up so early in his administration, it didn't have time to prepare a new position. He thought the state's privilege was too broad.[6] The Obama administration went forward with this case, along with others, as Bush had, anyway.

He lost 3–0. It was a great victory against excessive government secrecy but it would not last. At a subsequent hearing of a full eleven judge panel in the Ninth Circuit, the court reversed the decision, and Obama won 6–5.[7] The Supreme Court refused to hear the case.

Obama's hardline attitude on national security did not bode well for the future of a federal shield law. Many national security stories are based on classified leaks; for example, the Pentagon Papers, and indeed, the rendition stories. As Max Frankel pointed out, leaks of classified information are important for making public policy. If reporters could not protect their sources, leaks would diminish, and we would all be the worse off for it.

I had promoted a three-part test to protect reporters: materiality, relevance, and "unavailability from other sources." A weakness in this test was that in a leak case a reporter was the only source of information for the identity of the leaker. If the reporter was the only one who knew who the leaker was, it wouldn't do any good to find somebody else to supply that information. There was no such other person. My test did not work well in a leak case.

In the Judy Miller case, one of the judges, Tatel, suggested that a fourth part to the test would be in order. A court should weigh the benefit of disclosure of the leak against the harm of such disclosure. For example, in the case where the *San Francisco Chronicle* published a leak from a grand jury that baseball players were taking steroids, that information was beneficial in making public policy. It would impel the baseball team owners to change players' behavior. Without this leak, there would be no such changes. The benefit of the leak outweighed the damage, if any, to grand jury secrecy.

As a U.S. Senator, Obama had supported a shield law that generally would protect sources unless the three-part test plus the fourth component had been met. A bill protecting sources in this fashion made moves through the House of Representatives. Bush had threatened to veto the bill, but on October 16, 2007, the House voted for such a bill overwhelmingly 398 to 21.[8] The bill, however, would never reach the Senate floor. Obama and McCain both had backed this law during the 2008 election campaign.[9]

But when he came into office, Obama stunned everyone in the press. The bill was reintroduced in 2009, and it passed the House again by voice vote on March 31, 2009 in the 111th Congress. Obama said he would oppose the bill if it protected sources of national security leaks. Since a major purpose of the bill was to protect such sources, Obama had effectively killed it.

Arlen Spector, who at the time was a Republican member of the Judiciary Committee, called the proposed changes "totally unacceptable." He said: "If the President wants to veto it, let him veto it. I think it is different for the President to veto a bill than simply to pass the word from his subordinates to my subordinates that he doesn't like the bill."[10] Chuck Schumer, the Democrat senator from New York, said, "The White House's opposition to the fundamental essence of this bill is an unexpected and significant setback. It will make it hard to pass this legislation."[11]

Obama ultimately reached a compromise on the national security exception that he wanted in the bill. If the government could assert that disclosure of sources would prevent or instigate acts of terrorism, or other acts that are "likely to cause significant and articulable harm to national security," then the reporter would be required to disclose the source.[12]

This compromise was subsequently adopted by the Senate Judiciary Committee 14–5 on December 10, 2009. It never reached the Senate floor for a vote and died at the end of December, 2010 when the 111th Congress disbanded. When the 112th Congress convened in January 2011, the shield law bill was not reintroduced in the Senate. There would be no federal shield law under Obama.

At the same time that Obama proposed a watered down shield law, he began an unprecedented campaign under the Espionage Act against those who leaked to the press. There had been only three prosecutions under the Espionage Act for leaks in the history of the United States. During Obama's first term, he sent one leaker to jail and indicted five others. This was totally unprecedented.

Obama campaigned for stronger legal protection for whistleblowers. Under the title "Ethics" on his Web site, he vowed to "protect whistle-blowers," who are "[o]ften the best source of information about waste, fraud, and abuse," and who perform acts of "courage and patriotism."[13] After Obama was elected, the *Washington Post* headlined "Whistle-blowers May Have a Friend in the Oval office."[14] The *Post* said he campaigned on the promise he "will strengthen whistle-blower laws to protect federal workers...." He reneged on that promise too.

On April 14, 2010, the government indicted a former National Security Agency (NSA) official, Thomas A. Drake, for leaking evidence of government fraud and waste to the *Baltimore Sun* in 2006. Drake said the NSA had wasted over a billion dollars on a classified wiretapping program called "Trailblazer."[15]

Drake was a typical whistleblower. He went to his superiors to try to correct wrongdoing, but was ignored. Only then did he go to the press. Despite Obama's promise to protect a whistleblower such as Drake, his Justice Department went ahead and indicted him because the information leaked was classified.

Following the indictment of Drake, Obama went on an unprecedented rampage of pursuing leakers criminally. In the next eight months, he charged five leakers, including Private First Class Bradley Manning, who leaked information about the Afghanistan war to Julian Assange, the founder of WikiLeaks.

On May 24, 2010 Obama's Justice Department announced that former FBI linguist Shamai Kedem Leibowitz had been sentenced to twenty months in prison for leaking transcripts of wiretaps of Israeli diplomats to an anonymous blogger. The U.S. had apparently wiretapped the Israeli embassy. Leibowitz had leaked the transcripts because he wanted to prevent an attack by Israel on Iran. He thought the diplomats were improperly and illegally attempting to influence Congress with respect to such a threat.[16]

On August 27, Obama indicted yet another leaker, Stephen Jin-Woo Kim, a senior advisor to the State Department. Kim allegedly told Fox News that U.S. intelligence officials had warned that North Korea planned to respond to a new round of UN sanctions with another nuclear test.[17]

Later that year, on December 22, a grand jury indicted CIA employee Jeffrey Sterling for leaking "defense information" to a *New York Times* reporter. It was widely believed at the time that Sterling had leaked details of Iran's nuclear program to *Times* reporter James Risen.[18]

After this flurry of indictments in 2010, there were none for sixteen months, until April 5, 2012, when Obama indicted former CIA officer John Kiriakou for telling ABC News and other organizations about the waterboarding of terrorist suspects, and revealed the names of two CIA officers he accused of carrying it out.[19] Kiriakou, who was the first former official to label the practice of waterboarding torture, pled guilty and was sentenced on January 25, 2013 to 30 months in prison.[20]

These prosecutions and convictions are troubling because the whistleblowers are intent on providing information to the public which they believe that the public needs. In the past, leaks of this sort were tolerated by administrations, but not under Obama. Since these leaks are arguably in the public interest there is a question whether Obama can succeed in all of these cases.

In the Drake case he did not. Drake's prosecution attracted considerable attention, including a devastating article in the May 23, 2011 issue of *The New Yorker* by Jane Mayer. (In another *New Yorker* article, she had earlier taken Bush to task for his renditions.) After publication of the article on Drake, and perhaps because of it, Obama terminated the case on June 9, 2011. The judge in the case ridiculed the government for wasting thousands of dollars over two and a half years in prosecuting Drake.[21]

There is no easy way to explain why Obama the president is so different from Obama the candidate on national security matters. It may be because he wanted to placate the intelligence community after he declassified the so-called "torture memos." These memos have opened up intelligence officers to criminal liability.

Or it may be the case that he became especially concerned about national security after his initial briefing by CIA Director Mike McConnell. According to Bob Woodward in *Obama's Wars*, following such a briefing Obama said, "I am inheriting a world that could blow up any minute in half a dozen ways and I will have some powerful but limited and perhaps even dubious tools to keep it from happening."[22]

Whatever the reason, Obama became a national security hawk. His intimate involvement in the killing of bin Laden added to this image. Being tough on national security did not hurt him politically, either, since Republicans had always taunted Democrats for being "soft" on national security.

A clue to his hawkish stance on the Espionage Act may be found in a meeting he had with Danielle Brian of The Project of Government Oversight and four others representing the need-to-know community.[23] What he had to say was astounding. Brian was there in part to insure the Obama administration was providing sufficient information in order to satisfy the public's need to know.[24] They were particularly concerned about the case of Thomas Drake for the same reasons Mayer expressed in her article in *The New Yorker*.

Brian told Obama that the aggressive prosecution of national security whistleblowers was undermining his legacy. According to those present, the president practically jumped out of his skin at this remark.[25] Obama said that "anyone who leaks classified information is committing espionage." This response stunned Brian and the others. It was such a backward, antediluvian approach to leaking that it makes one wonder whether Obama learned anything from the Pentagon Papers case.[26]

Thomas Drake certainly was not committing espionage when he leaked information about waste at the NSA; nor were the others pursued by Obama. Obama apparently cannot distinguish between communicating information to the enemy and communicating information to the press. The former is espionage, the latter is not.

Obama's comments sound very much like those made to the *New York Times* by its lawyers Lord, Day & Lord in 1971 when they advised that it would be a crime to publish the Pentagon Papers. One would expect more of Obama, who was president of the *Harvard Law Review*, certainly one of the more prestigious positions in the undergraduate legal world.

There are more than four million individuals, including government employees and private contractors, who have been cleared for access to classified information. In 2010, the Obama administration classified an astounding 77 million documents, a 44 percent increase over the year before. It is inevitable that some of this information will leak to the press and, indeed, should leak to the press. In the real world, there is no way for Obama to pursue four million people on what they might say about 77 million documents to those of us without government clearance.[27]

As noted, when Obama came into office, there had only been three other prosecutions under the Espionage Act: one against Daniel Ellsberg, and one against Department of Defense employee Lawrence Franklin, who leaked information to AIPAC. The third was against Samuel Loring Morison, a Naval intelligence officer who was convicted of giving classified photographs of Soviet Naval shipbuilding facilities to *Jane's Fighting Ships* magazine. It was not clear at the time whether a conviction under the Espionage Act for leaks only applied to leaking tangible items like photographs, or to intangible information.

This ambiguity was cleared up in the decision rendered by the AIPAC court. It decided that the Espionage Act applied to "information," even though it was intangible. Lawrence Franklin was convicted for leaking information to the two lobbyists from AIPAC, Rosen and Weissman, who were also indicted.[28]

To Obama's credit, he dismissed the case against the two lobbyists when he came into office. But the decision in that case has proven useful to Obama. His Justice Department is now free to prosecute for leaks of information (and not just photos, for example, as in the Morison case).[29] It may explain in part the sudden increase of prosecutions for leaks.

In a sense one of the more shocking actions of the Obama presidency in the area of press freedom was the issuance of a subpoena on April 28, 2010 to James Risen, co-author of the Pulitzer Prize-winning series on the Bush wiretapping program. Under Justice Department guidelines, Attorney General Eric Holder personally had to approve the subpoena, which he did.

The subpoena sought the source of information relating to Iran's nuclear program in Risen's book, *State of War: The Secret History of the C.I.A. and Bush Administration*. Risen had written about a CIA mission that tasked a Russian defector in a plot to deceive Iran. The Russian was instructed to give Iran a false set of instructions for making a bomb. The hope was that Iran would follow these instructions and build an atomic bomb that was a total dud, thereby delaying its nuclear program for several years. The operation was botched and Iran ended up with the nuclear plans and the knowledge of where the flaw was.[30]

A similar subpoena had been issued by a grand jury to Risen during the Bush administration. The grand jury disbanded before Obama came into office, and Risen never had to answer that subpoena. These subpoenas were issued in connection with the prosecution of Jeffrey Sterling on the apparent belief that Sterling was the source for Risen's chapter.

Obama lost the first phase of his case against Risen when a federal judge ruled Risen could invoke a reporter's privilege in Sterling's trial.[31] Obama appealed this ruling to the Fourth Circuit. It was argued in May 2012 before a court which appeared to be highly skeptical that there was such a privilege.[32] It is likely if the court rules against Risen and if the Obama Administration chooses to pursue this subpoena, it will create another major hullabaloo like the Miller case.

Obama is no better than Bush in many aspects of the war against the press—and in some respects he is worse. He has used the criminal system to plug leaks to the press in an unprecedented fashion. He has watered down a proposed federal shield law. He has asked a *New York Times* reporter to disclose sources. But there may be more anti-press action to come from the Obama presidency.

Obama is presently pursuing Julian Assange for publishing information leaked to him by Bradley Manning. If he succeeds in this effort, he will have succeeded where Richard Nixon failed.

CHAPTER XXXIV

WILL OBAMA SUCCEED WHERE NIXON FAILED?

In late 2010, Obama convened a grand jury to consider indicting Julian Assange, the founder of the website WikiLeaks, for his role in publishing classified information leaked to him by Private First Class Bradley Manning, an intelligence analyst stationed in Iraq. Among other things, Assange had published information about the Afghanistan War, the Iraq War, and verbatim cables from the U.S. diplomatic corps. Should Obama or any other president successfully pursue this action or ones similar to it, she or he will have succeeded where Nixon failed.

WikiLeaks is a website started in 2006 by Julian Assange. It was set up to receive leaks with the assurance that the identity of the leaker would be kept secret. In its early years, it received scant publicity, although it published classified military documents detailing the United States' equipment expenditures and holdings in the Afghanistan and information regarding the corruption of the Kenyan leader Daniel Arap Moi.[1] In April 2010, it published a video of a helicopter raid in Iraq which showed the unnecessary killing of two Reuters journalists and Iraqi civilians. This video clip had been leaked to him by Manning.[2]

Later in 2010, Manning leaked 92,000 documents to Assange about the Afghanistan War, 77,000 of which became known as the Afghan War Logs. He subsequently leaked to Assange the same year 400,000 classified documents on the Iraq War and 250,000 classified diplomatic cables. The volume of these leaks was unprecedented.

Manning was a 22-year-old enlisted man in the intelligence service in Iraq who had met a group of hackers located in Boston while he was on leave. Through them, he was introduced to an online hacking community, including a hacker named Adrian Lamo, who became an FBI informant.

After Manning admitted online to Lamo that he had leaked documents to Assange, the FBI arrested Manning. The government later charged Manning with violating the Espionage and the Computer Fraud Acts.[3] All of the information Manning leaked was digitized. He was enabled by a lax security system, which the government subsequently changed.[4]

Since Manning could not have leaked this amount of information without a computer, his leak was a phenomenon of the digital age. Similarly, Daniel Ellsberg could not have delivered a copy of the Pentagon Papers without a Xerox machine. Technology has changed the way information is communicated. The publication of leaked information by WikiLeaks raises the same First Amendment issues as did the Pentagon Papers case.

When Assange received the Afghan War Logs, he contacted *Der Spiegel*, the *Guardian*, and the *Le Monde* to determine whether they would publish them. They agreed, and after separately vetting them, started publishing on June 25, 2010 along with the *New York Times*, which had been given a copy by *The Guardian*. Thereafter, WikiLeaks published unredacted versions on its Web site.

The War Logs disclosed for the first time the heavy involvement of Pakistan in the Afghan War on the side of the Taliban, the use of drones against insurgents, and NATO death squads.[5] When the War Logs were published, the Obama government was apoplectic. Admiral Mike Mullen, the U.S. military's top officer said, "Mr. Assange can say whatever he likes about the greater good he thinks he and his source are doing, but the truth is they might already have on their hands the blood of some young soldier or that of an Afghan family."[6] Secretary of Defense Robert Gates warned that "sources identified in the documents…risked being targeted for retribution by insurgents."[7]

On November 28, Assange cooperated with those publications, plus *El País*, to publish edited versions of the diplomatic cables. This time, Assange published the same cables on his website. These cables were more personal. They said President Dimitri Medvedev "plays Robin to Putin's Batman," North Korea's leader Kim Jong-II is "a flabby old chap," and that the Canadians had an inferiority complex.[8] The cables also described the corrupt lifestyles of Tunisia's Zine El Abidine Ben Ali and Libya's Muammar Gaddafi. These cables were thought to have played a part in the Arab Spring, particularly in Tunisia, which was the first Arab government to topple.[9]

Once again, there was a huge outburst against Assange. But this time Secretary of Defense Gates said, "Is this embarrassing? Yes. Is it awkward? Yes. Consequences for U.S. foreign policy? I think fairly modest."[10] Senators Joe Lieberman and Dianne Feinstein did not agree.

Feinstein said Assange should be prosecuted under the Espionage Act. Lieberman concurred and said all the publishers had "blood on their hands."[11] In addition, he persuaded Amazon to stop hosting WikiLeaks. After Lieberman publicly called on other companies to do the same, Visa and Mastercard stopped processing donations to WikiLeaks.[12]

The criticism of the publication of these documents was strikingly similar to criticism of publication of the Pentagon Papers. There was fear that lives would be lost and the publication of the cables would prove embarrassing to U.S. allies. In the Pentagon Papers case, William Butts Macomber testified that Australia was furious because the Papers said it had been muscled by the U.S. into providing troops to Vietnam. The Australian government had told its public it had sent troops there because of its treaty obligations under SEATO. This was not true.

Macomber also complained the Papers had embarrassed the Canadian government. The Papers disclosed the U.S. had used Blair Seaborn, a Canadian diplomat, to represent it at peace negotiations. The public story was that Seaborn represented the Canadian government alone. Macomber said that embarrassing disclosures of this sort jeopardized our relations with other countries, since they could not deal with us in confidence.

The courts were unimpressed. Supreme Court Justice Douglas said it best: "The dominant purpose of the First Amendment was to prohibit the practice of widespread government suppression of embarrassing information."[13] On the other hand, the fear that the publication of the War Logs disclosed sources who could be killed was troubling. It has now been some time, however, since the publication of that information, and there has not been a single instance of a life of an Afghan source being endangered.

It may be too early to tell whether this massive leak has in fact caused damage to national security. But thus far, there has not been a claim that has proven out. And so these leaks may be destined for the same fate as the claims made for national security in the Pentagon Papers. While the popular press referred to Assange as the one who leaked this information to the public, in fact he did not. It was Manning who leaked this information to Assange. Manning played the role of Daniel Ellsberg and Assange the role of the *New York Times* and the *Washington Post* in the Pentagon Papers case.

In addition to their role as traditional publishers of Manning's leaks, the *Times* et al. were digital publishers, too, since they published the leaks on their websites, as Assange did. Any action therefore taken against Assange under the Espionage Act could be taken against them too, since they published exactly as Assange had.

For some, Assange was only a data dumper, not a journalist. It is, however, hard to see how his actions were that much different from Neil Sheehan's. In reflecting on the Pentagon Papers in 2012, Max Frankel said that Ellsberg had "dumped" the Pentagon Papers on Neil Sheehan.

Whether Assange was carrying out other journalistic activities as well, such as being a journalist or an editor, became a matter of some dispute. The editor of the *New York Times*, Bill Keller, said, "I would hesitate to describe what WikiLeaks does as journalism."[14] But upon reflection, it should be clear Assange is carrying out the digital equivalent of editing and gathering news in the digital age.

Assange sought out secret information by setting up a private website for the anonymous transmission of information to him. Journalists asking sources to reveal secrets is the essence of journalism. The only thing that has changed is that online chats and a digital submissions system have replaced meeting over a cup of coffee and a PO box. Charging Julian Assange with conspiracy to commit espionage could be more accurately characterized as charging him with a conspiracy to commit journalism.

While Assange's role may seem to be passive compared with the image of hard-driving reporters of the past, journalism is quite different today. News is gathered through the use of the Internet with reporters sitting at their desks. Following the release of information by WikiLeaks, the *Wall Street Journal* set up a Web site to receive anonymous leaks, and the *New York Times* considered doing the same.

Assange acted as an editor, too. He held back (i.e., edited out) some of the information he shared with his fellow publishers. Later, when a series of mistakes by the *Guardian* and WikiLeaks allowed the unredacted cables to escape online, Assange was forced to release all his cables.[15]

In December 2010, Obama's Justice Department convened a grand jury in Alexandria, Virginia to consider indicting Assange. Since the Government had charged Manning with violation of the Espionage and Computer Fraud Acts, it was reasonable to assume that the Government would charge Assange under those Acts also.[16]

Soon after the grand jury was convened however, an unnamed Justice Department official told reporters it was not going to proceed under the Espionage Act, because to do so created problems. It became apparent thereafter, the government was going to charge Assange for conspiring with Manning to violate the Espionage Act.[17]

This was exactly the same approach Nixon had taken following publication of the Pentagon Papers. He concluded he would not prosecute the *Times* for violating the Espionage Act, but rather, indict Sheehan for conspiring with antiwar activists to publish the Papers in Boston. The government believed then that such activists had copies of the Papers, perhaps even before Sheehan did, and they had agreed (i.e., conspired) with Sheehan to publish the Papers. After a turbulent fight in Boston against these activists and reporters, which included jailing of Harvard Professor Sam Popkin following a Supreme Court decision, Nixon gave up on this approach. Obama has not.

According to information circulating on the Internet and elsewhere, the government has transcripts of conversations between Manning and Lamo, the FBI informant, that raised the possibility of a conspiracy between Manning and Assange.[18] The government's case would be that Assange had had conversations with Manning that caused Manning to leak to Assange. Assange has denied having any such conversations. If the government could prove that such conversations, if any, were more than usual news-gathering conversations, the government could assert that Assange had gone over the line from being a reporter to actually participating in Manning's crime.

The journalistic community was slow to perceive the danger from the government's approach. It did not realize that anytime it tried to obtain information for the publication of a national security story, it could be guilty of the crime of conspiracy. The government's theory would criminalize the news-gathering process.

While the grand jury proceedings were ongoing, Assange was accused by two Swedish women in Sweden of inappropriate sexual behavior. They complained to the Swedish authorities, who sought to have Assange extradited from England for questioning. While the matter might seem trivial on its face, Assange and his lawyers were convinced that if Assange were extradited to Sweden, he would be immediately extradited to the United States, where he would be indicted.[19]

In fact, Assange's lawyers had reason to believe that Assange had already been indicted. A leaked email from Fred Burton, vice president of intelligence at Stratfor Global Intelligence, a government contractor, published on WikiLeaks (ironically) said to his colleagues, "We have a sealed indictment on Assange. Pls protect."[20] Over 5 million other Stratfor emails were leaked and published on WikiLeaks. They indicate the Obama administration has had a secret indictment against Assange for more than twelve months.[21]

Assange fought his case against extradition in the UK courts, but on May 30, 2012, lost. Before he could be extradited to Sweden, however, he fled to the Ecuadorean Embassy, beyond the reach of UK authorities. He told supporters if he were extradited he would end up in the US, and would be tried under the Espionage Act and subject to the death penalty.[22]

In some respects, the Assange case may be typical of future cases involving leaks of classified information. There is a lesson in it, regardless of whether Obama pursues Assange or not. It may be too difficult with the speed of digital communication to stop the publication of information and to enjoin websites before publication happens. The only remedy for the government will be to prosecute those involved after publication for criminal violation of the Espionage Act.

The First Amendment should prevent such prosecution. As the constitutional scholar Geoffrey Stone has written, the government should be required under the First Amendment to show that such publication constitutes a clear and present danger to the United States.[23] If a publisher does not have significant First Amendment protection for such publication, the government will, through prosecution of publishers, be able to create a de facto Official Secrets Act. Furthermore, if the government were ever to succeed, it would intimidate others who might consider publication of leaks of classified information.

In the WikiLeaks case, the government cannot show that publication creates a "clear and present danger" to the United States. Secretary of Defense Gates said the publication of the cables was harmless, and there is no proof of any damage to national security from any of the other leaks published by WikiLeaks.

The way around Stone's First Amendment barrier is to indict Web journalists or publishers for conspiracy to violate the Espionage Act. If Obama or a future president chooses to pursue this case or a similar case in this fashion she or he will have succeeded where Nixon failed, since he pursued the same tactic against the *Times* and its reporter Neil Sheehan, but did not succeed.

The government should not be permitted to end-run the First Amendment in this fashion. If in fact someone like an Assange or Neil Sheehan actively urges a Manning to download information, or an Ellsberg to Xerox the Papers for their use, that is one thing. But barring that, the protection given to the Pentagon Papers before publication should be given after publication too.

There still is not much support for Assange in the journalistic community.[24] But that community should realize that the First Amendment protects against prosecution of someone like Assange, and such prosecution should be fought as tenaciously as it has fought for freedom of the press in other cases.

The fight for freedom of the press never ends, even under a president previously thought to be friendly to the cause. While Bush and Obama have taken aggressive actions against the press, they did not apparently ever consider trying to challenge the authority of the Pentagon Papers case. The case has taken on a mythic quality. It is a case for the ages.

CHAPTER XXXV
A CASE FOR THE AGES

The Pentagon Papers case was the first of its kind in American history. The United States Government tried and failed to use the courts to censor the press through the issuance of a prior restraint order. It will be very difficult for the government ever to succeed. The test adopted by the Supreme Court, that the government must show that a publication will surely cause direct immediate and irreparable damage to its nation or its people, is almost impossible to meet. The Pentagon Papers will never be overruled. It is a case for the ages.

Government claims that the publication of classified information damaged national security were unsubstantiated. Nixon tried to use these claims to destroy the *New York Times*. The government generally brings cases against the press for its political advantage, and that includes the *Caldwell* case. The only way to win cases such as these is to develop a rule of law which forces the government to desist. Failing that, the press must be prepared to go into contempt and to jail.

The government knows it cannot overturn the Pentagon Papers case. This is proved by what it does today when it learns of pending publication of classified information. It no longer attempts to get a court to enjoin the publication of stories such as a classified report discussing the surge of troops for Afghanistan, Bush's warrantless wiretapping program, or WikiLeaks.

In early 2010, journalist Bob Woodward published a story of a planned surge in Afghanistan. General Stanley McChrystal had written a classified report to President Obama requesting 40,000 troops for Afghanistan, and the report was leaked to Woodward by someone in the military. Woodward subsequently published a summary of the report in the *Washington Post* before it was adopted as U.S. policy by Obama.

Woodward and Marcus Brauchli, then the *Post*'s editor, told the government in advance that they were going to publish parts of the report. They did this, Woodward said, "because the government could not legally stop us from publishing the McChrystal assessment…"[1]

He said further: "[W]e had the upper hand in listening to the arguments for deleting passages from the report…. For the Pentagon Papers, the *Times* and the

Post did not consult the government in advance. To do so would have alerted the government and likely resulted in a court action to stop publication, which is exactly what the government did in federal court after the initial articles ran. The beauty of the Supreme Court's Pentagon Papers ruling—which forbids prior restraint—is that it encourages us to ask the government for their specific objections to the publication of classified documents."[2]

For the same reason, the *New York Times* met with President George W. Bush and others about the publication of its story by Eric Lichtblau and James Risen on warrantless wiretaps. Those conversations were not as pleasant as the ones with the government reported by Woodward in his book *Obama's Wars*. President Bush told the *Times* that if the newspaper proceeded to publish it would have "blood on its hands."[3] The *Times* published anyway. The government knew it couldn't stop the *Times* from publishing under the rule of the Pentagon Papers case.

The *Times* followed the same procedure with respect to information from WikiLeaks, where an army intelligence analyst had allegedly leaked details of the Afghanistan and Iraq wars to WikiLeaks. Before publication on its website, WikiLeaks shared its information with the *New York Times*. The newspaper then discussed the documents with the government. Consequently, the *Times* scrubbed the leak before publishing it. Again, the government knew it would not be able to stop the paper from publishing.

It has now been over forty years since the Pentagon Papers case was decided. There has not been a scintilla of proof that any of the 7,000 pages damaged national security. It's time to admit that the claims of breach of national security made in this case turned out to be hot air. The information in the Pentagon Papers may have been important for the government to keep confidential for its own purposes, but their release did not damage national security. As Erwin Griswold said, "In retrospect I know of no harm which was caused by the publication of the Pentagon Papers."[4] The "Pentagon Papers episode was a tempest in a teapot."[5]

Seventy percent of the items the government said it did not want published were published by the government itself a few weeks after the case. The other thirty percent have turned out to be trivial with the passage of time, particularly the claim made that the *New York Times* revealed North Vietnamese secret codes. Although it is probably true that classified materials may contain codes which only a trained eye can see, it was not true in the Pentagon Papers instance. Time after time, the government tried to persuade the courts it was true with unsupported allegations. It failed.

The Pentagon Papers should never have been classified as they were. Leslie Gelb, who was director of the Pentagon Papers project at the Department of Defense and Ellsberg's boss from 1967–1969, said at a discussion panel on March 16, 2010, that the classification of the Pentagon Papers was a "joke." I was sitting on the panel and had asked him how he could justify classifying newspaper articles as top secret. He replied:

The answer is a funny story: my first day at the Pentagon you had to get a classification briefing. That consisted of going to the auditorium and watching a World War II British spy movie.... So I went back to my office and I had to dictate a memo about Wheelus air force base in Libya, of all things. Most people didn't even know we had an air force base in Libya in the good old days.

So I finish dictating the memo and the secretary comes in and says to me, "How shall I classify it?" And I said, "what are my choices?" And she says, "there is 'official use only,' 'confidential,' 'secret,' 'top secret.'" So I said, "top secret!"

Then out of that the sergeants and the navy chiefs we had working on this [the Pentagon Papers], they started to stamp even the newspapers as top secret as kind of a joke.... There were some pages that should have been top secret sensitive because they came from top secret sensitive documents. But then we would have had go to through page by page to do it and it was too much work.[6]

The inappropriate classification described by Gelb led the government to take ridiculous positions in the case, such as requesting an injunction against re-publication of presidential speeches and *New York Times* articles.

Bob Woodward's highly acclaimed book *Obama's War* also suggests the claims of damage to national security were not substantive. His book is very much like the Pentagon Papers. It is a history of decision-making based almost entirely on classified information. It is much "worse" than the Pentagon Papers were in the sense that his disclosures are more immediate, and seem more "dangerous" and "damaging" to national security. *Obama's War* is, in effect, a massive national security leak. Apart from WikiLeaks, it may be one of the greater leaks in American history. I estimate that perhaps as many as 365 of the 390 pages in his book contain classified information.

In the Pentagon Papers case, Griswold said there were at least eleven items he sought to restrain. They included the exposure of U.S. decision making processes, embarrassment of foreign governments, disclosure of U.S. contingency plans, names of CIA agents, disclosure of secret bases and the disclosure of United States' ability to break North Vietnam's codes. Woodward's book publicizes the same type of information, but in greater detail.

His purpose in writing this book is to describe Obama's decision-making process to send 30,000 troops to Afghanistan. Woodward quotes officials saying highly unflattering and embarrassing things about Presidents Asif Zardari of Pakistan and Hamid Karzai of Afghanistan. Zardari says killing Pakistani civilians by drones does not worry him as long as they kill members of Al Qaeda.[7] Karzai is described as "delusional," "off his meds" and "high on weed."[8]

Woodward describes "one of the most sensitive and secret of all military" contingency plans: if the U.S. is attacked from terrorists within Pakistan, the U.S. would "bomb or attack" 150 suspected Al Qaeda locations.[9] He states flatly that Karzai's brother, Ahmad Wali, is a CIA agent.[10] He describes a secret CIA base in Quetta, Pakistan, and a secret 3,000 manned CIA army in Afghanistan.[11] Woodward describes the intelligence briefing by CIA Director Michael Hayden to Obama, obviously based on all kinds of intelligence, including Comint.[12]

The *Times* was excoriated in some part for publishing generically the same type of information as Woodward. It was enjoined and subjected to a grand jury investigation that lasted for fourteen months. Why shouldn't Woodward be subject to the same approbation when he did exactly the same thing as the *Times* did? Why shouldn't he be forced to disclose the source of his leaks or be subject to criminal investigation? The answer is that in Washington, D.C., leaks are used for political advantage. It was in the interest of the Obama administration to make all these leaks. It was very much to Nixon's advantage to stop them in the Pentagon Papers case.

Nixon knew it was a perfect case to smear the *Times*. He would be in a position very much like Senator Joe McCarthy was when he said that the State Department is infested with Communists: "I have here in my hand a list of 205...members of the Communist Party and who nevertheless are still working and shaping policy in the State Department."[13]

McCarthy never had to show the list to anybody. Nixon's lawyers knew assertions of damage to national security could not be challenged effectively, or at all. The American public had no way of knowing whether Nixon's claims of damage to national security were true or not. It was a perfect opportunity to smear his enemy, the *New York Times*, and he got Maxwell Taylor and others to do that for him.

Unfortunately, highly respected lawyers such as Mike Seymour and Erwin Griswold fell into the smear trap. They submitted unsupported assertions of damage to national security to the courts, including the Supreme Court, knowing full well the *Times* could not respond to them.

The only way the *Times* could overcome these smears was to up the ante as to what the First Amendment required. In order to understand the Pentagon Papers case, it is important to understand the history of how the *Times* developed its position as applied to prior restraints on the First Amendment.

In a sense, the Pentagon Papers was not a real case. There was huffing and puffing for no good reason other than for Nixon's political advantage. Political cases should be examined for what they are and not what they appear to be. This applies to the Caldwell and Judy Miller cases too. Nixon's lawyers fought the *Caldwell* case all the way to the Supreme Court for no purpose. They did this to vindicate the government's authority and for whatever political advantage would come out of it. The proof of that statement is that when the case was over, the government walked away from it. It never even bothered to follow up with Caldwell. That case too was full of hot air.

The same applies to journalist Judy Miller. If she had disappeared and become unavailable to federal prosecutor Patrick Fitzgerald, it would have made absolutely no difference to him. She only testified to a part of his case and then only to supplement what other witnesses had said. Her reward was jail time. No one else went to prison.

When the government brings these cases, the only thing to do is to fight like a tiger and risk going to jail if necessary. Anything less diminishes the freedom of the press. The Pentagon Papers case has become an international symbol of the resistance of the press to the government. If you mention the case anywhere in the world, most people recognize it. And there are many who know the particular facts of the case. It has become emblematic of a particular period in America's history, alongside the Dred Scott case (slavery) and *Roe v. Wade* (abortion). While the case itself sets out a rule that the government cannot enjoin the press from publishing information, even if it's classified, the case also stands for courage. It took courage for the press to stand up to the power of government and risk civil and criminal penalties. It took courage for the owners of the *New York Times* and the *Washington Post* to risk the viability of their institutions with the publication of classified documents. It stands as a worldwide example for institutions and others to fight government control of the press. It also serves as a reminder that the press can never give up its fight to be free of such control. It is indeed a case for the ages.

END NOTES

CHAPTER I: THE OTHER STORY THAT SUNDAY MORNING

1   Neil Sheehan, "Vietnam Archive: Pentagon Study Traces Three Decades of U.S. Involvement," *New York Times*, June 13, 1971.
2   *The Pentagon Papers: Secrets, Lies, and Audio Tapes: Audio Tapes from the Nixon White House*, "Telephone Conversation with Alexander Haig." June 13, 1971. National Security Archive. Available at http://www.gwu.edu/~nsarchiv/NSAEBB/NSAEBB48/nixon.html.
3   Ibid.
4   Ibid.
5   Ibid., "Telephone Conversation with William Rogers." June 13, 1971.
6   Ibid., "Telephone Conversation with Henry Kissinger." June 13, 1971.
7   H.R. Haldeman and Joseph DiMona, *The Ends of Power*. New York: New York Times Book Company, 1978, 110.
8   "35 Women Picket the Gridiron Dinner." *New York Times*, March 14, 1971.
9   Ibid.
10 Robert E. Bedingfield. "Times Acquiring Family Circle and Six Other Cowles Properties." *New York Times*, October 29, 1970.
11 "Gridiron Club Stages Spoof on Politicians." *Reading Eagle*, March 14, 1971.
12 Ibid.
13 *New York Times v. Sullivan*, 376 U.S. 254 (1964).
14 I had worked briefly on the case. It was my first experience with a high-publicity First Amendment case. I discovered that in such cases judges frequently make up the law. The trial judge's name was Walter B. Jones. He had written a book on how lawyers could dismiss cases in Alabama courts if they were from out of state.
    The *Times* followed the directions in his book. It argued that since it only had 354 subscribers in Alabama, its case should be dismissed. Judge Jones refused to dismiss. He decided the *Times* had waived its right to object to his court's jurisdiction. Yet the *Times* had followed the directions in his book as to how to object to jurisdiction. In other words, Jones the judge overruled Jones the author to "get" the *New York Times*.

CHAPTER II: NIXON'S WAR AGAINST THE PRESS

1   Stanley I. Kutler. *Abuse of Power: The New Nixon Tapes*. New York: Simon & Schuster, 1997.
2   "Two Hiss Brothers Deny Red Charges." *New York Times*, August 4, 1948.
3   Hiss also worked at the predecessor firm of Cahill, Gordon & Reindel, the firm that represented the *New York Times* in the Pentagon Papers case.
4   Private communication with Bret Carlson, a partner of Debevoise & Plimpton, early 1980.

5   Bill Hare. "Robo Calls Throwback to Early Nixon Campaign Tactic," *Political Cortex*, October 19, 2008, http://www.politicalcortex.com/story/2008/10/19/181225/83.
6   Greg Mitchell. *Tricky Dick and the Pink Lady.* New York: Random House, 1998.
7   My view of Nixon remains the same. In light of Johnson's lies about Vietnam and Kennedy and Clinton's sexual peccadilloes, however, I have a more nuanced attitude today about presidents. Not all wrongdoing lies with the GOP.
8   "Mr. Agnew's Fitness." Editorial, *New York Times*, October 26, 1968.
9   "Nixon Assails The Times For Editorial on Agnew." *New York Times*, October 28, 1968.
10   Eberstadt's legendary career was chronicled in the biography *The Will to Win: A Biography of Ferdinand Eberstadt: Contributions in Economics and Economic History* (New York: Greenwood Press, 1989) by Robert C. Perez and Edward F. Willett. He was a counselor to presidents and drafted the bylaws and guidelines for the CIA when it was first organized. See "Letter to the editor from his son, Frederick Eberstadt," *New York Review of Books*, October 14, 2010.
11   "Agnew Presses *Times* to Retract Critical Comments." *New York Times*, October 30, 1968.
12   Homer Bigart. "Agnew Charges 'Blooper' By Times." *New York Times*, October 29, 1968.
13   "GOP Officials Continue Their Attacks on The *Times* for Criticism of Agnew and Nixon," *New York Times*, October 31, 1968.
14   In the *New York Times* files, there is an anonymous undated report from an unnamed U.S. publisher saying: "The threat of the lawsuit remained, however, and our reporters who were covering the campaign were told in no uncertain terms that the suit would be brought."
15   "Agnew Takes Gibe at Some in the Press." *New York Times*, December 7, 1968.
16   "Transcript of Address by Agnew Criticizing Television for its Coverage of the News." *New York Times*, November 14, 1969.
17   In Houston, Agnew referred to "the liberal news media of this country, those really illiberal, self-appointed guardians of our destiny who would like to run the country without ever submitting to the elective process as we in the public must do." The press, or as he called them, the "hell raisers," were "enemies" of the Constitution, and "isolationists," who used the First Amendment "as its own preserve." (Don Oberdorfer, "Agnew Hits Press, 'Hell Raisers,' 'Isolationists' in New Offensive," *Washington Post*, May 23, 1970.) In Jackson, Mississippi, Agnew implored "the great majority of thoughtful Americans" to reject "editorial double-think" of the "Seaboard media." (Philip D. Carter, "Agnew Exhorts the Majority: Reject Editorial Doublethink," *Washington Post*, May 19, 1971.) In Los Angeles, Agnew called a specific report on the Vietnam War by *Life* magazine a "hatchet job" while decrying the "preponderantly negative" coverage of the war in general. If the press continued to criticize American policy, he said, then "it will destroy us as a nation." (Carl Greenberg, "Agnew Assails Media on Vietnam Coverage," *Washington Post*, April 8, 1971.)
18   "Traveler Agnew Volubly Verbalizes Viewpoints." *New York Times*, September 20, 1970.
19   Don Oberdorfer, "Agnew Hits Press, 'Hell Raisers,' 'Isolationists' in New Offensive." *Washington Post*, May 23, 1970.
20   Herbert Lawrence Block is also known as Herblock.
21   Ibid.
22   James M. Naughton. "Agnew Criticizes CBS Over a TV Documentary." *New York Times*, March 18, 1971.
23   "Agnew Criticism of CBS Renewed." *New York Times*, March 25, 1971.
24   Richard Halloran. "House Subpoena Is Rejected by CBS." *New York Times*. April 21, 1971.
25   Christopher Lydon. "House Vote Kills Move to Cite CBS on Pentagon Film." *New York Times*, July 14, 1971.

CHAPTER III: NIXON FIRES A SALVO

1   Actually, Caldwell received his subpoena on January 15, 1971. However, he did not tell Turner about it until Febuary 2.
2   Jack Gould. "CBS Will Comply With Subpoenas on Panthers." *New York Times*, January 27, 1970.
3   Henry Raymont. "Magazines' Files Under Subpoena." *New York Times*, February 1, 1970.
4   Ibid.
5   Gould. *NYT*, Jan. 27, 1970.
6   Raymont. *NYT*, Feb. 1, 1970.
7   Ibid.
8   Sanford J. Ungar. *The Papers & The Papers*. New York: E.P. Dutton, 1972, 121.
9   See generally, Chris Argyris. *Behind the Front Page: Organizational Self-Renewal at a Metropolitan Paper*. San Francisco: Jossey-Bass Publishers, 1974.
10 Nick Ravo. "Marie Torre, 72, TV Columnist Jailed for Protecting Source." *New York Times*, January 5, 1997.
11 Ibid.
12 Personal communication between Arthur J. England, Jr., former Justice of the Florida Supreme Court and former law school contemporary of Amsterdam, and James Goodale, circa April 1980.
13 *U.S. Constitution*, amend. 1.

CHAPTER IV: WHICH FIRST AMENDMENT?

1   Robert D. McFadden. "A.M. Rosenthal, Editor of the Times, Dies at 84." *New York Times*, May 11, 2006.
2   In *New York Times v. Sullivan,* the *Times* argued newspapers could be held liable if they had reason to know what they were printing was not true but published anyway, or if they published "with reckless disregard of whether it was false or not." This was a qualified view of the First Amendment. The precise First Amendment position the *Times* took in this case was not subject to debate among the editors and executives of the *Times*. It was left to be articulated by Professor Herbert Wechsler of Columbia Law School, who argued the case in the Supreme Court.
3   "News Media Heads Cite Their Concern on U.S. Subpoenas." *New York Times*, February 4, 1970.
4   Ibid.
5   Ibid.
6   Specifically, the three-part test the *Times* and Caldwell proposed was: "1) The 'information sought' must be demonstrably relevant to a clearly defined, legitimate subject of governmental inquiry;... 2) It must affirmatively appear that the inquiry is likely to turn up material information;... 3) The information sought must be unobtainable by means less destructive of First Amendment freedoms" (Memorandum of Points and Authorities at 19–22, Application of Caldwell, 311 F. Supp. 358 (N.D. Cal. 1970).
7   Ibid. at 9. "Mr. Caldwell does not object to affirming before the grand jury—or any other place—the authenticity of quotations attributed to Black Panther sources in his published articles. But he respectfully declines to give testimony or produce materials relative to unpublished interviews with the Panthers because these are confidential..."
8   An "*amicus curiae*" is a legal term for someone outside the parties in dispute who voluntarily offers to present evidence, in the form of legal precedent and arguments, to assist the court in making its decision.
9   It could be argued, however, that there is an advantage to having at least one *amicus* take a more radical, absolutist position. It can have the effect of making an argument such as the *Times*' appear to be more centrist.
10 In broadcast cases, the ACLU favored viewer rights over broadcaster's rights. It backed the "Fairness Doctrine." That Doctrine required that anytime a controversial issue was

broadcast, time had to be given up to the proponent of an opposing view so as to make the program fairly balanced. This was different from the well-known equal time doctrine. There, a station was required to give time to a political candidate to equal the time given to his opponent.

The networks had had a furious fight with the government over the Fairness Doctrine. They took a case called *Red Lion v FCC* to the Supreme Court claiming their First Amendment rights had been violated. The ACLU supported the Fairness Doctrine. The Supreme Court upheld the Fairness Doctrine in *Red Lion*. Ultimately the networks won their fight to outlaw the Fairness Doctrine. I caused the *New York Times* to support the networks in this battle.

Another instance where the ACLU and the *Times* disagreed was whether there was a First Amendment right to publish information of grand jury proceedings when the jury does not hand down a formal indictment. When the *Times* published a story based on a transcript of a runaway jury (*see infra* chapter 8 & 9), Mel Wulf of the ACLU wrote a letter to the *Times* and complained. He said the information amounted to "gossip" and inferred the story violated the Sixth Amendment rights of those named in the transcript. ("Letter from Melvin Wulf, Legal Director of the ACLU to the *New York Times*," from the *New York Times* files, July 2, 1970.

The ACLU would subsequently take a different position than the *Times* on prior restraints, as well. After oral argument in Supreme Court in the Pentagon Papers case, the ACLU submitted a brief to the Court saying it disagreed with Alex Bickel's statements to the Court regarding his proposed test for prior restraints (*see infra* chapter 27).

11   Zirpoli decided, "…such power shall not be exercised in a manner likely to do so until there has been a clear showing of a compelling and overriding national interest that cannot be served by alternative means." "A compelling and overriding interest" was stronger than the "clearly defined, legitimate subject of government inquiry" test proposed by the *Times*. (Application of Caldwell, 311 F. Supp. 358, 360 (N.D. Cal. 1970)).

12   Ibid.

13   "Limiting the Subpoena." Editorial. *New York Times*, April 7, 1970.

14   "Judge Puts a Limit on Disclosure Subpoenaed Writer Must Make." *New York Times*, April 4, 1970.

15   *Caldwell v. United States*, 434 F.2d 1081 (9th Cir. 1970).

16   Caldwell was subpoenaed twice by the grand jury—once for his notes on February 2, 1970, and then to appear before the grand jury on March 17, 1970. Even though a second subpoena was issued, the first was never withdrawn.

17   *Branzburg v. Hayes*, 408 U.S. 665 (1972).

18   Branzburg was subpoenaed by two separate grand juries. He had written two stories, one talking about the manufacture of hashish and a second about general drug use in Frankfort. In the second case, he refused to disclose the names of those who told him drugs were being used in Frankfort. The Kentucky shield law statute protected such disclosure. Branzburg refused, however, to appear before the grand jury to claim a privilege of non-disclosure available under such shield law.

19   *Air Transport Ass'n v. PATCO*, 313 F.Supp. 181 (E.D.N.Y. 1970).

CHAPTER V: DRESS REHEARSAL FOR THE PENTAGON PAPERS

1   *In re Grand Jury*, 315 F.Supp. 662 (D.C. Cir. 1970).

2   *Near v. Minnesota*, 283 U.S. 697 (1929).

3   Fred W. Friendly. *Minnesota Rag: Corruption, Yellow Journalism, and the Case That Saved Freedom of the Press.* Minneapolis: University of Minnesota Press, 2003.

4   Ibid.

5   "The fact that the public officers named in this case, and those associated with the charges of official dereliction, may be deemed to be impeccable cannot affect the conclusion that the statute imposes an unconstitutional restraint upon publication," the Court held (*Near*, 283 U.S. at 723).

6   Note: in *Times v. Sullivan*, Douglas joined the majority opinion, and Black wrote a concurring opinion taking an absolutist position, at least when it came to public officials. He said newspapers should be completely immune from libel suits from public officials.

7   For a more detailed explanation of disobeying state court prior restraints prior to 1970, see James C. Goodale, "The Press Ungagged: The Practical Effect on Gag Order Litigation of *Nebraska Press Association v. Stuart,*" *Stanford Law Review* 29 (February 1977): 23.

8   U.S. Attorney Stephen H. Sachs agreed with the grand jury's findings, but Attorney General John Mitchell issued an order to Sachs not to sign any indictment implicating the congressmen because there was not enough evidence against them. Further, Mitchell reasoned that their names should not even be mentioned in the indictment, as their reputations would be damaged by the publicity. Sachs, while disagreeing with the Justice Department, followed their orders and refused to sign the indictment. (Robert M. Smith, "6 on Capital Hill Figure in Secret Inquiry On Builder's Action in $5-Million Claim," *New York Times, June 21, 1970.*)

9   Ibid.

CHAPTER VI: HAS CLASSIFIED INFORMATION BEEN PUBLISHED BEFORE?

1   Conversation with George Wilson, former *Washington Post* reporter, August 2010.

2   Sherman Kent. *Strategic Intelligence for American World Policy.* Princeton: Princeton University Press, 1949.

3   David E. Pozen. "The Mosaic Theory, National Security, and the Freedom of Information Act." *Yale Law Journal* 116 (2005): 630.

4   Stewart Alsop and Charles Bartlett. "In Time of Crisis." *Saturday Evening Post,* December 8, 1962.

5   Ibid.

6   Ibid.

7   Tania Long. "Anti-Castro Units Trained to Fight At Florida Bases." *New York Times,* April 7, 1961.

8   Ibid.

9   "Cuban Alarums." *New York Times,* April 9, 1961.

10   Ibid.

11   James Reston. *Deadline: A Memoir.* New York: Times Books, 1991, 142, 244–252.

12   Gabriel Schoenfeld. *Necessary Secrets: National Security, the Media, and the Rule of Law.* New York: W.W. Norton & Company, 2010, 163.

13   Ibid.

14   Ibid.

15   Katrina Vanden Heuvel. "The Nation and NY Times: Bay of Pigs Déjà vu." *The Nation,* July 6, 2006, http://www.thenation.com/blog/nation-and-ny-times-bay-pigs-deja-vu.

16   R. W. Apple Jr. "James Reston, A Giant of Journalism, Dies at 86." *New York Times,* Dec. 7, 1995.

17   Alsop and Bartlett, *Saturday Evening Post,* Dec. 8, 1962.

CHAPTER VII: CAN CLASSIFIED INFORMATION BE PUBLISHED LEGALLY?

1   *Espionage Act,* 18 U.S.C., § 793 (1917).

2   Exec. Order No. 10,501, 3 C.F.R. 398 (1949–53).

3   18 U.S.C., § 641. This law covered the theft of tangible property such as Jeeps. It did not cover the Xeroxing of documents.

4   "Mitchell Issues Plea on F.B.I. Files." *New York Times,* March 24, 1971. The reason no one took him seriously was that no one believed the "Espionage Act" applied to publications.

5   *McKinney's Constitutional Laws of New York,* Ch. 20, Art. 21., Sec. 330.

6   Among other things, the Espionage Act did not cover "classified information." It covered "information relating to national defense." Everything the *Times* published on stories covering defense fit that definition. That was too vague.

7   The "confidential" classification is for information or material that, if disclosed, could be "prejudicial to the defense interests of the nation." The "Secret" classification is for information or material that, if disclosed, could result in "serious damage to the Nation." The "Top Secret" classification is for information or material that, if disclosed, could result in "exceptionally grave damage to the Nation," which means, among other things, "a definite break in diplomatic relations affecting the defense of the United States, an armed attack against the United States or its allies, [or] a war" (Exec. Order No. 10501, 3 C.F.R. 398 (1949–53)).

8   Under the theory of separation of powers, Congress makes laws that apply to everyone, while the Executive branch can only make laws that apply to itself, unless Congress has passed a law supporting the application of such Executive Orders to the general public. Accordingly, Executive Order 10501 applied only to the Executive Branch, since there was no Congressional action authorizing the order. It did not apply to the general public, of which the *Times* was a member.

9   *Comint Act*, 18 U.S.C. § 798 (1953).

10   *Atomic Energy Act*, 42 U.S.C. § 2274 (1976).

11   "Week of Protests on War to Start." *New York Times*, April 19, 1971.

12   R.W. Apple, Jr. "10,000 Gather at Rhode Island's Capitol for Start of 'Dump Nixon' Campaign." *New York Times*, April 19, 1971.

13   The *New York Times* online archives show forty-two articles that mention Vietnam from April 19 through April 21, 1971.

14   Richard Halloran. "House Subpoena is Rejected by CBS." *New York Times*, April 21, 1971.

15   "Summary of Actions Taken on Cases Before the Supreme Court." *New York Times*, May 4, 1971.

16   *Memorandum from James C. Goodale*, from *New York Times* files, July 6, 1971, 5.

17   Ibid., 5–6.

18   Leslie H. Gelb. "Foreign Affairs; The 100 Questions." *New York Times*, June 16, 1991.

19   Daniel Ellsberg. *Secrets: A Memoir of Vietnam and the Pentagon Papers.* New York: Viking Penguin, 2002, 323–329.

20   Ibid., 356–364.

21   Ibid.

22   Ibid., 206.

23   Ibid., 206–209.

24   Ibid., 375.

25   Gold temporarily brought Sheehan's original copy back to New York in the second week of April to make two additional working copies. He drove them back down to Washington in his car a few days later. (*Memorandum prepared by Counsel to Neil Sheehan*, addressed to James C. Goodale, from personal files, October 14, 1971, 5.)

26   *Memorandum from James C. Goodale*, from *New York Times* files, July 6, 1971, 6–7.

27   Ibid., 7–8.

CHAPTER VIII: A STRATEGY TO PUBLISH

1   "Louis M. Loeb, 80; Was *Times* Counsel." *New York Times*, March 17, 1979.

2   Ibid.

3   Lord, Day & Lord was particularly known for its tax group headed by Harry Rudick, which once included Randolph Paul, who later founded the well known firm of Paul, Weiss, Rifkind, Wharton & Garrison.

4   When the Republicans sought a candidate to run for president in 1952, Brownell was the one who convinced General Dwight D. Eisenhower to run as a Republican candidate. There was a famous picture of Brownell rowing on a lake in Europe to reach Eisenhower's villa, which was accessible only by water. The visit resulted in Eisenhower saying "yes." Michael Bak. "Herbert Brownell, GOP Civil Rights Hero." *American Thinker*, February 20, 2007, http://www.americanthinker.com/blog/2007/02/

herbert_brownell_gop_civil_rig.html. See generally Herbert Brownell with John P. Burke, *Advising Ike: The Memoirs of Attorney General Herbert Brownell*. Kansas: University of Kansas, 1993.

5   *Memo from James C. Goodale*, from personal files, July 6, 1971, 9.

6   Ibid., 9–10.

CHAPTER IX: A FIRST LOOK AT THE PENTAGON PAPERS

1   Eric Pace. "Harrison E. Salisbury, 84, Author and Reporter, Dies." *New York Times*, July 7, 1993.

2   President John F. Kennedy, 8th News Conference, March 23, 1961, http://www.youtube.com/watch?v=ioYdAuiXJLM.

3   E.W. Kenworthy. "Katzenbach Says Congress Cleared Wide War Power." *New York Times*, August 18, 1967.

4   Ibid.

5   *The Pentagon Papers: The Defense Department History of United States Decision-making on Vietnam*, The Senator Gravel Edition (Boston: Beacon Press, 1971), Vol. 1, Ch. 1.

6   Ibid., Vol. 1, Ch. 3–4.

7   "Top Secret Talks: Daniel Ellsberg, Leslie Gelb, James Goodale, Nick Lemann and Victor Navasky." Presented by USC Annenberg's Center on Communication Leadership & Policy, March 16, 2010, http://communicationleadership.usc.edu/presentations/top_secret_talks_daniel_ellsberg_leslie_gelb_james_goodale_nick_lemann_and_victor_navasky.html.

8   Sanford J. Ungar. *The Papers & The Papers: An Account of the Legal and Political Battle Over the Pentagon Papers*. New York: E.P. Dutton & Co., Inc., 1972, 149–152.

CHAPTERS X: LORD, DAY & LORD SINKS THE SHIP

1   This is the correct date of this meeting. Rudenstine wrote I had stated that the meeting occurred on April 22nd. He may have been misled because the source he cites for that fact was "James Goodale, *Communications Policy and Law: The Pentagon Papers* (available from Benjamin N. Cardozo Law School, Yeshiva University, New York, photocopy)." This is a citation to materials on the Pentagon Papers I used in a course I taught at Yale University School of Law, 1977–80, New York University Law School, 1982–85, and Fordham School of Law, 1986–2010. These materials, which covered the Pentagon Papers litigation, were in fact prepared by Anthony Lewis, a former columnist for the *New York Times*. He used them for a course he taught at Harvard University Law School, Harvard's Kennedy School of Government, and to the Columbia University Graduate School of Journalism. I used his materials as part of a larger set of materials covering the First Amendment which I had prepared for the course I taught, "Communications Policy and Law."

This meeting was also the only meeting with Lord, Day & Lord. Both Salisbury and Rudenstine incorrectly assert there was a second meeting on May 12.

2   "Lord, Day & Lord Firm to Close." *New York Times*, September 2, 1994. There are many reasons, of course, for a law firm's closure, but I believe Lord, Day & Lord's failure to represent the *Times*, which became notorious in the legal community, substantially led to its demise.

3   R.W. Apple Jr. "James Reston, A Giant of Journalism, Dies at 86." *New York Times*, December 7, 1995.

4   *Memorandum from Abe Rosenthal to James Reston and Max Frankel*, from the *New York Times* files, June 1, 1971.

CHAPTER XI: WE WILL PUBLISH AFTER ALL

1   *Remarks by A.O. Sulzberger at Sydney Gruson's funeral*, March 26, 1998.

2   "The Covert War." *New York Times*. June 13, 1971.

3   Ibid.
4   Neil Sheehan. "Vietnam Archive: A Consensus to Bomb Developed Before '64 Election, Study Says." *New York Times*, June 14, 1971.
5   "McNamara Report to Johnson on the Situation in Saigon in '63." *New York Times*, June 13, 1971.
6   "McGeorge Bundy Memo to Johnson on 'Sustained Reprisal Policy.'" *New York Times*, June 15, 1971.
7   Ibid.
8   Ibid.
9   *Memorandum from Harding Bancroft to A.O. Sulzberger*, from the *New York Times* files, June 10, 1971.
10 Harrison E. Salisbury. *Without Fear or Favor*. New York: Times Books, 1980, 202–204. Salisbury details Gruson and Rosenthal's conversations and subsequent events that evening. He does not report, however, that such conversation was precipitated by Brancroft's memo, which is newly discovered.
11 *Memorandum from Abe Rosenthal to A.O. Sulzberger*, from the *New York Times* files, June 11, 1971.

CHAPTER XII: NIXON THREATENS: LORD, DAY & LORD QUITS

1   *Memorandum from Gene Roberts*, *New York Times* files, June 14, 1971.
2   Max Frankel. "Court Step Likely: Return of Documents Asked In Telegram to Publisher." *New York Times*, June 15, 1971.
3   *The Pentagon Papers: Secrets, Lies, and Audio Tapes: Audio Tapes from the Nixon White House*. "Oval Office Metting with H.R. Haldeman," June 14, 1971, National Security Archive (June 13–15, 1971), http://www.gwu.edu/~nsarchiv/NSAEBB/NSAEBB48/nixon.html.
4   Ibid.
5   Ibid., "Telephone conversation with John Mitchell, 7:19 p.m.," June 14, 1971.
6   While the conversation between Nixon and Mitchell discussing what actions the Justice Department should take against the *Times* on Sunday night is somewhat unclear, Nixon almost certainly knew that he was giving the go ahead to pursue a prior restraint.
    Admittedly, when Nixon and Mitchell spoke at 7:19 p.m. that night, the conversation was confusing, at best. Nixon first asked Mitchell, "Has the government ever done this to a paper before?" He seemingly is asking Mitchell if the government have the legal ability to enjoin a publication. Mitchell responds, "Oh yes—advising them of their— yes, we've done this before." In reality, a newspaper had never been enjoined in federal court the history of the country.
    This conversation has led some to argue that Nixon may not have known he was actually approving the prior restraint (Gabriel Schoenfeld. *Necessary Secrets: National Security, the Media, and the Rule of Law*. New York: W.W. Norton & Company 2010, 177–78). When looking at the conversation in the context of the surrounding evidence, however, this argument does not hold water. What else could Nixon have been approving? Criminal action against the newspaper had barely been discussed in the White House and Justice Department. Was Nixon just saying a warning telegram should be sent if he did not plan on following through on court action? That is highly doubtful, considering later in the conversation he is adamant in his belief that the *Times* is his "enemy" and decisive action was needed.
    Furthermore, in his memoirs, Nixon stated he had ample reasoning for suing the *Times*, including that the Papers could "provide code breaking clues" or CIA "informants would be exposed." He also said that the State Department had maintained that the Papers would expose current SEATO contingency war plans and that the international community would be shaken given the secret roles various government had been playing as diplomatic go-betweens.

Nixon's belief was that if the government did not act against the *Times* "it would signal to every disgruntled bureaucrat in the government that he could leak anything he pleased while the government stood by" (Richard Nixon, *Memoirs of Richard Nixon*, New York: Grosset & Dunlap 1978, 509). Such belief is borne out by White House conversations in which Nixon appears as angry or even angrier at the leak itself than the actual contents of the leak. And there is no evidence that Nixon was surprised or was under the impression anything different was happening when the Justice Department followed through on its threat to sue the *Times* the next morning.

Nixon's explicit approval at that time, however, may have been unnecessary because, according to Mardian's sworn affidavit, Mardian made the phone call and read the telegram to Harding Bancroft at 7 p.m., although Mitchell did not talk to Nixon until 7:19 p.m. (Annexed affidavit of Robert C. Mardian, Order to Show Cause by the United States, June 15, 1971). In his book, David Rudenstine argues that Nixon had already given his approval when this conversation took place, as Nixon had discussed his reasons for approving the suit during unrecorded White House meetings earlier that afternoon (David Rudenstine, *The Day the Presses Stopped.* Los Angeles: University of California Press, 1996 89–92).

But there appears to be no direct evidence to support such contention either. While Robert Mardian said in an interview with Rudenstine that he persuaded Haldeman to talk to Nixon that afternoon to try to convince him of the need for a prior restraint, Rudenstine does not say explicitly when—or to whom—Nixon approved the suit. Rudenstine assumes Nixon told Kissinger his reasons for suing the *Times* during their meeting an hour prior to his phone call with Mitchell, but there is no evidence of this specific conversation occurring, either. Rudenstine says that Mitchell "likely" used the 7:19 p.m. telephone conversation with Nixon to "inform" him the telegram had been sent, but it's clear from the transcript Mitchell is not "informing"—he is asking for permission.

7   *The Pentagon Papers: Secrets, Lies, and Audio Tapes: Audio Tapes from the Nixon White House.* "Telephone conversation with John Mitchell, 7:19 p.m." June 14, 1971, National Security Archive (June 13–15, 1971), http://www.gwu.edu/~nsarchiv/NSAEBB/NSAEBB48/nixon.html.

8   Ibid.

9   Frankel, *New York Times*, June 15, 1971.

10 Ibid.

11 Exec. Order No. 10,501, 3 C.F.R. 398 (1949–53).

12 Rudenstine, *The Day the Presses Stopped*, 100–101.

13 Abrams' recollection and mine differ on this point. His recalls that he never called back to say his firm would represent the *Times*. Later, in the middle of the case, as a joke, he said Cahill Gordon would indeed represent the *Times*.

CHAPTER XIII: NIXON STOPS THE PRESSES

1   The Affidavit of J. Fred Buzhardt can be found in James C. Goodale, *The New York Times Company versus United States: A Documentary History*, 2 vols., New York: Arno Press 1971, 1–4.

2   Ibid.

3   The Memorandum of Law submitted by the United States in favor of a Temporary Restraining Order can be found in James C. Goodale, *The New York Times Company versus United States: A Documentary History*, 2 vols., New York: Arno Press 1971, 16–22.

4   Floyd Abrams. *Speaking Freely.* New York: Viking Penguin, 2005, 22.

5   It turns out Seymour was at the Annual Conference of U.S. Attorneys in Washington, D.C. and couldn't get back in time for the initial court appearance. Whitney North Seymour, Jr. *United States Attorney: An Inside View of "Justice" in America Under the Nixon Administration.* New York: Morrow, 1975, 190–191.

6   There was no transcript made of this proceeding. The description of the hearing comes from notes I made during and directly after the hearing.

7   Ibid.

8   Patricia Sullivan. "Robert Mardian; Attorney Caught Up in Watergate Scandal." *Washington Post*, June 21, 2006.

CHAPTER XIV: NIXON HAS THE PRESS WHERE HE WANTS IT

1   "Transcript of Nixon's News Conference on His Defeat by Brown in Race for Governor of California." *New York Times*, November 8, 1962.

2   Haldeman Notes, Box 43, June 1971, as cited in Rudenstine, *The Day the Presses Stopped*.

3   David E. Rosenbaum, "Opponents of War in Congress Decry U.S. Suit on Study," *New York Times*, June 17, 1971.

4   Leslie Gelb. "The Secretary of State Sweepstakes." *New York Times*, May 23, 1976.

5   These affidavits are available in James C. Goodale, *The* New York Times *Company versus United States: A Documentary History*, 2 vols. New York: Arno Press 1971, 423–440.

6   Ibid., 414–422.

7   Ibid., 396, 403–404.

8   Ibid., 397.

9   Ibid., 397–398.

10   "Sulzberger Terms Documents 'History.'" *New York Times*, June 17, 1971.

11   Mark Singer. "Talk of the Town: The Pentagon Suitcases." *The New Yorker*, December 9, 1996.

CHAPTER XV: NIXON'S LAWYERS WANT OUR SOURCE

1   Hedrick Smith. "Mitchell Seeks to Halt Series on Vietnam but *Times* Refuses." *New York Times*, June 15, 1971.

2   Bickel wrote, "The Court of Appeals in Caldwell…held that the Government cannot obtain disclosure of materials before a grand jury which could lead to the disclosure of a confidential source absent proof of a crime, proof that the information sought is essential to prove the crime, and that it has made unsuccessful efforts to obtain the information elsewhere." (*Memorandum of Defendant New York Times Company In Opposition to Issuance of Preliminary Injunction*, available in Goodale, *New York Times v. U.S.: A Documentary History*, 387.)

3   *Memorandum of Defendant New York Times Company In Opposition to Issuance of Preliminary Injunction*, available in Goodale, *New York Times v. U.S.: A Documentary History*, 390–391. This statement is from Bickel's Brief to the District Court for the trial on Friday, June 18, 1971. Bickel inserted the statement on the assumption that the issue of compelling disclosure of a source would still be undecided at the time he delivered his brief to the court on late Thursday afternoon, June 17. But because the pace of litigation was so fast, that statement, as good as it was, never reached Gurfein in time. The issue had already been decided by the time Gurfein received the brief. This was typical of the Pentagon Papers case. Events moved so fast that no one could keep up with them.

4   Oral Argument before United States District Judge Murray I. Gurfein, Southern District of New York, in the action of the *United States of America* v. *The New York Times Company et al.*, 71 Civ 2662, June 17, 1971, 10 A.M., 27–28. The transcript is available in Goodale, *The New York Times Company versus United States: A Documentary History*.

5   "Excerpts From Oral Arguments on U.S. Effort to Obtain Documents From *Times*." *New York Times*, June 18, 1971.

6   Seymour, *United States Attorney*, 201–204.

CHAPTER XVI: THE REPUBLIC STILL STANDS

1   Chalmers M., Roberts. "Documents Revealed, U.S. Effort in '54 to Delay Viet Election." *Washington Post*, June 18, 1971.
2   Geoffrey Cowan and Leroy Aarons. *Top Secret: The Battle for the Pentagon Papers*, 29.
3   *Telecommunications & Information Revolution with James Goodale*, Guest Ben Bradlee, "A Good Life," Part I, WNYE TV/Ch. 25–October 1995.
4   Unpublished Transcript of Hearing before United States District Judge Murray I. Gurfein, Southern District of New York, in the action of the *United States of America v. The New York Times Co.*, 71 Civ. 2662 19 (June 18, 1971). This transcript is available in Goodale, *New York Times v. U.S.: A Documentary History*, hereinafter known as "*New York Times* Public Hearing."
5   Ibid., 19.
6   Ibid., 20.
7   Richard M. Nixon, *The Memoirs of Richard Nixon,* 508 (1978).
8   New York Times Public Hearing, 124–5.
9   Ibid., 104–5.

CHAPTER XVII: WHAT SECRETS DOES THE GOVERNMENT HAVE?

1   Unpublished Transcript of *In Camera* Hearing before United States District Judge Murray I. Gurfein, Southern District of New York, in the action of the *United States of America v. New York Times Company et al.*, 71 Civ. 2662, June 18, 1971, 28, hereinafter "*New York Times* Secret Hearing."
2   *New York Times* Secret Hearing, 40.
3   Ibid., 5–6.
4   Ibid., 6.
5   Ibid., 6.
6   Ibid., 41.
7   *New York Times Public* Hearing, 159.
8   *New York Times* Secret Hearing, 159.
9   Ibid., 160.
10 Seymour, *United States Attorney,* 199–200.
11 *New York Times Secret* Hearing, 55.
12 Ibid., 55–6.
13 Ibid., 62.
14 Ibid., 54.
15 Ibid., 39, 49.
16 Ibid., 39.
17 Ibid., 76.
18 Ibid., 77.

CHAPTER XVIII: ALEX MAKES A CONVINCING CASE

1   *New York Times* Secret Hearing, 117.
2   Ibid., 121.
3   Memorandum of Defendant *New York Times* Company In Opposition to Issuance of Preliminary Injunction, in the action of the *United States of America v. The New York Times Company et al.*, 71 Civ. 2662, June 18, 1971, 45–46, quoting from 55 Cong. Rec. 2004. This memorandum is available in Goodale, *NYT v. U.S.: A Documentary History*.
4   Ibid., 51.
5   Ibid., 53.
6   *New York Times* Secret Hearing, 133.
7   Ibid., 139–40.
8   Ibid., 132.

9   Ibid.,156.
10   Ibid., 160.
11   *New York Times* Public Hearing, 193.

CHAPTER XIX: THE POST SURPRISES NIXON BY PUBLISHING

1   Seymour has a different view on why the government used different lawyers in D.C. He says that Mardian took a more hardline position in respect to classified documents than he did and didn't like how he argued the case. Mardian believed if the government said it was "top secret" then the argument ended there and newspapers couldn't print it. Seymour claims he had a more nuanced position and only wanted the prior restraint to apply to the most sensitive documents in the study, not all of them. He wrote in his memoirs that "When the *Washington Post* took up publication of the study after the Times had been stayed by the district court's order, Mardian saw his chance to get the case under his control...Mardian started a separate injunction action in Washington using his own staff, where he could be free to present his hard-line position." Seymour, *United States Attorney*, 203.
2   Bruce Lambert. "Judge Gerhard Gesell Dies at 82; Oversaw Big Cases." *New York Times*, February 21, 1983.
3   Ungar, *The Papers & The Papers*, 147.
4   Unpublished Transcript of Hearing before United States District Judge Gerhard A. Gesell, D.C. District Court, in the action of *United States v. Washington Post*, 71 Civ. 1235, (D.D.C. June 18, 1971): 23.
5   Ibid., 20.
6   "Gesell Ruling on *Post,*" *New York Times*, June 19, 1971.
7   Ibid.
8   *United States v. Washington Post*, 446 F.2d 1322 (D.C. Cir. Ct. 1971).
9   Ibid., 1323.
10   Ibid., 1325.

CHAPTER XX: GURFEIN SETS THE TIMES FREE

1   *United States v. New York Times*, 328 F. Supp. 324, 329 (S.D.N.Y. 1971).
2   Ibid., 330.
3   Ibid., 331.
4   Ibid.
5   Rudenstine, *The Day The Presses Stopped*, 169.
6   Ibid.
7   *Correspondence from Mel Barkan to James Goodale,* August 23, 2001.

CHAPTER XXI: GESELL SAYS "ABSOLUTELY NO" TO NIXON

1   Unpublished Transcript of Hearing before United States District Judge Gerhard A. Gesell, D.C. District, *United States v. Washington Post*, 71 Civ. 1235 (D.D.C. June 21, 1971): 23, hereinafter "*Washington Post* Public Hearing."
2   *New York Times* Public Hearing, 80.
3   Unpublished Transcript of In Camera Hearing before United States District Judge Gerhard A. Gesell, D.C. District, *United States v. Washington Post Company et al.*, 71 Civ. 1235 (D.D.C. June 21, 1971): 56–7, hereinafter "*Washington Post* Secret Hearing."
4   *Washington Post* Secret Hearing, 59.
5   *Central Intelligence Agency v. Sims*, 471 U.S. 159, 178 (1985).
6   David Pozen, "The Mosaic Theory, National Security, and the Freedom of Information Act," *Yale Law School Journal*, 116 (2005) 628.
7   *Washington Post* Secret Hearing, 112.
8   Ibid., 106.

9   Ibid., 105.
10 Ibid., 151–152.
11 Affidavit of Vice Admiral Noel Gayler, June 21, 1971, *United States v. Washington Post*, 446 F.2d 1322 (D.C. Cir. Ct. 1971).
12 *Washington Post* Secret Hearing, 216.
13 Ibid.
14 *Memorandum from Harding F. Bancroft*, from the *New York Times* files, June 21, 1971.
15 Rudenstine, *The Day the Presses Stopped*, 201.
16 *Washington Post* Secret Hearing, 251.
17 Ibid., 266.
18 Ibid., 267.

CHAPTER XXII: SEYMOUR CUTS AND PASTES THE POST'S PAPERS

1   Transcript of Hearing before the *United States Court of Appeals for the Second Circuit*, in *United States v. New York Times*, Docket No. 71–1617 (June 21, 1971): 6.
2   Ibid.
3   Ibid., 6–7.
4   Ibid., 7.
5   Ibid., 8.
6   Seymour, *United States Attorney*, 199–200.
7   Unpublished Transcript of the Hearing before United States Court of Appeals, *en banc*, in *United States v. New York Times*, Docket No. 71–1617 (June 22, 1971): 38. This transcript is available in Goodale, *New York Times v. U.S.: A Documentary History*.
8   Ibid., 39.
9   John Prados & Margaret Pratt Porter, eds. *Inside the Pentagon Papers*. Lawrence: University Press of Kansas, 2004. Prados has analyzed the merits of the claims listed in the Special Appendix. Prados also states which items in the Special Appendix were not made public and which were not in the subsequent government publication of the Pentagon Papers. In the footnotes that follow this statement appears as "not made public," "made public," or "not made public except for…"
    There are some discrepancies in the Special Appendix re-printed by Prados and the Special Appendix submitted to the Second Circuit. Such Appendix does not, for example, specifically refer to the Rolling Thunder campaign or the Tonkin Gulf Incident. Prados' Appendix does.
10 The Lodge cable was dated November 30, 1966. Prados contends the underlying document contains none of the material claimed in this section of the Special Appendix. Made public. The other message from the Secretary of State to an unknown source was dated June 10, 1967. The Appendix claimed there were other cables interspersed throughout the documents just like this one. Not made public.
11 These SEATO contingency plans, according to the Appendix, were "still in effect" and listed the costs of "an all out effort to take all of Southeast Asia." The documents are dated October, 1961. Made public except for a few "occasional words."
12 The two contingency plans from 1964 and 1965 detailed deployments for use against the People's Republic of China if it decided to get involved in the conflict. The Special Appendix conceded that the plans were no longer in use. Prados contends no details were revealed on troop size, strength, sequence, movement, or any other description besides the initial appearance of troops in South Vietnam conformed to their provisions.
13 These "current contingency plans" for an escalating bombing campaign in 1967 against the North Vietnamese, according to the Special Appendix, included details about the major ports, destroying bridges, and lines of communications. Prados contends no such details were revealed. Made public.
14 The National Intelligence Estimate was dated October 1961. Made public except for a few lines from one paragraph of this seven page NIE.
15 The sets of chronologies detailed U.S. force buildup from 1961–67. Made public.

16   The two other references from the Special Appendix not included in this chapter were a CINCPAC assessment of the strength of North Vietnamese forces from 1966, and a set of statistics covering the years 1965 to 1967 of operational and intelligence nature. The CINCPAC assessment, however, was dated more than five years before publication of the Pentagon Papers and represented a snapshot of the U.S. estimate of North Vietnamese strength. Made public. By 1971, conditions on the ground had changed dramatically and it was no longer accurate. This assessment also had no relevance to the war in 1971. Prados contends these statistics were typical of those high ranking military personnel use at congressional hearings to report on the progress of the war. Made public.

17   This item focused on the U.S. frustrations with the South Vietnamese government and U.S. criticism of Vietnamese actions, specifically their inability to control drug trafficking in their own country. Made public.

18   This item details the weaknesses in the South Vietnamese leadership and U.S. attempts to influence their actions, as well as speculation on possibility of the collapse of its government. Made public except for two minor sentences.

19   This item describes the Pacification program, and specifically, details on U.S. involvement in the program that was "essentially Vietnamese in character." It also documents the friction between the U.S. and Vietnamese government. Made public.

20   This item discusses U.S. decisionmaking in the Vietnamization process and contained information that could lead the enemy to learn about domestic pressures as well as U.S. "fiscal restraints" which could embolden enemy actions. Made public except for two minor sentences.

21   A cable from Ambassador Thompson to the Under Secretary of State detailed Thompson's assessment of his opinion of Soviet attitudes and possible countermoves towards U.S. military actions. Made public.

22   There were many examples listed of third party negotiations that could bring embarrassment to nations involved. This item, however, mainly details the "Marigold" negotiations that arguably portrayed the Polish government in a disparaging light. Made public.

23   In addition to President Diem's assassination in 1963, this item reveals frank conversations discussing the South Vietnam government's weaknesses. This revelation diminished "the status" of many South Vietnamese officials. Made public.

24   Rudenstine, *The Day the Presses Stopped*, 8.

25   Ibid.

26   Ibid, 9.

CHAPTER XXIII: GRISWOLD ENTERS THE FRAY

1   Dennis Hevesi. "Erwin Griswold Is Dead at 90; Served as Solicitor General." *New York Times*, November 21, 1994.

2   Ibid.

3   Rudenstine, *The Day the Presses Stopped*, 243.

4   Unpublished Transcript of the Hearing before the Court of Appeals for the D.C. Circuit, *United States v. Washington Post* (June 22, 1971): 4–12, hereinafter "*Washington Post* Court of Appeals Hearing."

5   *Washington Post* Court of Appeals Hearing, 5.

6   "U.S. Brief Appealing Judge Gesell's Rejection of Injunction," *Washington Post*, June 23, 1971.

7   *Washington Post* Court of Appeals Hearing, 33–54.

CHAPTER XXIV: ALEX BICKEL QUITS

1   Abrams, *Speaking Freely*, 36.

2   *Memorandum from Harding Bancroft*, from *New York Times* files, June 23, 1971.

3   Conversation with Robert Phelps, Washington bureau of the *New York Times*, June 23, 1971.
4   George Wilson, "Hey, hey, LBJ, got any secrets to give away?" *Nieman Watchdog*, July 26, 2006, available at http://www.niemanwatchdog.org/index.cfm?fuseaction=showcase.view&showcaseid=0044
5   George Wilson conversation, August 10, 2010.
6   Ibid.
7   Affidavit of Noel Gayler, June 20, 1971.
8   George Wilson, *Nieman Watchdog*, July 26, 2006.
9   This analysis is based on a comparison of the original Gayler affidavit filed with Gesell and the message printed by the Senate Foreign Relations Committee. This message, according to Wilson was set out verbatim in the Gayler affidavit submitted to Bazelon. The original affidavit has not been fully released. The affidavit submitted to Bazelon has not been released either. It may be when these two affidavits are fully released, this analysis will have to be revisited.
10   *United States v. New York Times*, 444 F.2d 544 (2nd Cir. 1971).
11   Floyd Abrams, *Speaking Freely*, 34–35.
12   *United States v. Washington Post*, 446 F.2d 1327 (D.C. Cir. 1971).

CHAPTER XXV: A RUSH TO THE SUPREME COURT
1   Petition for a *Writ of Certiorari* to the United States Court of Appeals for the Second Circuit, *New York Times v. United States*, (June 24, 1971).
2   Memorandum for the United States in Opposition to Application for Vacatur of Stay Ordered by The Court of Appeals and Stay of Mandate of that Court, in *New York Times v. United States* before the Supreme Court (June 24, 1971). "In cases dealing with such vital matters of national security, the outcome cannot depend upon the *legal nicety* that, due to the short deadline under which the government was required to operate in presenting its proof to the district court in the present case, it was unable to prepare as complete a submission as it could present with the additional time it had available in the *Washington Post* case." (Emphasis supplied.)
3   *United States v. Washington Post*, 446 F.2d 1327, 1331 (D.C. Cir. 1971).
4   "Government Plea to the Supreme Court," *Washington Post*, June 26, 1971.
5   Ibid.
6   "Text of The Post's Memorandum Opposing Stay of Publication," *Washington Post*, June 26, 1971.
7   Fred P. Graham, "Times Asks Supreme Court to End Restraints on Its Vietnam Series; U.S. Loses in Move to Curb Post: Action Today Seen," *New York Times*, June 25, 1971.
8   Order by the Supreme Court of the United States, in *New York Times v. United States* (Oct. Term 1970, No. 1873).
9   Brief for the *Washington Post* (Secret) filed in *United States v. Washington Post*, 403 U.S. 943 (1971), in the Supreme Court.
10   Ibid.
11   Max Frankel. *The Times of My Life and My Life with the Times*. Random House: New York, 1999, 341–342. The secret brief written by Frankel and Hegarty has been lost along with the Supplemental List of forty-four items. The secret brief of the *Post* was not lost however. The *Post* quoted part of the list of forty-four in that brief and I have used that quote in this chapter to describe the items on the list. Taking that quote, Frankel's recollection and the eleven items in Griswold's secret brief to the Court (which was not lost), the list of forty-four items can be substantially reconstructed. When release of the *Times'* secret brief and the government's Supplemental List was sought from the Defense Department years later by public interest groups, the Defense Department said it could not find them.
12   Max Frankel, e-mail to James Goodale, May 19, 2010.

13 Max Frankel, e-mail to James Goodale, August 15, 2010.
14 First, it had to respond to a Special Appendix which covered 400 pages of the Pentagon Papers. Next, it had to respond to the Supplemental List which named at least forty-four items including one entire volume. Since these items incorporated references to other pages of the Pentagon Papers, a fair estimate is that such references totaled 1,000 pages of the Pentagon Papers. Additionally, the government had expanded the response to the seventeen items in Seymour's Special Appendix and these references totaled an additional 1,000 pages. The above response had to be prepared in the period from 5:00 Friday night until 10:30 the next morning.
The *Post* counted 100 items and Frankel counted forty-four. The *Post* probably added the items in the Special Appendix and counted them differently than the *Times* did. The *Post* said in its secret brief: "[It] is clear from its Supplemental List of Special Items that the government continues to tilt at windmills. In addition to designating some 100 items, including one entire volume, the Supplemental List would bar publication of all documents that fall in 13 broadly defined categories." Brief for the *Washington Post* (Secret) filed in *United States v. Washington Post*, 403 U.S. 943 (1971), in the Supreme Court.

CHAPTER XXVI: ALEX TO THE RESCUE

1 The appropriate First Amendment test for prior restraints took different forms in the two cases. In its brief to Gurfein, the *Times* said any restraint would have to meet the examples set out in *Near v. Minnesota* (e.g. troop ships) or to analogous examples. The government agreed with this position. In his closing argument *in camera* Bickel said, "The standards in a prior restraint case are the highest. I don't know how to define it except... [by] narrowing it down by picking one or another example. We have the troop ship example (*New York Times* Secret Hearing, 64). Judge Gurfein, although he did not set forth a specific test, suggested a restraint could only be issued if the information to be published causes "serious security breaches vitally affecting the interests of the Nation" (*United States v. New York Times*, 328 F. Supp. at 330). On appeal to the Second Circuit, the *Times* did not suggest a test as such in its open brief. It focused on a separation of powers position. Under this position a prior restraint could only be granted if there was a national emergency. (Brief submitted by the *New York Times* in *United States v. New York Times*, 444 F.2d 544 (2d Cir., 1971), filed in the United States Court of Appeals for the Second Circuit). The Court of Appeals, in remanding the case to Gurfein, used the standard of "grave and immediate danger." *New York Times*, 444 F.2d 544.
In the *Post* case initially before Gesell, he asserted the First Amendment was absolute when he said "Congress appears to have condemned any pre-existing restraining or censorship of the press...and the Supreme Court...has outlined the historic reasons supporting the total freedom of the press to publish as guaranteed by the First Amendment." ("Gesell Ruling on Post," *New York Times*, June 19, 1971). The D.C. appellate court remanded the case to Gesell using the standard "prejudice the defense interests of the United States and result in irreparable injury to national security." It also used a standard "vitally affecting national security." (*United States v. Washington Post*, 446 F.2d 1322, 1323–25 (D.C. Cir. 1971). The *Post*'s trial brief proposed a "grave and irreparable injury" test ("*Post*'s Brief Against Barring Series," *Washington Post*, June 22, 1971). At the *Post* trial (as distinct from the first hearing before Gesell), Gesell used the "irreparable harm" test set by the Court of Appeals (*Washington Post* Secret Hearing, 266). On appeal, the *Post* used *Near v. Minnesota* as a guidepost and argued for an "immediate, grave threat to national security" standard. (WP Brief to Court of Appeals, 19). On appeal, the government argued Gesell had erred by being "arbitrary and capricious" in rejecting its position that its classification system could be challenged. (U.S. Government Brief to the Court of Appeals, 13). On the appeal, the D.C. Court used "irreparable injury" and "gravely prejudice the defense interests of the United States." (*United States v. Washington Post*, 446 F.2d 1327, 1328 (D.C. Cir. 1971).

2   Brief for the *New York Times* (Public Brief) filed in *New York Times v. United States* (Oct. Term, 1970, No. 1873), in the Supreme Court, 58.

3   Ibid., 59.

4   Ibid., 60.

5   Brief for the United States (Public Brief) filed in the *New York Times v. United States*, 403 U.S. 713 (1971) and *United States v. Washington Post*, 403 U.S. 943 (1971), in the Supreme Court.

6   Brief for the *Washington Post* Company (Public Brief), *United States v. Washington Post*, 403 U.S. 943, 8 (1971).

7   Ibid.

8   Erwin N. Griswold, *Ould Fields, New Corne: The Personal Memoirs of a Twentieth-Century Lawyer* (St. Paul: West, 1992), 303.

9   Ungar, *The Papers & The Papers,* 228.

CHAPTER XXVII: THE DAY THE PIN DROPPED

1   The State and Defense Department briefs were each entitled "Sealed List of Additional Items to the Special Appendix," dated June 26, 1971. The Supreme Court's order set the deadline for such "Supplemental Lists," Friday, June 25 at 5:00 p.m.

2   Griswold, *Ould Fields, New Corne*, 303–4.

3   Transcript of the Oral Argument in the Supreme Court in the *New York Times v. United States* (Oct. Term, 1970, No. 1873), and *United States v. Washington Post* (Oct. Term, 1970, No. 1885), reprinted in James C. Goodale, *The New York Times Company versus United States: A Documentary History, 2 vols* (New York: Arno Press, 1971), hereafter "Transcript, Supreme Court Oral Argument."

4   Transcript, Supreme Court Oral Argument, 1220.

5   Ibid., 1219.

6   Ibid.

7   Ibid., 1222.

8   Ibid.

9   Erwin N. Griswold, *Ould Fields, New Corne*, 307.

10 In fact, Bickel could not agree with that statement since, among other things, the reason I decided to appeal the case was that standard was inadequate to meet the First Amendment.

11 Memorandum in Support of Government's Motion for a Preliminary Injunction, in *New York Times v. United States*, 71 Civ. 2662 (June 17, 1971).

12 Bickel said perhaps there were some items under the definition that could be enjoined. He did not say which. Perhaps he was thinking of a publication that leads to "an armed attack against the United States." In answering one of the questions asked by Stewart, he said an event that could trigger a prior restraint need not be "cosmic."

13 Transcript, Supreme Court Oral Argument, 1226.

14 Ibid.

15 Motion of Amicus Curiae to file post Argument Memo, in *New York Times v. United States*, 403 U.S. 943 (1971).

16 Motion to Intervene as Defendants: American Civil Liberties Union Memorandum in behalf of Amici Curiae, U.S. District Court, Southern District of New York (June 18, 1971).

17 Transcript, Supreme Court Oral Argument, 1227.

18 Ibid., 1230.

19 Ibid.

20 Ibid.

21 Gesell used "irreparable harm." Gurfein did not articulate a specific standard. *See supra*, chapter 26 (part II), footnote 1.

22 Letter from James Goodale to Floyd Abrams, October 26, 1971.

23 Since the Gayler affidavit has not been fully released, there may be assertions of damage to national security not fully reflected in this analysis.

24 Prados and Porter, eds., *Inside the Pentagon Papers*, 171.
25 The estimate that spoke in generalities was dated 1967 and the Pentagon Papers only quoted one paragraph from that estimate. The other estimate asserted hypothetically the U.S. would consider the nuclear option if China invaded Thailand. For this event to occur, however, the U.S. and Vietnam would have to invade Cambodia, North Vietnam would send more troops to Laos, which would cause the U.S. to send more troops to Thailand and finally, China would then have to attack Thailand. Ibid., 172–3.

CHAPTER XXVIII: THE HISTORIC VICTORY

1   Ungar, *The Papers & the Papers*, 250.
2   Ibid., 315–16.
3   *New York Times v. United States*, 403 U.S. 703, 730 (1971) (J. Stewart, concurring).
4   Ibid., 717 (J. Black, concurring).
5   Ibid. 714–715.
6   Ibid., 722.
7   Ibid., 723–724.
8   Black, Douglas, Brennan also emphasized that there was no statute that applied.
9   *New York Times v. United States*, 403 U.S. at 725 (J. Brennan, concurring).
10 Ibid., 726–727 (J. Brennan, concurring).
11 *Nebraska Press Association v. Stuart*, 427 U.S. 539, 591–95 (1976) (J. Brennan, concurring).
12 *Bernstein v. U.S. Department of State*, 176 F.3d 1132, 1144 (1999).
13 Ben Bradlee. *A Good Life: Newspapering and Other Adventures.* New York: Simon & Schuster, 1995, 321–2.
14 Ungar (1972), 242.
15 *New York Times v. United States*, 403 U.S. at 751 (J. Berger, dissenting).
16 Ibid., 762 (J. Blackmun, dissenting).

CHAPTER XXIX: MITCHELL LICKS HIS CHOPS

1   I was told this by several lawyers who knew Mitchell. I am not, however, able to pinpoint these lawyers. As such, this statement could be deemed unconfirmed gossip.
2   "Mitchell Will Prosecute Law Violations in Leaks," *New York Times*, July 2, 1971.
3   From the beginning, Nixon wanted to indict the *Times* as quickly as possible. After the first articles were printed, Nixon asked Haldeman to check the "statute of limitations" for a criminal prosecution. *The Pentagon Papers: Secrets, Lies, and Audio Tapes: Audio Tapes from the Nixon White House* "Nixon Oval Office meeting with H.R. Haldeman," June 14 1971, 3:09 p.m., National Security Archive *available at* http://www.gwu.edu/~nsarchiv/NSAEBB/NSAEBB48/nixon.html.
    Later, Nixon told Haldeman he was "not sure Mitchell should delay [the] Grand Jury [investigation]" and they "must play boldly—don't be afraid of risks." H.R. Haldeman, *The Haldeman Diaries: Inside the Nixon White House.* New York: G.P. Putnam, 1994.
4   Ungar, *The Papers & The Papers*, 309.
5   *Memo from James Goodale*, from *personal files*, July 28, 1971. The two objectionable matters were 1) information about communist governments that acted on behalf of the U.S. and 2) U.S. ability to intercept communications between foreign governments. These were similar to claims listed on Griswold's list of eleven items.
6   This consent was set out in a Stipulation and Order between the government and the Times dated October 12, 1971. In addition to the "Sealed Special Appendix filed in the Second Circuit Court of Appeals" and "Sealed List of Additional Items to the… Appendix filed with the Federal District Court for the Southern District of New York," the documents listed in the Stipulation included the "Sealed State Department List of Supplemental Items to the … Appendix," the "Sealed Defense Department List of Supplemental Items to the … Appendix," and "Sealed Brief the Solicitor General served on June 26, 1971 at the United States Supreme Court." From personal files.

7   Mardian earlier told Michael Hess he was going to set up three grand juries to determine who received the Papers. They would be in New York, Los Angeles, and Boston. Hess was offered the job of coordinator. Hess turned him down. Whitney North Seymour Jr., *United States Attorney,* 203–204.

8   Ken Clawson. "Jury Weighs Indictment of *New York Times.*" *New York Post,* July 13, 1971.

9   Ibid. Clawson wrote the story for the *Washington Post* which syndicated to the *New York Post.*

10   "U.S. Said to Be Planning to Seek Indictment of a *Times* Reporter," *New York Times,* July 15, 1971.

11   According to Judge Garrity's decision in *United States v. John Doe,* 332 F.Supp 932, on page 93, "The crimes being investigated by the grand jury include the retention of public property or records with intent to convert (18 U.S.C. § 641), the gathering and transmitting of national defense information (18 U.S.C. § 793), the concealment or removal of public records or documents (18 U.S.C. § 2071), and conspiracy to commit such offenses and to defraud the United States (18 U.S.C. § 371), as is indicated in the prosecuting attorneys' oaths of office on file with the Clerk."

12   Remarks by Daniel Ellsberg at ABA Communications Law Section meeting in Palm Springs, California, January 16, 2006.

13   Prados and Porter, eds., *Inside the Pentagon Papers,* 188.

14   *Memorandum from Mitchell Rogovin to James Goodale,* from personal files, October 14, 1971, 1.

15   Ibid.

16   Ibid., 3.

17   Ibid.

18   Ibid., 4.

19   Ibid., 5.

20   Ibid., 6.

21   Ibid., 5.

22   Ibid., 10.

23   Ibid., 11–12.

24   On December 6, 1971, while the Grand Jury was still meeting, Scotty Reston met with Daniel Ellsberg at Ellsberg's request. Ellsberg said he had been angry at the *Times* for a long time. He said he never gave Sheehan permission to copy the Pentagon Papers. While he let Sheehan see the Papers and take notes, when Sheehan asked him if he could copy the documents, Ellsberg told him "no." *Memo from James Goodale,* from personal files, December 6, 1971.

25   *Gravel v. United States,* 408 U.S. 606 (1972).

26   *Text of Proposed Statement of A.O. Sulzberger,* from *JCG personal files,* February 14, 1972.

27   *Unofficial Transcript of the Testimony of Samuel Popkin,* Boston Grand Jury, from JCG personal files, March 24, 1971.

28   Bill Kovach. "Harvard Professor Jailed in Pentagon Papers Case." *New York Times,* November 22, 1972.

29   Bill Kovach, "Popkin Freed in a Surprise As U.S. Jury Is Dismissed," *New York Times,* November 29, 1972.

30   Peter Kihss, "The *Times* Wins a Pulitzer For the Pentagon Papers," *New York Times,* May 2, 1972.

CHAPTER XXX: NIXON'S REVENGE

1   Rehnquist told Mitchell when he was in the Justice Department that the *Times* could be enjoined. *See supra,* page 97–98.

2   The *Times* was no longer directly involved in the case. Our interest initially was to protect Caldwell from Nixon because we owned his notes. Since we disagreed with

Caldwell about his tactics in his case, we dropped our claim of interest in his notes and supported him solely through our amicus brief. In retrospect, that was a wise decision since many years later we discovered Caldwell had destroyed his notes.

Had we continued to tell the Supreme Court we were part of his case through our ownership of his notes, we would not have been telling the Supreme Court the truth, although we didn't know it at the time.

3   "It is quite clear that he accepts the relevance test, since he would quash the subpoena if the newsman is called upon to give information bearing only a remote and tenuous relationship to the subject of the investigation.... Dealing...with the requirement of compelling state interest, it can be said that Justice Powell adopts the test to the extent that he requires the state to seek only information required by a legitimate law enforcement inquiry.... What of the exhaustion of alternate sources test suggested by Justice Stewart, by Caldwell and by Bickel? Justice Powell is silent on this point, and the most that can be said is that he does not explicitly exclude exhaustion from the 'balancing' he favors. However, the test, which requires that the newsman be called to testify only as a last resort, would seem to be a common sense way to accommodate First Amendment interests with the interest of the state in seeking testimony." James Goodale, *Branzburg v. Hayes* and the Developing Qualified Privilege for Newsmen," 26 *Hastings Law Journal* 26 (1975): 717–18.

4   The essence of my argument in the *Hastings Law Journal* can be summed up in the following two paragraphs taken from it: "First, it is submitted that Justice Powell did adopt a qualified privilege for newsmen: 'The Court does not hold that newsmen, subpoenaed to testify before a grand jury, are without constitutional rights with respect to the gathering of news or in safeguarding their sources.' It follows that if reporters when subpoenaed to testify do have constitutional rights as to gathering news and protecting their sources, then they have a qualified privilege not to testify." Ibid., 716. "The rule of a numerical majority of the justices in *Branzburg v. Hayes* can therefore be said narrowly to be that reporters have a qualified testimonial privilege, dependent on a showing by the newsman that (a) the testimony would be irrelevant, (b) the testimony would further no compelling state interest (e.g., when the testimony is sought for purposes of harassment, not in good faith, or not for a legitimate purpose of law enforcement), or (c) the testimony is not required by other unspecified forms of balancing (e.g., exhaustion of alternate sources)." Ibid, 718.

5   A listing of these cases can be found in essays I wrote in each of the years 1973–2008 for the Practising Law Institute's annual seminar, "Communications Law." In each of those years the title of each essay is "Recent Developments in the Law of the Reporter's Privilege."

6   Ibid.

7   John M. Crewdson. "F.B.I. Warns Staff on Leaking Data; Tells All Employees to Sign a Statement Recognizing Possible Penalties," *New York Times*, August 26, 1973.

8   Joe Califano and Ed Williams called this approach "the Gray-Haired Widow Defense." The gray-haired widow was, of course, Kay Graham. The point of Califano and Williams' remark was that no court was going to order a gray-haired lady to jail when she wanted to protect her reporters' sources. (Ben Bradlee, *A Good Life: Newspapering and Other Adventures*, 371.)

9   Martin Arnold. "Resignation Ends a Court Test on Disclosure of News Sources." *New York Times*, October 12, 1973.

10   Ibid.

11   Ibid.

CHAPTER XXXI: THE POWER OF CONTEMPT

1   *New York Times v. United States*, 403 U.S. at 715 (Black, J., concurring).

2   *See supra*, chapter 4, footnote 10.

3   Lesley Oelsner, "Justice Postel, at Persico Trial, Warns Reporters on Coverage," *New York Times*, Nov 12, 1971.

4   *Oliver v. Postel*, 30 N.Y.2d 171 (N.Y. 1972).
5   Ibid.
6   Postel was attempting to protect Persico's right to a fair trial under the Sixth Amendment. The clash between the First Amendment right to publish information about a criminal defendant and that defendant's right to a fair trial is typically accommodated by a searching *voire dire*, a warning not to follow the case in the press, and if all else fails, by sequestering a jury.
7   Paul Thomasch. "Madoff assaulted by another inmate in December: report." *Reuters*, March 17, 2010.
8   Friendly appeared as a panelist of my seminar, held under the umbrella of the Practising Law Institute, for many years. I suggested to him after the first seminar that the Ford Foundation sponsor a seminar to consider the press–government issues I had encountered. I was particularly concerned that § 798 of the Espionage Act which prevents the publication of codes was overbroad and unconstitutional. I wanted that issue discussed by a distinguished group—it never was. The hypotheticals were written in large part by Stuart Sucherman of the Ford Foundation.
    Friendly took my idea and turned it into a TV–like production, which I couldn't have possibly imagined. Indeed, the seminars were so successful that he later turned them into a TV series on Media & Society, which runs to this very day as Fred Friendly Seminars.
    The genius of Friendly's approach was to create hypotheticals that all participants read. He then invited law professors with extraordinary dramatic talent, such as Arthur Miller of Harvard, to ask participants questions based on the hypothetical. The seminars were hugely successful.
    I persuaded Sucherman (and the Ford Foundation) to initiate a Media Law Studies Program for journalists at Yale Law School in 1977. It provided an MLS degree for one year of legal studies to journalists who attended. Linda Greenhouse, the Supreme Court reporter for the *Times*, and others, were graduates of this program.
9   Stewart referred to *Walker v. Birmingham*, 388 U.S. 307 (1967), a Supreme Court case. In that case, the city of Birmingham had denied civil rights protestors the right to parade. They paraded anyway. They were held in contempt because they had not tried to appeal the case before the parade was scheduled. Stewart was not advising me what to do, as such. He was talking to a group of three. The other two were observers at the conference. They were civil rights lawyers.
10 *New York Times v. Starkey*, 51 A.D.2d 60 (N.Y. App. Div. 2d Dep't 1976).
11 Ibid. The quote in full is: "Whether undue frenetic activity of the press should be curbed should never be a matter for court decision." In *New York Times Co. v United States* (403 U.S. 713), the "Pentagon papers" case, Mr. Justice Brennan clearly indicated that any "gag" of the press must be limited to one area, and one alone—that of national security. He there said: "Our cases, it is true, have indicated that there is a single, extremely narrow class of cases in which the First Amendment's ban on prior judicial restraint may be overridden. Our cases have thus far indicated that such cases may arise only when the nation "is at war," *Schenck v. United States*, 249 U.S. 47, 52 (1919), during which times "no one would question but that a government might prevent actual obstruction to its recruiting service or the publication of the sailing dates of transports or the number and locations of troops. *Near v. Minnesota*, 283 U.S. 697, 716 (1931)." That narrowly defined exception to the ban to the First Amendment on any prior restraint order is not really an exception, for every government has the inherent right to take measures against its own self-destruction." *New York Times Co. v. Starkey*, 51 A.D. 2d at 68. "If there is to be such authorization it should come from the people through an amendment of *their* Constitution and by *their* choice and not by court limitation on the purpose and intent of the First Amendment to permit the American people to enjoy the benefits—and sometimes the detriments—of a free and untrammeled press." Ibid.
12 *In re Providence Journal Co.*, 820 F.2d 1354 (1ˢᵗ Cir. 1986).

13   James C. Goodale, Bruce P. Keller, Lee Levine. *Communications Law in the Digital Age 2009.* New York: Practicing Law Institute, 2010, 262–318. The only exception was *United States v. Noriega (In re Cable News Network, Inc.)*, 917 F.2d 1543 (11ᵗʰ Cir. 1990). In 1990, CNN had obtained copies of recorded conversations between General Manuel Noriega, the former military leader of Panama, and his lawyer. Noriega had been in prison in Miami for drug violations. CNN broadcast part of the tapes. Noriega's lawyer obtained a restraining order against CNN for further publication of those Noriega tapes. CNN, attempting to follow the *Providence Journal*'s case, asked for any emergency appeal in the next highest court. The appeal was set for two days later, but CNN went ahead and published before the appeal could be heard. What CNN did wrong was that it should have told the court it wanted an immediate hearing so that it could broadcast the tapes. This is what I had done in the Starkey case. CNN opted for the formal procedures set out for appeals, rather than following my informal reinvention of those procedures. But once it involved those procedures, it did not follow them. As a consequence, CNN was held in contempt, fined and it never appealed the court's action. This case may have scared off press lawyers from disobeying orders not to print. Indeed, it was dangerous, as Floyd Abrams pointed out, to disobey orders not to print—if you did it the wrong way.

14   *Associated Press v. District Court for the Fifth Judicial District of Colorado*, 542 U.S. 1301 (2004).

15   *United States v. Progressive, Inc.*, 467 F. Supp. 990 (W.D. Wis. 1979).

16   Schoenfeld, *Necessary Secrets*, 216.

17   There have been six cases of courts issuing temporary restraining orders since the Starkey case in New York. Four have been disobeyed. In none of those four cases did the court believe it was appropriate to hold the publication in contempt. *See* James C. Goodale, Bruce P. Keller, Lee Levine, *Communications Law in the Digital Age 2009* (New York: Practising Law Institute, 2010), 262–318.

18   Deirdre Carmody. "Courts and the Process of News Gathering." *New York Times*, July 28, 1978.

19   Lesley Oelsner, "*Times* Reporter Jailed as Marshall Refused to Extend Stay of Penalties," *New York Times*, August 5, 1978.

20   Communication from Floyd Abrams to James C. Goodale at the time of the Farber trial.

21   Goodale, *Communications Law 2012*, 12.

22   Goodale, *Communications Law 2001*, 793–856.

23   Ibid., 681–1124.

24   Eric Pfanner, "E.U. Laws Shielding Journalist's Sources Limited," *New York Times*, September 19, 2010.

CHAPTER XXXII: BUSH'S WAR AGAINST THE PRESS

1   Jay Rosen, "Bush to Press: 'You're Assuming That You Represent the Public. I Don't Accept That,'" Pressthink.org, http://archive.pressthink.org/2004/04/25/bush_muscle.html.

2   Tony Snow, "White House scribe asks for the remote," CNN.com, April 28, 2006.

3   After Dana Priest of the *Washington Post* and Eric Lichtblau and James Risen of the *New York Times* won Pulitzer Prizes for their stories on CIA secret prisons and Bush's warrantless wiretapping program, Bennett said they were not worthy of the prizes. Instead, he said, "I think what they did is worthy of jail, and I think an investigation needs to go forward." David Carr, "The Pulitzer, Now a Badge of Controversy," *New York Times*, April 24, 2006.

      After the *New York Times* printed a story about the Bush administration monitoring international banking transactions in July of 2006, Kristol said, "I think it is an open question whether the *Times* itself should be prosecuted for this totally gratuitous revealing of an ongoing secret classified program that is part of the war on terror."

Then a few weeks later he was more adamant, "I think the Justice Department has an obligation to consider prosecution [of The *Times*]." Faiz Shakir, "Kristol: The *New York Times* 'Should Be Prosecuted; Isn't A First Rate Newspaper,'" *Think Progress*, December 29, 2007, http://thinkprogress.org/2007/12/29/kristol-v-nyt/.

4   In *McKevitt v. Pallasch*, 339 F.3d 530 (7th Cir. 2003), Posner wrote, "A large number of cases conclude, rather surprisingly, in light of *Branzburg*, that there is a reporter's privilege." Posner, after discounting the theory Powell's concurring opinion left the door open for such a privilege, said all of the other court decisions "can certainly be questioned."

5   Adam Liptak. "A Justice's Scribbles on Journalists' Rights." *New York Times*, October 7, 2007.

6   Ibid. Powell wrote in his notes "there is a privilege analogous to an evidentiary one which courts should recognize and apply" on case by case basis "to protect confidential information." In my *Law Review* article on *Branzburg*, I say, "Indeed if there is any solution to the problems presented by subpoenas, it is to let them be resolved on a case-by-case basis, so that, in effect, a common law of subpoenas may develop." James Goodale, "*Branzburg v. Hayes* and the Developing Qualified Privilege for Newsmen," *Hastings Law Journal* 26 (1975): 709.

7   James C. Goodale, "Was Judith Miller's Trip to Jail Necessary?" *New York Law Journal*, April 6, 2007.

8   Miller was the last witness subpoenaed to testify before the grand jury. Fitzgerald had already built his case before she testified. A key part of Miller's testimony was excluded from the trial because it was not relevant. Miller's testimony was not essential to Fitzgerald's case. It did not go to the heart of Fitzgerald's case. James Goodale, "Was Judith Miller's Trip to Jail Necessary?" *New York Law Journal*, April 6, 2007.

9   Adam Liptak. "Time Inc. to Yield Files on Sources, Relenting to the U.S." *New York Times*, June 1, 2005.

10   Pearlstine set out his disagreement with me in his book *Off the Record* (Norman Pearlstine, *Off the Record,* New York: Farrar, Straus and Giroux, 2007, 135–136). My own view was that Pearlstine was in a corporate dilemma. *Time* had been purchased by Warner Communications which had a vast portfolio of diverse interests, of which *Time* was only one small part. I think it would have been very difficult to persuade a board of such a diverse company to go into contempt. Pearlstine has told me this was not so. He didn't think the law protected Cooper. He characterized my view of the law as a "diatribe." Ibid.,136.

11   The specific information Franklin leaked to the AIPAC officials was a presidential directive and deliberations on foreign policy relating to Iran.

12   This was the first time the Espionage Act had been applied to private citizens in a leak case. Ronald K.L. Collins. "AIPAC, Espionage Act, and the First Amendment." *First Amendment Center*, September 4, 2006, http://archive.firstamendmentcenter.org/analysis.aspx?id=17318.

13   James Risen and Eric Lichtblau. "Bush Lets U.S. Spy on Callers Without Courts." *New York Times,* December 16, 2005.

14   Charlie Savage and James Risen. "Federal Judge Finds N.S.A. Wiretaps Illegal." *New York Times*, March 31, 2010.

15   Joe Hagan. "The United States of America v. Bill Keller." *New York Magazine*, September 10, 2006.

16   Substitution for the Testimony of Khalid Sheikh Mohammed, *United States. v. Moussaoui*, 333 F.3d. 509, 517 (4th Cir. 2003). Further, as the *Washington Post* made clear four months before the *New York Times* published the warrantless wiretapping story, Khalid Sheikh Mohammed was already using "great creativity" to avoid eavesdroppers in the United States government in 2001. He employed a technique called virtual "dead drop" where he would open a simple, public email account, write a message, and save it as a draft. Then, instead of sending it, he would give the name

and password to an associate manually or through a secure message board, who could then read the e-mail's contents without the message being transmitted. Steve Coll and Susan B. Glasser, "Terrorists Turn to the Web as Base of Operations," *Washington Post*, August 7, 2005.

17   "Source Steps Up, lets BALCO Reporters off the Legal Hook." Associated Press, February 15, 2007.

CHAPTER XXXIII: IS OBAMA ANY BETTER?

1   *Mohammed v. Jeppesen Dataplan Inc.*, 579 F.3d 943 (9th Cir. 2009).

2   Jane Mayer. "Outsourcing Torture: The Secret History of America's 'Extraordinary Rendition' Program." *The New Yorker*, February 14, 2005.

3   *Mohammed*, 579 F.3d 943 (9th Cir. 2009).

4   Glenn Greenwald. "The 180-degree reversal of Obama's State Secrets Position." Salon.com, February 10, 2009, http://www.salon.com/2009/02/10/obama_88.

5   John Schwartz, "Obama Backs Off a Reversal on Secrets," *New York Times*, February 9, 2009.

6   "Transcript of Obama's 100th day Press Conference." *Wall Street Journal*, April 30, 2009, http://blogs.wsj.com/washwire/2009/04/30/transcript-of-obamas-100th-day-press-conference.

7   *Mohammed*, 579 F.3d 943 (9th Cir. 2009).

8   The bill was passed again by a voice vote in March 2009.
     More precisely, the bill required: 1) that the compelling party must have exhausted all other alternative sources; 2) that there must be reasonable ground that a crime occurred and the testimony or document sought must be "critical" to the investigation or prosecution; 3) if the document or testimony would reveal a confidential source, then there are only certain situations that it could ever be compelled, such as preventing terrorism, preventing imminent death or harm, or situations where someone has leaked classified information that would cause "significant and articulable" harm to national security; 4) the court must conduct the aforementioned balancing test, weighing the public interest in compelling the disclosure versus the public interest in gathering or disseminating the news. The burden of proof is on the party seeking to compel production, e.g., a prosecutor.
     This bill combines parts one and two of the test, "relevance" and "materiality" into one requirement—the need for the information must be critical. It retained the "alternate source" part of the test and added a balancing test. It also provided protection for sources except in enumerated circumstances and it covered unpublished material including notes. (Free Flow of Information Act, H.R. 965, 111th Congress (2009)).

9   David Jackson. "McCain, Obama back law shielding reporters." *USA Today*, April 15, 2008, http://www.usatoday.com/news/politics/election2008/2008-04-14-shield-law_N.htm.

10   Charlie Savage. "White House Proposes Changes in Bill Protecting Reporters' Confidentiality." *New York Times*, September 30, 2009.

11   Ibid.

12   As part of the compromise between the Senate and the president, protection for notes and other non-confidential material was removed from the bill. The Senate bill states the same test as the House bill for civil cases. For criminal cases, the burden of proof shifts to the journalist, making it much harder for newspapers to quash subpoenas. Instead of the issuer of the subpoena having to prove necessity by a preponderance of the evidence, the journalist would have to prove it, by an even higher standard of "clear and convincing" evidence. If the criminal case involves classified national security issues, the balancing test goes out the window, as long as the information sought would help prevent or mitigate a terrorist attack, or acts that would "likely cause significant and articulable harm to national security." (Free Flow of Information Act of 2009, S.448, 111th Congress (2009)).

The Judy Miller case and the *New York Times* wiretapping cases (Risen and Lichtblau) might very well have fallen under the "significant and articulable harm to national security" exception because they were about protecting the identification of a covert agent and the existence of a communications intelligence program, respectively. Because the Senate bill also would not protect journalists if they were an eyewitness to a crime, even Earl Caldwell would have been forced to testify under the new bill, as the government could have alleged he witnessed the Black Panthers conspired to incite a riot.

13   Ethics Agenda, Obama Administration, http://change.gov/agenda/ethics_agenda.

14   Joe Davidson. "Whistleblowers May Have a Friend in the Oval Office." *Washington Post*, December 11, 2008.

15   Siobhan Gorman. "NSA Killed System that Sifted Phone Data Legally." *Baltimore Sun*, May 18, 2006.

16   Joel Stashenko. "Lawyer Who Disclosed Classified FBI Information Is Suspended." *New York Law Journal*, April 14, 2010.

17   Spencer S. Hsu, "State Dept. contractor charged in leak to news organization," *Washington Post*, August 28, 2010.

18   Charlie Savage. "Ex-C.I.A. Officer Named in Disclosure Indictment, *New York Times* January 6, 2011.

19   Dylan Blaylock. "Obama Indicts Sixth Whistleblower Under the Espionage Act." Whistleblower.org, April 5, 2012.

20   Charlie Savage. "Former C.I.A. Operative Pleads Guilty in Leak of Colleague's Name." *New York Times,* October 23, 2012.

21   Ellen Nakashima. "Judge: Government's Treatment of Alleged Leaker Thomas Drake Was 'Unconscionable.'" *Washington Post*, July 29, 2011.

22   Bob Woodward. *Obama's Wars.* New York: Simon & Schuster, 2010, 11.

23   Also attending were OMB Watch Executive Director Gary Bass, OpenTheGovernment. org Director Patrice McDermott, National Security Archive Executive Director Tom Blanton and Lucy Dalglish, Executive Director, Reporters Committee for Freedom of the Press.

24   The stated purpose of the meeting was to present Obama with the "Transparency Award." After the meeting, twenty-four whistleblowers including Daniel Ellsberg and twenty-five open government organizations sent a letter to *The Guardian* asking that the award be vacated. ("Rescind President Obama's 'Transparency Award' Now," Open Letter, *The Guardian,* June 14, 2011).

25   Daniel Brian. "Open Government Advocates Meet with POTUS: A Firsthand Account." Project on Government Oversight, March 29, 2011.

26   Statement made by Lucy Dalglish, Executive Director of The Reporters Committee on Freedom of the Press, on November 11, 2011 at a seminar in New York City, sponsored by the Practicing Law Institute, "Communications Law in the Digital Age."

27   Editorial, "Why Is that a Secret?" *New York Times* (August 24, 2011); see also Jennifer Lynch and Trevor Timm, "The Dangers in Classifying the News," Electronic Frontier Foundation, October 18, 2011, https://www.eff.org/deeplinks/2011/10/dangers-classifying-news.

28   *United States v. Franklin, Rosen & Weissman*, No. 1:05cr225 (E.D. Va.) (Superseding Indictment); *United States v. Rosen*, 557 F. 3d 192 (4th Cir. 2009).

29   The case itself decided that the government would have to prove three things beyond a reasonable doubt: 1) that the AIPAC officials intended to harm the United States with its participation in the leaks; 2) that the persons whom the AIPAC officials gave the information to were not entitled to receive it; 3) that they communicated the information with a "bad purpose to either disobey or disregard the law." It may be that one of the reasons that Obama dropped the case was it would be difficult to prove the intent required of "three" above.

30   James Risen. *State of War: The Secret History of the CIA and the Bush Administration.* New York: Free Press, 2006, 193–219.

31 *United States v. Franklin, Rosen & Weissman*, No. 1:05cr225 (E.D. Va.) (Superseding Indictment); *United States v. Rosen*, 557 F. 3d 192 (4th Cir. 2009).

32 Charlie Savage. "Appeals Panel Weights Question on Press Rights." *New York Times*, May 18, 2012, http://www.nytimes.com/2012/05/19/us/politics/appeals-panel-weighs-press-rights-in-case-involving-reporter-james-risen.html?_r=0.

CHAPTER XXXIV: WILL OBAMA SUCCEED WHERE NIXON FAILED?

1 Joseph Channing. "Wikileaks Releases Secret Report on Military Equipment." *The New York Sun*, September 9, 2007; Xan Rice. "The Looting of Kenya." *The Guardian*, August 31, 2007.

2 Chris McGreal. "US Private Bradley Manning charged with leaking Iraq killings video." *The Guardian*, July 6, 2010.

3 Kevin Poulsen and Kim Zetter. "U.S. Intelligence Analyst Arrested in Wikileaks Video Probe." *Wired*, June 6, 2010. Also, James Goodale, "Blame the Defense Department for Wikileaks," *The Daily Beast*, March 18, 2011.

4 Matt Williams and Ed Pilkington. "Bradley Manning hearing told of lax security at military intelligence unit." *The Guardian*, December 18, 2011.

5 Declan Walsh. "Afghanistan war logs: Secret war along the Pakistan border." *The Guardian*, July 25, 2010; Rob Evans and Richard Norton-Taylor. "Afghanistan war logs: Reaper drones bring remote control death." *The Guardian*, July 25, 2010; Nick Davies. "Afghanistan War logs: Task Force 373–special forces hunting top Taliban." *The Guardian*, July 25, 2010.

6 Adam Levine. "Top military official: WikiLeaks founder may have 'blood' on his hands." CNN, July 29, 2010.

7 Robert Winnett. "Wikileaks Afghanistan: Taliban 'hunting down informants.'" *The Telegraph*, July 30, 2010.

8 "Medvedev's Address and Tandem Politics." WikiLeaks, August 30, 2011; "Deputy Secretary Steinberg" May 30, 2009. "Conversation with Singapore Minister Mentor Lee Kuan Yew," CablegateSearch.net, November 30, 2010; "The U.S. in the Canadian Federal Election—Not!" WikiLeaks, August 30, 2011.

9 Judy Bachrach. "WikiHistory: Did the Leaks Inspire the Arab Spring?" *World Affairs*, July/August 2011.

10 Elisabeth Bumiller. "Gates on Leaks, Wiki and Otherwise." The *New York Times*, November 30, 2010.
    For a view that publication of diplomatic cables harm the United States, see Floyd Abrams, "Don't Cry for Julian Assange: Julian Assange put many people at risk, which may have already cost lives," *Wall Street Journal*, December 8, 2011. Also, in connection with Abrams' article: James C. Goodale, "We Should Support Julian Assange," Letter to the Editor, *Wall Street Journal*, December 20, 2011, and Floyd Abrams, "WikiLeaks to Blame for Envoy Expulsions," Letter to the Editor, *Wall Street Journal* (December 24, 2011).

11 Philip Dorling. "US senator calls to prosecute Assange." *Sunday Morning Hearld*, July 2, 2012; News, "Lieberman Condemns New Wikileaks Disclosures," Lieberman. Senate.gov, November 28, 2010.

12 Ryan Singel. "Key Lawmakers Up Pressure on WikiLeaks and Defend Visa and Mastercard." *Wired*, December 9, 2010.

13 New York Times, 403 U.S. at 723–24 (1971).

14 Bill Keller. "Dealing with Assange and the WikiLeaks Secrets." The *New York Times*, January 26, 2011.

15 Robert Johnson. "How Julian Assange Totally Lost Control of 250,000 Diplomatic Cables." *Business Insider*, September 1, 2011.

16 Presumably the government could have considered indicting Assange under the Espionage Act for receiving classified information under the authority of the AIPAC case. However, since Obama had decided to terminate that case, he could not resurrect it again for use against Assange.

17   Mike Masnick. "U.S. Looking to Use Computer Hacking Law Against Assange."
      Techdirt, December 16, 2010; Ellen Nakashima and Jerry Markon. "WikiLeaks
      founder could be charged under Espionage Act." The *Washington Post,* November 30,
      2010.
18   Charlie Savage. "U.S. Prosecutors Study WikiLeaks Prosecution." *New York Times,*
      December 7, 2010; *see also* the subpoenas issued to witnesses at the WikiLeaks grand
      jury. Glenn Greenwald. "FBI serves grand jury subpoena likely related to WikiLeaks."
      Salon, April 27, 2011.
19   Jack Mirkinson. "Julian Assange Granted Asylum by Ecuador; Britain Vows to
      Extradite Him To Sweden." *The Huffington Post,* August 16, 2012.
20   Leaked e-mail of Vice President of Stratfor published on Wikileaks. "Fw: [CT]
      Assange-Manning Link Not Key to WikiLeaks Case." WikiLeaks, February 28, 2012,
      http://wikileaks.org/gifiles/docs/375123_fw-ct-assange-manning-link-not-key-to-
      wikileaks-case-.html.
21   Press Release. "Global Intelligence Files." Wikileaks, February 27, 2012, http://
      wikileaks.org/the-gifiles.html.
22   "Assange 'faces death penalty' in US." *Al Jazeera,* January 12, 2011; Provisional
      Skeleton Argument on Behalf of Mr. Assange (Draft), *Swedish Prosecution Authority v.
      Julian Assange*.
23   Geoffrey R. Stone, "WikiLeaks and the First Amendment," *Federal Communications
      Law Journal* 64 (2012): 478. Stone equates a clear and present danger test with the test
      in the Pentagon Papers. His conclusion in this regard is debatable. The *Times* rejected
      the clear and present danger test in the Pentagon Papers case. This was because the test
      had no requirement of immediacy. Instead the *Times* urged a test, which the Supreme
      Court substantially adopted, that an injunction can be granted only if publication, in
      the words of Justice Stewart, "will surely result in direct, immediate and irreparable
      damage to our Nation and its people."
24   For examples of lack of support from the journalism community see: Marc Thiessen,
      "WikiLeaks must be stopped," the *Washington Post,* August 3, 2010; Ben Adler, "Why
      Journalists Aren't Standing Up for Wikileaks," *The Daily Beast,* January 4, 2011;
      Susan Milligan, "Why WikiLeak's Julian Assange Isn't a Journalist," U.S. *News,*
      January 31, 2011; Jason Stverak, "WikiLeaks Isn't Journalism," the *Washington Times,*
      January 7, 2011.

CHAPTER XXXV: A CASE FOR THE AGES

1   Woodward, *Obama's Wars,* 179.
2   Ibid., 179.
3   Joe Hagan. "The United States of America v. Bill Keller." *New York Magazine,*
      September 10, 2006.
4   Griswold, *Ould Fields, New Corne,* 312.
5   Ibid.
6   "Top Secret Talks: Daniel Ellsberg, Leslie Gelb, James Goodale, Nick Lemann
      and Victor Navasky." Presented by USC Annenberg's Center on Communication
      Leadership & Policy, March 16, 2010, http://communicationleadership.usc.edu/
      presentations/top_secret_talks_daniel_ellsberg_leslie_gelb_james_goodale_nick_
      lemann_and_victor_navasky.html.
7   Woodward, *Obama's Wars,* 26.
8   Ibid., 128.
9   Ibid., 46.
10   Ibid., 66.
11   Ibid., 286, 160.
12   Ibid., 3–11.
13   Griffith, Robert. *The Politics of Fear: Joseph R. McCarthy and the Senate.* University
      of Massachusetts Press, 1970, 49.

SELECTED BIBLIOGRAPHY

Abrams, Floyd. *Speaking Freely: Trials of the First Amendment*. New York: Viking Penguin, 2005.

Ackland, Len, complied. *Credibility Gap: A Digest of the Pentagon Papers*. Philadelphia: The National Peace Literature Service, 1972.

Argyris, Chris. *Behind the Front Page: Organizational Self-Renewal at a Metropolitan Paper*. San Francisco: Jossey-Bass Publishers, 1974.

Bamford, James. *The Puzzle Palace: A Report on America's Most Secret Intelligence Organization*. New York: Penguin, 1983.

Barendt, Eric. *Freedom of Speech*. New York: Oxford University Press, 1987.

Barnett, Stephen R. "The Puzzle of Prior Restraint," *Stanford Law Review* 29, (1977): 539–60.

Bernstein, Carl and Bob Woodward. *All the President's Men*. New York: Simon & Schuster, 1974.

Bickel, Alexander M. *The Morality of Consent*. New Haven: Yale University Press, 1975.

Bickel, Alexander M. *The Supreme Court and the Idea of Progress*. New York: Harper and Row, 1970.

Blasi, Vincent, ed. *The Burger Court: The Counter Revolution That Wasn't*. New Haven: Yale University Press, 1983.

Bradlee, Benjamin C. *A Good Life: Newspapering and Other Adventures,* New York: Simon & Schuster, 1995.

Campbell, Geoffrey A. *The Pentagon Papers: National Security Versus the Public's Right to Know*. San Diego: Lucent Books, 2000.

Cowan, Geoffrey and Leroy Aarons. *Top Secret: The Battle for the Pentagon Papers,* L.A. Theater Works, Audio Cassette, 1999.

Edgar, Harold and Benno C. Schmidt, Jr. "The Espionage Statutes and Publication of Defense Information," *Columbia Law Review*, 73 no. 5 (1973): 929–1087.

Exec. Order No. 10501: "Safeguarding Official Information in the Interests of the Defense of the United States," 3 C.F.R. 398 (1949–53).

Ellsberg, Daniel et al. "Top Secret Talks: Daniel Ellsberg, Leslie Gelb, James Goodale, Nick Lemann and Victor Navasky." Presented by USC Annenberg's Center on Communication Leadership & Policy, March 16, 2010.

Ellsberg, Daniel. *Secrets: A Memoir of Vietnam and the Pentagon Papers*. New York: Viking Penguin, 2002.

Emerson, Thomas I., "The Doctrine of Prior Restraint," *Law and Contemporary Problems* 20 (1955): 648–71.

Fainaru-Wada, Mark and Lance Williams. *Game of Shadows: Barry Bonds, BALCO, and the Steroids Scandal That Rocked Professional Sports.* New York: Gotham Books, 2006.

Farber, Myron. *Somebody Is Lying: The Story of Dr. X.* New York: Doubleday, 1982.

Frankel, Max. *The Times of My Life and My Life with the Times.* Random House: New York, 1999.

French, Peter A., ed. *Conscientious Actions: The Revelation of the Pentagon Papers.* Cambridge: Schenkman Books, 1994.

Friendly, Fred W. *Minnesota Rag: Corruption, Yellow Journalism, and the Case That Saved Freedom of the Press.* University of Minnesota Press, 2003.

Gelb, Arthur. *City Room.* G.P. New York: Putnam Sons, 2003.

Gelb, Leslie H. "The Pentagon Papers and the Vantage Point." *Foreign Policy* 6 (Spring): 25–41, 1972.

Gold, Susan Dudley. *The Pentagon Papers: National Security or the Right to Know.* New York: Benchmark Books, 2004.

Goldstein, Gordon M. *Lessons in Disaster, McGeorge Bundy And The Path To War In Vietnam.* New York: Henry Holt, 2008.

Goodale, James C., "*Branzburg v. Hayes* and the Developing Qualified Privilege for Newsmen," *Hastings Law Journal* 26 (1975): 709.

Goodale, James C. "The Press Ungagged: The Practical Effect on Gag Order Litigation of *Nebraska Press Association v. Stuart*," *Stanford Law Review* 29, (February 1977):497–513.

Goodale, James C. *Communications Policy and Law: The Pentagon Papers* (available from Benjamin N. Cardozo Law School, Yeshiva University, New York, photocopy).

Goodale, James C. *Cowles Acquisition.*, 7 vols. The New York Times Company, 1971.

Goodale, James C. *State of New Jersey v. Jascalevich. Myron Farber and the New York Times Company Charged With Contempt of Court.* New York: The New York Times Company, 1978.

Goodale, James C. *The New York Times Company versus United States: A Documentary History* (2 vols). New York: Arno Press, 1971.

Goodale, James C. *United States of America v. Earl Caldwell. Application Of Earl Caldwell and the New York Times for An Order Quashing Grand Jury Subpoenas.* The New York Times Company, 1972.

Goodale, James C. et al. Practising Law Institute's annual seminar. *Communications Law* 1973–2008. In each of those years the title of each essay is "Recent Developments in the Law of the Reporter's Privilege." New York: Practicing Law Institute.

Goodale, James C., Bruce P. Keller, Lee Levine. *Communications Law in the Digital Age 2009.* New York: Practicing Law Institute, 2010.

Goodale, James C. *Communications Law 2001*, New York: Practising Law Institute, 2001.

Goodwin, Richard N. *Remembering America: A Voice from the Sixties.* Boston: Little Brown, 1988.

Graber, Mark A. *Transforming Free Speech: The Ambiguous Legacy of Civil Libertarianism.* Berkeley: University of California Press, 1991.

Graham, Katherine. *Personal History,* New York: Alfred A. Knopf, 1977.

Greenwald, Glenn. "The 180-degree reversal of Obama's State Secrets Position." *Salon,* February 10, 2009.

Griffith, Robert. *The Politics of Fear: Joseph R. McCarthy and the Senate* University Press of Kentucky, 1970.

Griswold, Erwin N. *Ould Fields, New Corne: The Personal Memoirs of a Twentieth-Century Lawyer.* St. Paul: West, 1992.

Hagan, Joe. "The United States of America v. Bill Keller," *New York Magazine,* September 10, 2006.

Halberstam, David. *The Best and Brightest.* New York: Random House, 1972.

Haldeman, H.R. *The Haldeman Diaries: Inside the Nixon White House.* New York: G.P. Putnam, 1994.

Haldeman, H.R. and Joseph DiMona. *The Ends of Power.* New York: New York Times Book Company, 1978.

Halperin, Morton H. and Daniel Hoffman. *Freedom versus National Security: Secrecy and Surveillance.* New York: Chelsea House, 1977.

Hentoff, Nat. *The First Freedom: The Tumultuous History of Free Speech in America,* New York: Delcorte, 1980.

Herring, George C., ed., *The Pentagon Papers.* New York: McGraw-Hill, 1993.

Herring, George C. *America's Longest War: The United States and Vietnam, 1950–1975.* New York: Alfred A. Knopf, 1985.

Hersh, Seymour M. *The Price of Power: Kissinger in the Nixon White House.* New York: Summit, 1983.

Heuvel, Katrina Vanden. "The Nation and NY Times: Bay of Pigs Déjà vu." *The Nation,* July 6, 2006.

"Historical Notes: The Pumpkin Papers." *Time,* August 11, 1975.

Kalven, Harry, Jr. "The Supreme Court 1970 Term," *Harvard Law Review* 85 (1971): 3–36.

Kent, Sherman. *Strategic Intelligence for American World Policy.* Princeton: Princeton University Press, 1966.

Kurland, Philip B., ed. *Free Speech and Association: The Supreme Court and the First Amendment.* Chicago: University of Chicago Press, 1975.

Lewis, Anthony. *Make No Law: The Sullivan Case and the First Amendment.* New York: Random House, 1991.

Liebovich, Louis, W. *Richard Nixon, Watergate, and the Press.* Westport: Praeger Press, 2003.

Mayer, Jane. "Outsourcing Torture." *The New Yorker,* February 14, 2005.

McKinney's Consolidated Laws of New York.

Mitchell, Greg. *The Age of WikiLeaks: From Collateral Murder to Cablegate (and Beyond),* New York:Sinclair Books, 2011.

Mitchell, Greg. *Tricky Dick and the Pink Lady.* New York: Random House, 1998.

Murphy, Paul L. "*Near v. Minnesota* in the Context of Historical Developments." *Minnesota Law Review* 66 (1981): 95–160.

Nixon, Richard, *Memoirs of Richard Nixon.* New York: Grosset & Dunlap, 1978.

Oakes, James L. "The Doctrine of Prior Restraint since the Pentagon Papers." *Journal of Law Reform,* 15 (1982): 497–519.

Pearlstine, Norman. *Off The Record: The Press, The Government, and the War over Anonymous Sources.* New York: Farrar Strauss & Giroux, 2007.

Perez, Robert C. and Edward F. Willett. *The Will to Win: A Biography of Ferdinand Eberstadt: Contributions in Economics and Economic History,* Greenwood Press, 1989.

Powe, Lucas A. Jr. *American Broadcasting and the First Amendment.* Berkeley: University of California Press, 1988.

Powe, Lucas A., Jr. *The Fourth Estate and the Constitution: Freedom of the Press in America.* Berkeley: University of California Press, 1991.

Pozen, David E., "The Mosaic Theory, National Security, and the Freedom of Information Act." *Yale Law Journal,* 115, 2005.

Prados, John and Margaret Pratt Porter. *Inside the Pentagon Papers.* Lawrence: University Press of Kansas, 2004.

Prados, John. *President's Secret War: CIA and Pentagon Covert Operations since World War II.* New York: William Morrow, 1986.

Reston, James. *Deadline: A Memoir.* New York: Times Books, 1991.

Risen, James. *State of War: The Secret History of the CIA and the Bush Administration,* New York: Free Press, 2006.

Rudenstine, David, "The Pentagon Papers Case: Recovering Its Meaning Twenty Years Later," *Cardozo Law Review,* 12 (1991): 1869–1913.

Rudenstine, David. *The Day The Presses Stopped: A History of the Pentagon Papers Case.* Los Angeles: University of California, 1996.

Safire, William. *Before the Fall: An Inside View of the Pre-Watergate White House.* New York: Da Capo Press, 1975.

Salisbury, Harrison E. *Without Fear or Favor: An Uncompromising Look at The New York Times.* New York: Times Books, 1980.

Schoenfeld, Gabriel. *Necessary Secrets: National Security, the Media, and the Rule of Law,* New York: W.W. Norton & Company, 2010.

Schwab, Nikki. "QA: The Father of the Reporter's Privilege." *U.S. News & World Report,* Oct 25, 2007.

Seymour, Whitney North, Jr., *United States Attorney: An Inside View of "Justice" in America Under the Nixon Administration.* New York: Morrow, 1975.

Shakir, Faiz. "Kristol: The *New York Times* Should Be Prosecuted; It 'Isn't A First Rate Newspaper.'" *Think Progress,* December 29, 2007.

Shapiro, Martin, ed. *The Pentagon Papers and the Courts: A Study in Foreign Policy-Making and Freedom of the Press.* San Francisco: Chandler Publishing Co., 1972.

Shepard, Richard F. *The Paper's Paper: A Reporter's Journey Through The Archives of The New York Times.* New York: Times Books, 1996.

Sifry, Micah L. *WikiLeaks and the Age of Transparency,* New York: OR Books, 2011.

Simons, Howard and Joseph A. Califano Jr., ed. *The Media and the Law,* New York: Praeger Publishers, 1976.

Sims, John Cary. "Triangulating the Boundaries of the Pentagon Papers," *William and Mary Bill of Rights Journal,* 2 (Winter 1993): 341–53.

Singer, Mark. "Talk of the Town: The Pentagon Suitcases," *The New Yorker*, December 9, 1996.

Stone, Geoffrey R. *Perilous Times: Free Speech in Wartime from the Sedition Act of 1798 to the War on Terrorism.* New York: W.W. Norton, 2004.

Talese, Gay. *The Kingdom and the Power.* New York: Dell, 1981.

The New York Times Edition of the Pentagon Papers. New York: Bantam, 1971.

The Pentagon Papers: The Defense Department History of United States Decision-making on Vietnam, The Senator Gravel Edition. Boston: Beacon Press, 1971.

Tifft, Susan E. and Alex S. Jones. *The Trust: The Private and Powerful Family Behind The New York Times.* New York: Little, Brown, 1999.

Ungar, Sanford J. *The Papers & The Papers: An Account of the Legal and Political Battle Over the Pentagon Papers.* New York: E.P. Dutton, 1972.

Wells, Tom. *Wild Man: The Life and Times of Daniel Ellsberg.* New York: Palgrave, 2001.

White, Theodore. *The Making of the President 1968.* New York: Atheneum Publishers, 1969.

Wilson, George. "Hey, hey, LBJ, got any secrets to give away?" *Nieman Watchdog,* July 26, 2006.

Woodward, Bob. *Obama's Wars*, New York: Simon & Schuster, 2010.

INDEX